IMAGES
of America

Hamilton County

On the Cover: This 1950s photograph depicts a group of dancers practicing in front of the Stephen Foster Museum before their performance during the Florida Folk Festival. This is an example of swing dancing, one of the many genres of dance and music that can be seen and heard at the festival. Others include folk, blues, gospel, country, jazz, bluegrass, and zydeco. Concerts and performances are given throughout the day and into the night. Visitors are often encouraged to join in while the performers dance on the old marble stage. (Florida Development Commission.)

IMAGES
of America

HAMILTON COUNTY

Marsanne Petty

ARCADIA
PUBLISHING

ISBN 978-0-7385-6813-3

Published by Arcadia Publishing
Charleston, South Carolina

Printed in the United States of America

Library of Congress Control Number: 2008941222

For all general information contact Arcadia Publishing at:
Telephone 843-853-2070
Fax 843-853-0044
E-mail sales@arcadiapublishing.com
For customer service and orders:
Toll-Free 1-888-313-2665

Visit us on the Internet at www.arcadiapublishing.com

To my mother, who has done nearly as much work on this project as I have, and to my family, who has listened to me ramble on about the various subjects covered in this book for quite some time. It seems the more research I do, the more I want to discover. I could not have completed this work without their help, patience, and understanding.

Contents

ACKNOWLEDGMENTS

The Early History of Hamilton County, Florida, compiled and written under the guidance of Cora Hinton (1907–1999), has proven to be a useful instrument of preliminary research for many of the subjects covered in this book. Without that first publication, and the subsequent editions, it would have been nearly impossible to determine what should be included.

Dozens of individuals have assisted me with this project in one way or another. Some have contributed photographs, in which case the credit for each can be found below the caption. Others have contributed information or guided me to the appropriate person to answer my questions. Still others have sat by quietly listening to me stress over the photographs, the captions, and the deadlines. All of those who provided the smallest tidbit of information are equally important, as it was many times those people who prodded me to think of something else that needed to be included or another question that needed to be answered. I would also like to thank my employer and coworkers for their patience with me while working on the manuscript.

Arcadia editor Luke Cunningham has been a fount of enthusiasm for me. When I became too stressed and panicky, he provided the push I needed to continue. Those who contributed photographs—Paul Marion, Alan Fouraker, Marian Deas, Cliff Adams, Evelyn Singletary, Tracy Woodard, Mildred Shepherd, Marion Turner, Hamilton County High School, Hamilton County Clerk's Office, William S. Mitchell IV, Florida Development Commission, Florida Photographic Collection of the State Archives of Florida, Malcolm Greene, Phyllis Whitaker, Richard McCulley, Sudie Kelley Selph, and those who wish to remain unnamed—have been overwhelmingly supportive and helpful to me.

One of the most uplifting people throughout the whole process has been my mother. She has provided me with guidance when needed, inspiration when down, and editing skills beyond belief. After reading and rereading a caption a million times, I could never find all of the errors, but she did. She has been my editor at home, prompting me to continue when I faltered and pushing me to succeed when I thought I could not.

Finally, to my husband and my children—thank you. It will never be possible for you to realize how much your patience and understanding has meant to me.

INTRODUCTION

Situated on the north Florida–south Georgia state line, Hamilton County offers a natural setting of scenic rivers and lakes, forests and bogs, and dazzling sunsets through the branches of trees. Surrounded by rivers—the Withlacoochee River on the west and the Suwannee River on the east and south—dozens of small towns and communities cropped up along them. As with all communities, there is growth and decline, and many of those towns have vanished from the maps and remain only as distant memories of old-timers.

Not all of those communities that have vanished were situated on riverbanks. Some of them were around lumber and sawmills, turpentine stills, and family homesteads. Some of the names that are no longer well known include Avoca, Wallburg, Micco, Rosseters Ferry, Hooker's Ferry, Baker's Mill, Blacks Still, Benton, Avrietville, Hollywood, West Lake, Marion Station, and Smithville. There are other areas, such as Genoa, Bellville, and Facil, that once had shops and larger communities but have dwindled to nearly nothing. The county's main communities—Jasper, Jennings, and White Springs—have remained, weathering great declines of population and community businesses.

The area where Hamilton County is located was first a portion of Leon County, which was then divided further, and the area fell into Jefferson County. In 1827, Hamilton County was created as the 15th in the territory of Florida, 18 years before statehood was an issue. At that point, Daniel Bell, two years after he first settled in the area, became the first senator from the county, while Israel Stewart acted as the first representative to the state legislature.

It is believed that there were settlements at the location of Jasper in the late 1820s or early 1830s, but no substantiated evidence can be found. By 1892, there was a community of fair size, but the Thompkins fire destroyed nearly all the records, including those of the city. What records were not completely turned to ash were unsalvageable.

In 1839, the county commissioners purchased 40 acres of land from William M. Reed. This property was surveyed into 25 blocks, allowances were made for streets, and the Old Town of Jasper was born, nearly a mile from its current location. The following year on February 27, the Town of Jasper was incorporated by an act of the Legislative Council of the Territory of Florida. William Roberts, Josiah Baisden, Joseph B. Watts, John Whitehurst, and William M. Hunter were appointed as officers of the new town. By 1841, a post office had been established, with postmaster William Roberts. In that same year, a school was officially established by another act of Legislative Council.

Eighteen years later, another incorporation of Jasper was deemed necessary on March 2, 1858. All the voters were in favor of incorporation: W. A. Alford, James R. Bass, I. L. Brooks, Lewis P. Dunn, L. B. McTyer, John Parr, I. H. Stephens, William R. Tuten, T. J. Zipperer, F. M. Ayers, H. B. Blount, George W. Cooper, R. L. Ivy, William M. Mitchell, Solomon Rouse, Henry J. Stewart, and John W. Umstead. The population of the community had grown to nearly 300 by then. The railroad came to town in 1865, drawing in additional merchants, which in turn drew families closer to the core of town, nearer to its current center.

It was felt necessary that a third incorporation of the area be performed. On February 25, 1878, a full 38 years after the initial incorporation, Henry J. Stewart, Sam McInnes, Elisha P. Smith, Irvin R. Swilley, James H. Ancrum, James P. Watson, Lucian Frink, John C. Lee, W. H. Greene, and W. F. Staten were appointed officers of the "new" town of Jasper.

The Jasper Normal Institute was established as the first formal school in 1890, although there had been other country schools that taught local children. Hotels, boardinghouses, and restaurants sprang up, as well as a new courthouse, jail, town hall, and artesian well. By 1900, the population had grown to almost 1,000.

The community continued to blossom. Hotels, restaurants, millinery, stables, and two railroad depots were added. In 1912, a city hall and fire station were constructed. More businesses opened, catering to the population that swelled to 2,200 in 1976. However, as with all three main communities in the county, the new interstate built in the later 1960s put a hardship on businesses. Tourists were no longer driving straight through Jasper. Now they were being detoured around it. The economy has suffered; businesses have shut their doors. The current population remains stable at nearly 1,800 citizens, the largest area in the county.

In 1825, the Jennings area was sparsely populated but had plenty of fertile soil—a prime area for pioneers to settle. Some of those early settlers included Dixon T. Cross, James S. Lewis, and Jeremiah B. Smith. Perhaps the most well known was George Jennings, who established the town of Jennings Station in 1860. After losing all of his belongings in the Alapaha River on the way through the area, Jennings built a homestead. The family developed the nearby land and built another house, which they used for boarders, establishing the first boardinghouse in the area.

Later a post office was established 10 miles west of Jasper, with postmaster James Avriett. The town was a stop on the railroad, and a telegraph office was located there. The town soon became known as only Jennings; the "Station" was dropped. By 1900, the population had grown enough to support seven cotton gins and several turpentine stills and lumber mills.

In 1909, the Jennings Hotel Company decided to construct a hotel in the city. Stockholders included J. R. Jennnings, B. F. McCall, K. K. Powell, W. C. Clayton, J. B. Shiver, Wolf Lipsitz, J. L. McDaniel, A. C. Stephens, and W. B. Avriett. For more than a year, the group delayed building the hotel, until J. B. Shiver bought the lots and completed the hotel himself, operating it until 1939.

In 1914, Jennings High School was established, and most of the country schools were closed. The two-story building had an auditorium upstairs where the student body held chapel on a daily basis. More rooms were added to the school in the following years. The school eventually fell into disrepair, and the building currently in use was completed on January 28, 1928.

The Georgia Southern Railroad allowed for shipping of cotton, lumber, and other merchandise from Jennings to outlying areas. In addition, passengers could ride the train to Valdosta, Georgia, for a day of shopping or to White Springs for a day of relaxation at the Spring House.

By 1920, the population of Jennings had grown to 1,200, supporting a small city of 36 businesses. It was during this time that John Bradshaw, who owned the department store, grew the first crop of tobacco in the county. The wonder crop was quickly established and became one of the highest-ranking crops in the county.

Throughout the years, the population of Jennings has slowly dwindled. Businesses have closed their doors, leaving only a few locally owned businesses. The current population of the area is a mere 830 citizens.

Incorporation was not a big issue for the citizens of White Springs. In 1885, on Christmas Day, they finally incorporated the town that had been in existence for nearly 50 years, since Bryant Sheffield first settled there in 1835. He bought 1,000 acres, developed the springs into a tourist feature, and sold lots to newcomers to build upon. Nearly two-thirds of his property became the basis of White Springs. By the time of incorporation, the population of the town had reached nearly 350, supporting quite a business core: four stores, a steam saw, gristmill and cotton gin, two private schools, a few churches, a newspaper (the *Echo*), several hotels, and other businesses. Crops grown in the area included sea island cotton, trees for lumber, fruit and vegetables, and sugar cane.

The elected officers of the incorporation included R. W. Adams, William Robarts, John Powell, O. K. Paxton, Francis Adams, A. C. Bell, and Calvin Buckels. The mail had been delivered to the area for nearly 50 years as well, with a post office located in a general store for many of those years.

Dr. J. L. Skipworth established the Florida Normal College in 1883 for the education of teachers. Shortly after, the Camp family established a lumber mill in the area. In order for them to ship their products to the nearest seaport in Jacksonville, Florida, they first had to send it to Valdosta, Georgia, and then back to Jacksonville. The Camps petitioned for and received permission to build a railway line called the Florida and Georgia Railroad. The small company constructed an 8-mile section from White Springs to Wellborn, Florida. Lumber and produce could then be shipped from Wellborn to Jacksonville, thus eliminating the need for interstate commerce. In the late 1900s, the lumber mill and associated basket factory caught fire and burned, and the Camps abandoned the venture.

Fire was a prevalent disaster in the early 1900s—one after another plagued the small town. Three fires struck the Spring House hotel alone, and Sheffield replaced it each time. The Camps' operation was destroyed. Then in 1911, on the last day of hunting season, a massive fire that spread for blocks destroyed 35 buildings, including the Baptist parsonage, livery stables, Dr. D. N. Cone's office, the High Hotel, the Oaks Hotel, a cotton warehouse, and several other residences and businesses.

The population of White Springs at the time of the fire had increased to 1,177 citizens. The double tragedy of the great fire and the closing of the Camps' mill and factory put a tremendous hardship on citizens to find gainful employment. By 1920, the population had dropped to 984. After a few rises and falls in the numbers, the population remains fairly stable at about 800 citizens.

The history of Hamilton County has been filled with many ups and downs, tragedies and pitfalls, joys and happiness. A single book could never relay all those that have left their imprint on the communities or all those that have stayed for a moment before leaving the area. It is the hope of the author that this book will allow the memories of some to live on a while longer.

One

Scenes

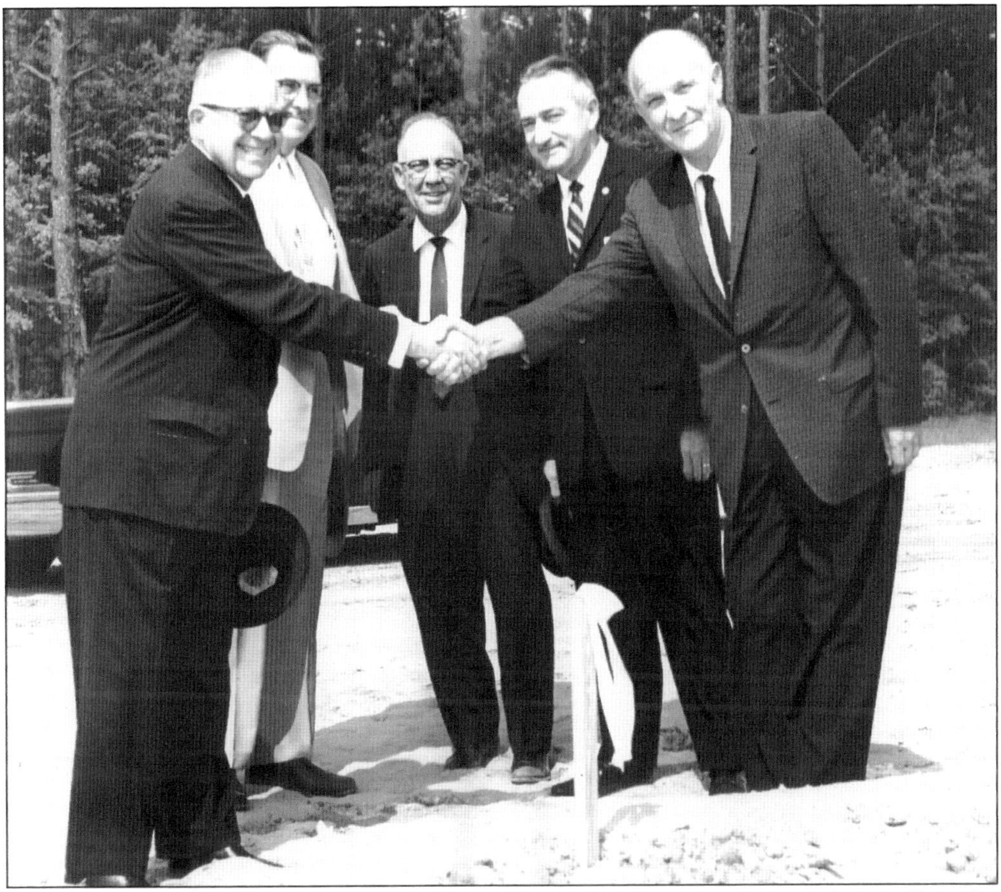

In late 1961, a portion of Interstate 75, from Lake City to Genoa, was opened to traffic. The section from Genoa to the Florida-Georgia state line was still under construction at the time of this photograph (1962) but was completed in 1963. Paving of the segment between State Road 6 and the state line was done in two sections, beginning in April 1962. The first section from State Road 6 to County Road 141 cost $695,547. The second section between County Road 141 and the state line cost $865,379. Both sections of the work in Florida were completed by Couch Construction Company of Dothan, Alabama. Paving on the Georgia side of the state line did not begin for another week or two. Pictured from left to right are the following: Lonnie A. Pope, executive assistant of the highway department; M. L. Shadburn, state highway engineer for Georgia; W. T. Mayo, Florida interstate administrator; Ralph Powers, second district member of the Florida Road Board; and John R. Phillips, chairman of the Florida Highway Board. (Florida Photographic Collection, State Archives of Florida.)

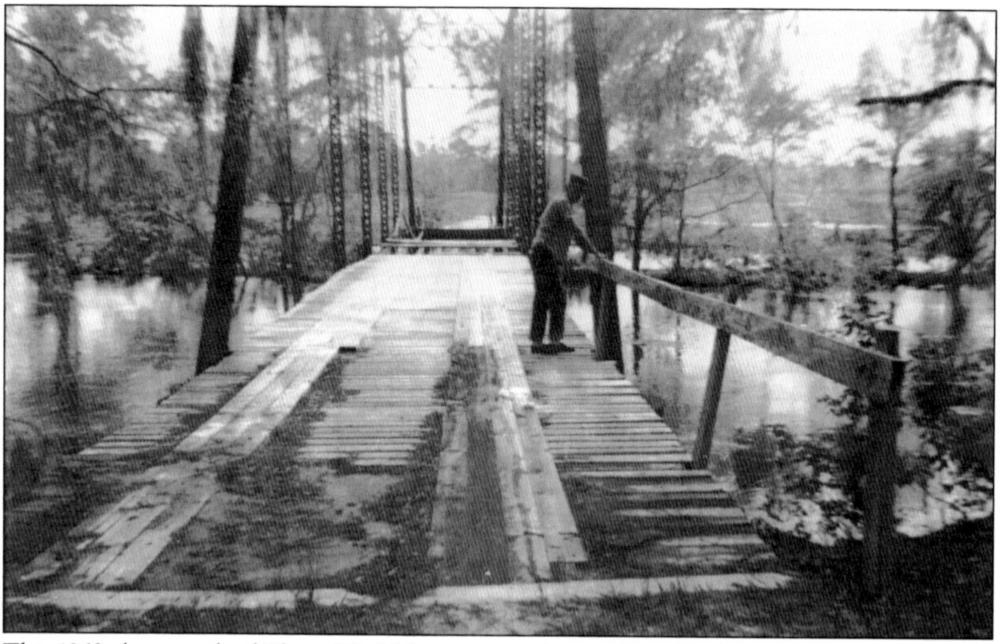

This 1963 photograph of Glenn "G. P." Rogers was taken at Cone Bridge on the Suwannee River near Highway 441. Semitrucks commonly used the bridge to bypass the agriculture station on Highway 41, near White Springs. The bridge was damaged during the 1970s when an overloaded truck attempted to cross it. It was never repaired and was eventually torn down. Rogers worked for the Florida Forestry Department. (Malcolm Greene.)

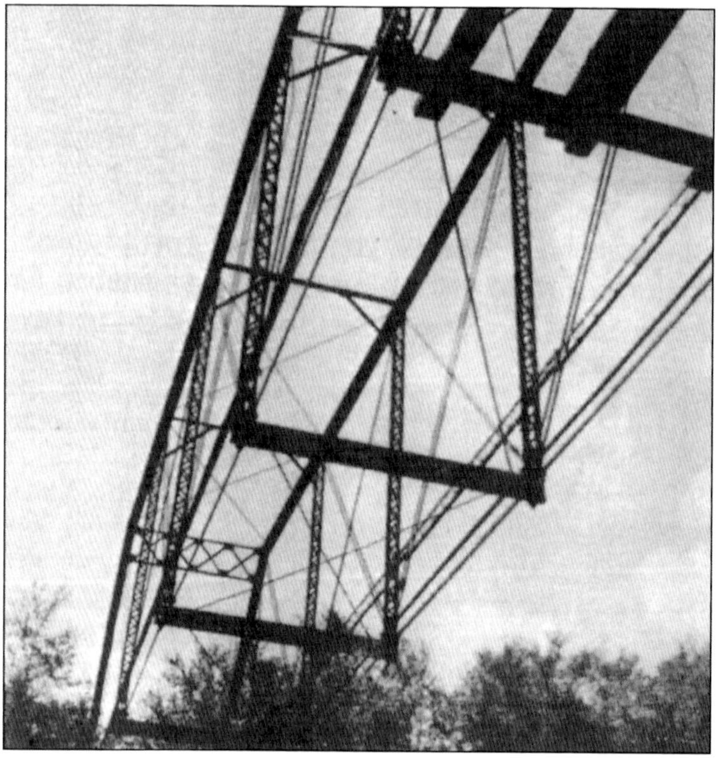

The Jennings Bridge, approximately half a mile downstream from County Road 150, was built in the early 1900s. The Board of County Commissioners approved the steel truss bridge over the Alapaha River on December 3, 1901. The American Bridge Company, from New York, constructed the bridge for $2,788. It was later abandoned and the frame washed away during a flood in the 1990s. (Florida Photographic Collection, State Archives of Florida.)

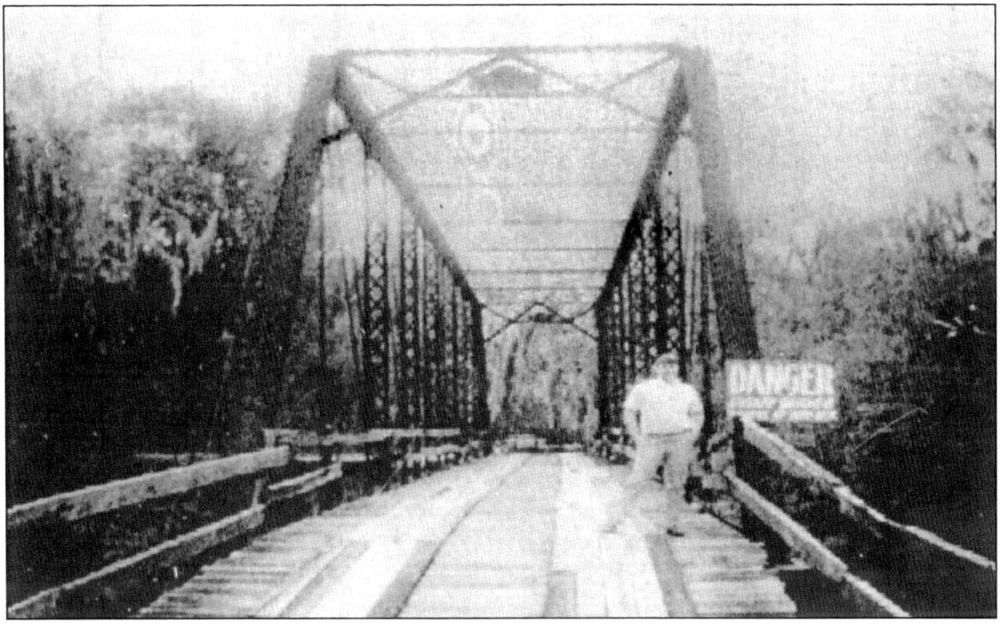

Spanning the Withlacoochee River on State Road 6 between Hamilton and Madison Counties stood a wooden and steel-framed bridge. When the bridge was built, it did not need to be extraordinarily sturdy, but the advent of heavier vehicles and more traffic demanded a new bridge. The wooden bridge was later replaced with a new one. No information about the gentleman in the photograph is known. (Marian Deas.)

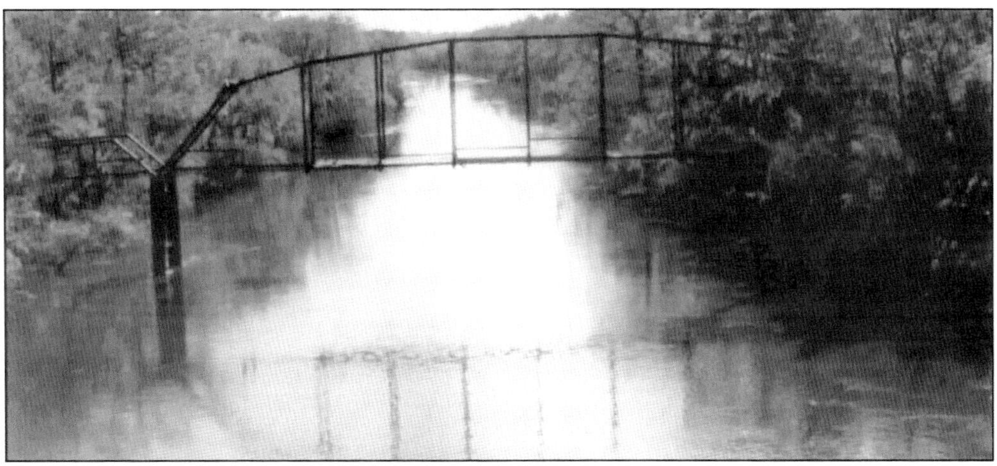

The Bellville Bridge on the Withlacoochee River was constructed in 1912 by the Converse Bridge Company of Chattanooga, Tennessee, at a cost of $4,297. This was the only pin-connected Camelback steel-truss bridge in Florida at the time. This 1987 photograph was taken a week before the bridge was washed away by the rising river, leaving only wreckage. The pieces were later pulled from the river, but the bridge was never restored. (Richard McCulley.)

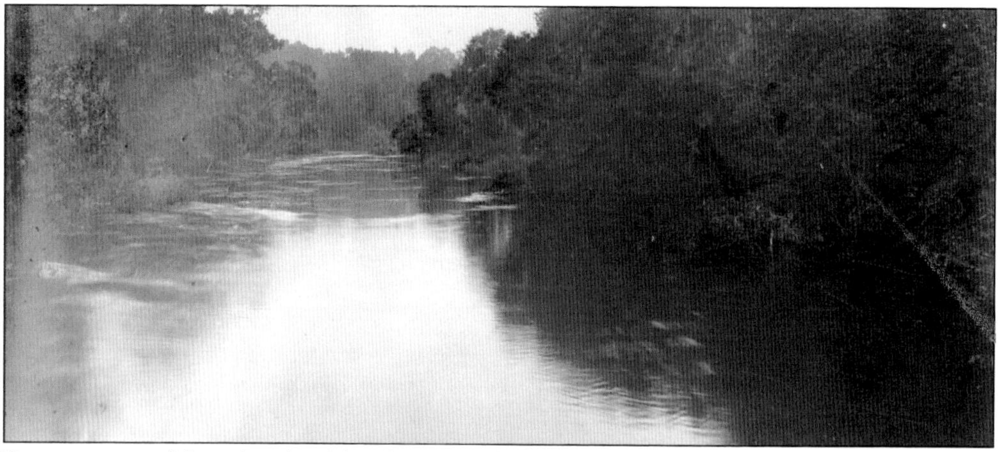

During times of drought, the Alapaha River disappears underground into sinkholes about 2 miles south of Jennings. For this reason, it is called the "River of Sand." It reemerges about 900 feet from the Suwannee River in a dark-colored spring, the Alapaha Rise. The other extreme of the river can cover everything up to a mile away from the riverbed in some areas. Several times, the flooded river has caused concern for nearby farmers, as their land would be underwater. At times, it was possible to pull fish from the ditches and out of fields as a result of a flood. The river itself is only 190 miles long, stretching from southeastern Dooly County, Georgia, to the Suwannee River about 10 miles southwest of Jasper. This 1928 photograph shows the Alapaha River flooded out of its banks. This particular flood was the first one documented by the Suwannee River Water Management District, even though the agency was not created until 1972. Earlier floods and droughts were documented using historical data contributed by area citizens. (Florida Photographic Collection, State Archives of Florida.)

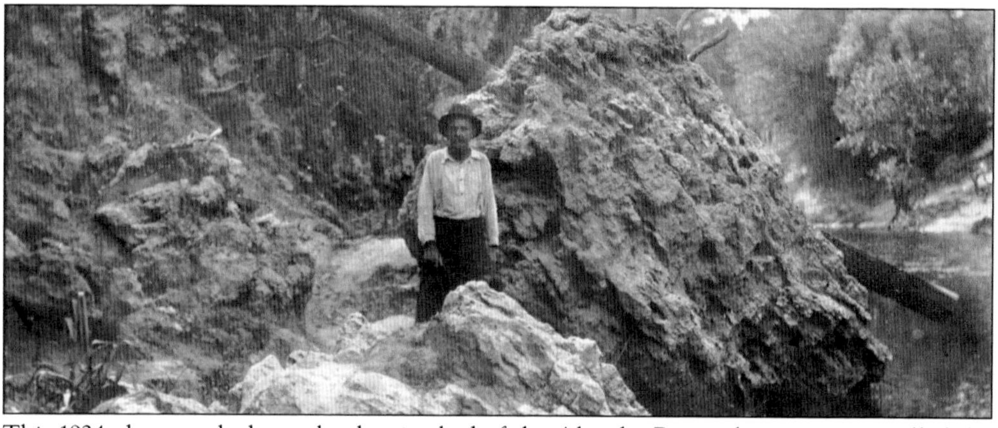

This 1924 photograph shows the dry riverbed of the Alapaha River, also sometimes called the "Disappearing River." The water in the river often runs underground between County Road 150 and Highway 41. When it dries up, fish are left in holes of water for local fishermen to catch. Decar Scaff, Sump Smith, and J. D. Lasiter thought they had caught an alligator in one of the holes and decided to wrestle it out of the hole for dinner. Imagine their surprise when they found they really had a huge fish. They carried the 5.5-foot fish to H. D. Smith, the local game warden, who identified it as a 73-pound sturgeon, believed to be the largest caught in Hamilton County. This unidentified man is standing on an outcrop of Glendon Limestone, exposed by the receding water. Glendon Limestone is characterized by cream-colored crystalline weathering, with irregular tubular-shaped cavities. It is generally 15 to 40 feet in height, although many times the entire piece cannot be seen. (Florida Photographic Collection, State Archives of Florida.)

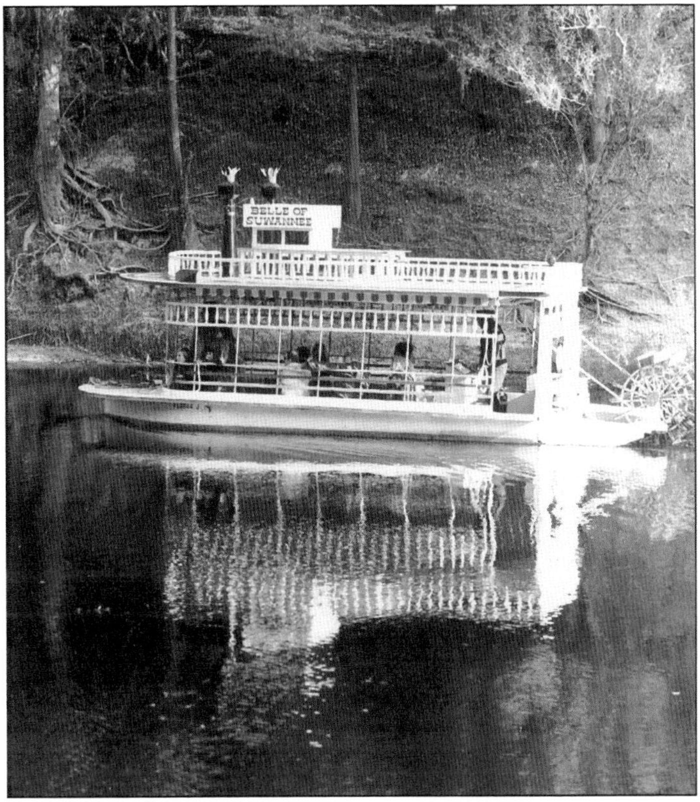

This 1972 photograph of the *Belle of Suwannee* shows one of the paddle steamboats that frequented the Suwannee River. Evidently, the *Belle of Suwannee* was a popular name for steamboats, as there is evidence of many of them being so named. A letter from R. H. Knapp, dated 1947, claims that his father, L. C. Knapp, built the first stern-wheeler steamboat that operated on the Suwannee River, at the town of Branford, Florida, in 1883. Regardless of which *Belle of Suwannee* this photograph depicts, it declares the beauty of a time gone by. (Florida Photographic Collection, State Archives of Florida.)

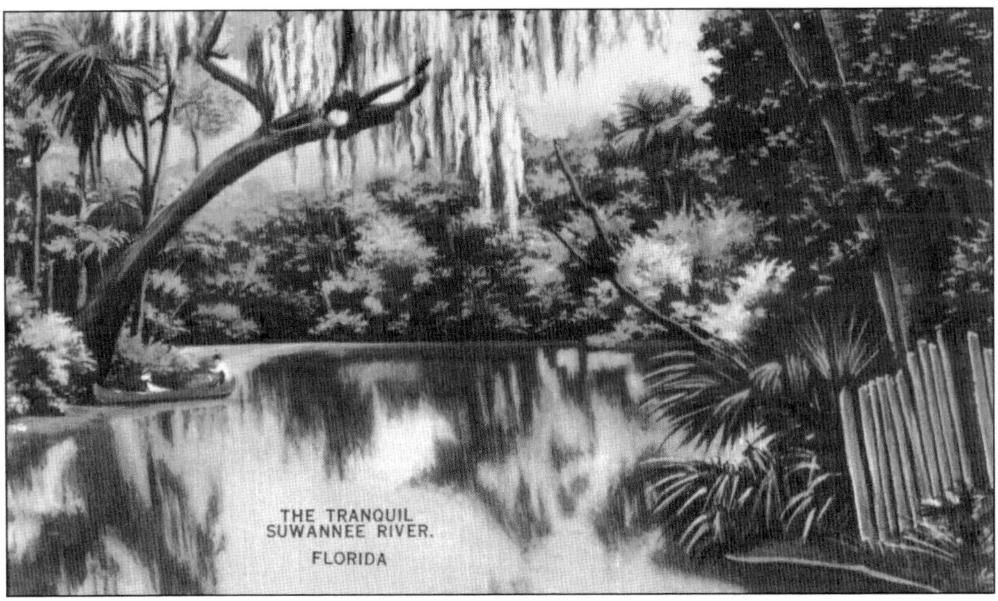

Beginning in the Okeefenokee Swamp, 60 miles above the Florida-Georgia state line, the Suwannee River winds for nearly 250 miles before emptying into the Gulf of Mexico. This early-1960s postcard shows an artist's rendition of the Suwannee River. The Spanish moss in the upper foreground relies on its host for nutrients, often killing the host tree from over-shading the leaves and the weight of the moss. (Author's collection.)

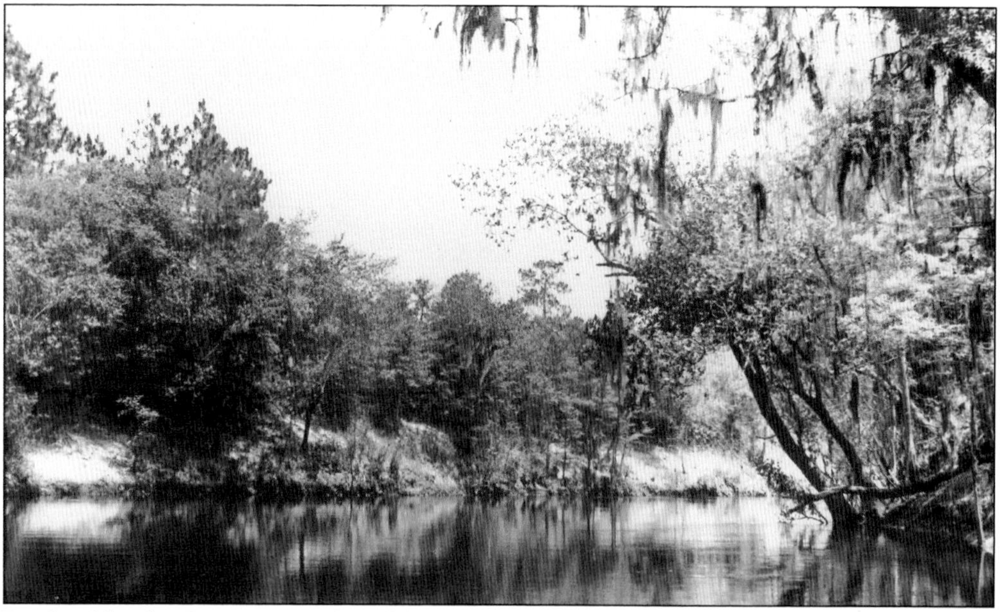

Bordered by the Suwannee and Withlacoochee Rivers on three sides, Hamilton County has as its north side the state line determined in 1854. Georgia maintained it should run from the Flint-Chattahoochee River junction to Lake Spalding or Lake Randolph. Florida preferred the line marked by Daniel F. McNeil in 1825 from the rivers' junction to Ellicott's Mound, near St. Mary's River. Had Georgia prevailed, Florida would have lost approximately 1.2 million acres. (Author's collection.)

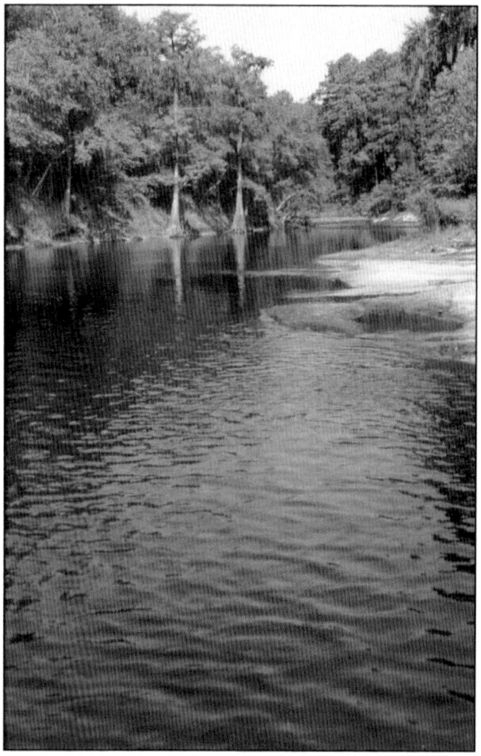

Outcrops of sand such as this one on the Suwannee River, near White Springs, present an excellent opportunity for an array of outdoor activities, including sunbathing, swimming, camping, and grilling. Rather than paying the high prices of materialistic entertainment, many citizens of rural areas opt for entertainment of the natural kind instead. Canoeing is especially popular, both with citizens of the county and those who are not local. The Suwannee River boasts the Big Shoals, the only Class III whitewater rapids in Florida. The canoe trip is generally calm and peaceful above the Big Shoals, then thrilling when traveling through the 1-mile stretch of whitewater rapids, and back to peaceful and serene afterward. Canoes can be rented or purchased from businesses in nearby White Springs. (Florida Photographic Collection, State Archives of Florida.)

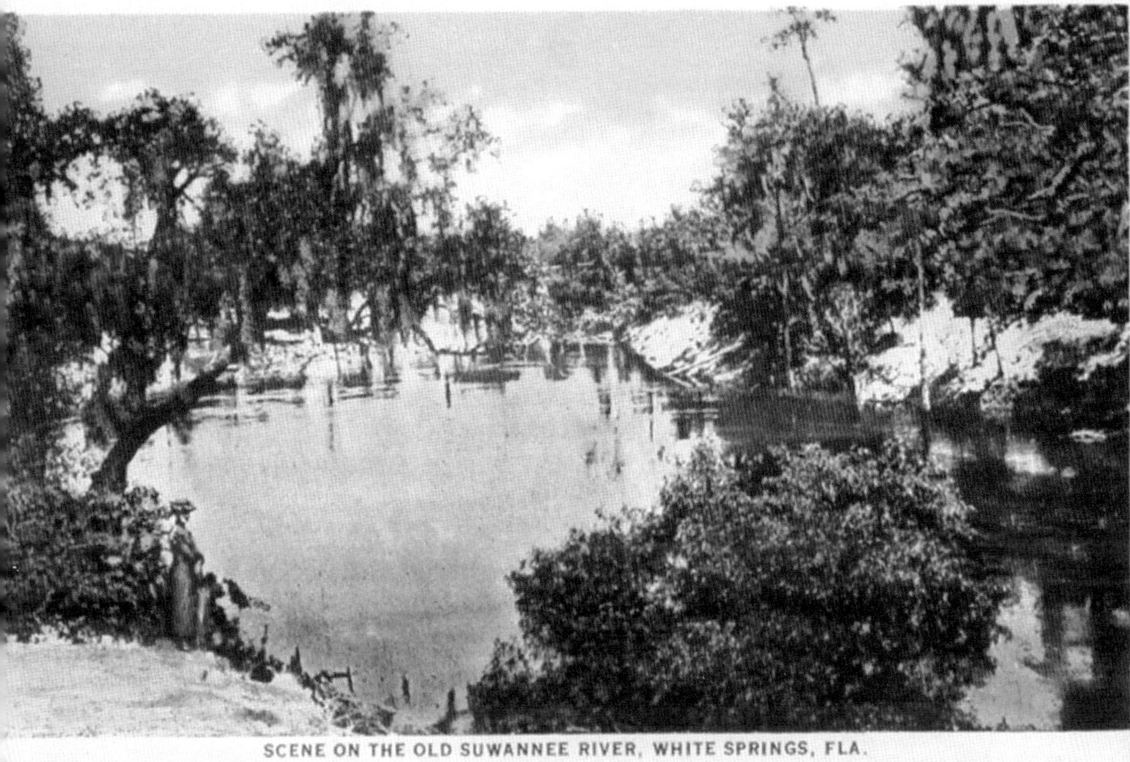

This 1928 photograph of the Suwannee River shows the delicate balance of upland mixed forests that line the naturally occurring levees and plateaus paralleling the river. Common wildlife that can be seen from within the confines of a boat while traveling the river include timber rattlesnakes, white-tailed deer, moccasins, gopher tortoises, frogs, alligators, and snapping turtles, not to mention a multitude of bird species. With luck, gar, mullet, or sturgeon may be seen jumping along the river, although it is advised to proceed with caution as the large sturgeon can harm boaters if they jump into the boat. (Author's collection.)

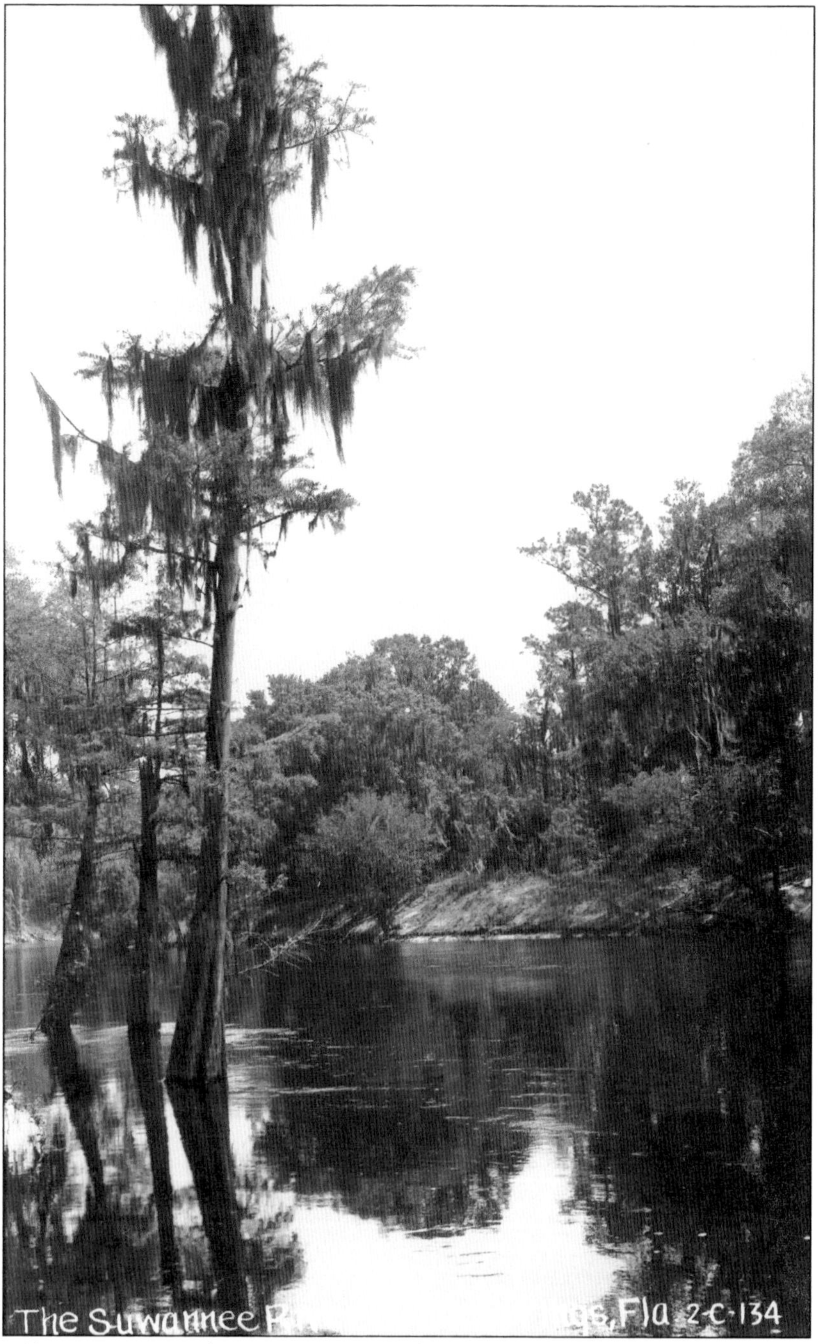

Fishing and hunting are popular pastimes in Hamilton County, with a multitude of areas accessible to either sport, including Bienville Plantation and Wildlife Management Areas such as Holton Creek, Big Shoals, Suwannee Ridge, PotashCorp, and Cypress Creek. In addition to hunting white-tailed deer, foxes, hogs, and turkeys, avid sportsmen can catch largemouth bass, bluegill, channel and bullhead catfish, bream, and gar in the rivers and lakes located throughout the county, including the Alapaha, Suwannee, and Withlacoochee Rivers. This early view of the Suwannee River shows a nice bend where several species of fish likely bed down. (Tracy Woodard.)

Madison Blue Springs State Park is a popular swimming and picnicking area on the Madison County side of the Withlacoochee River at State Road. It was purchased by the state in 2000 and reopened to the public after being restored. This 1950s photograph shows two unidentified young men enjoying the first magnitude spring that emerges 25 feet below the surface into a limestone basin approximately 82 feet in diameter. (Contributor.)

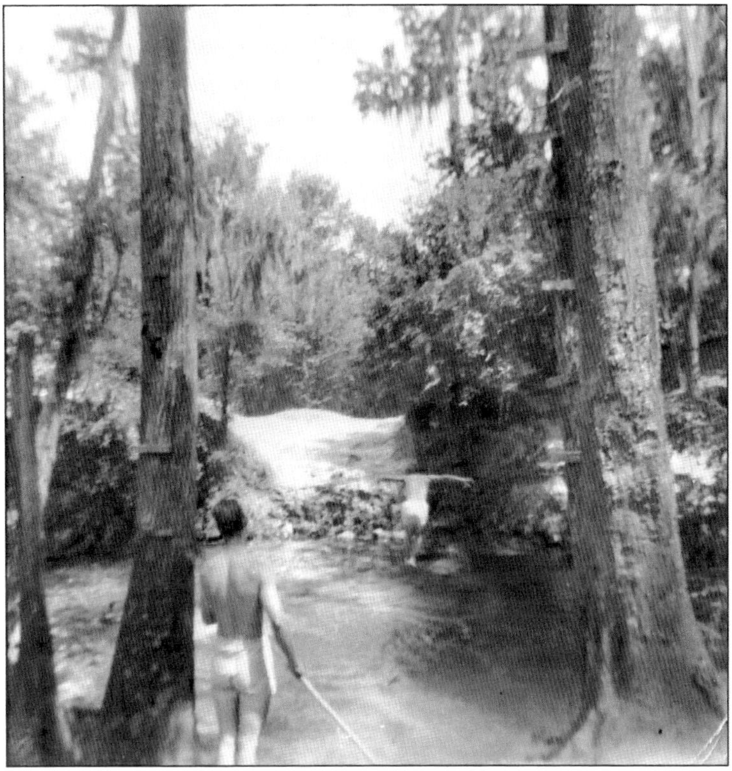

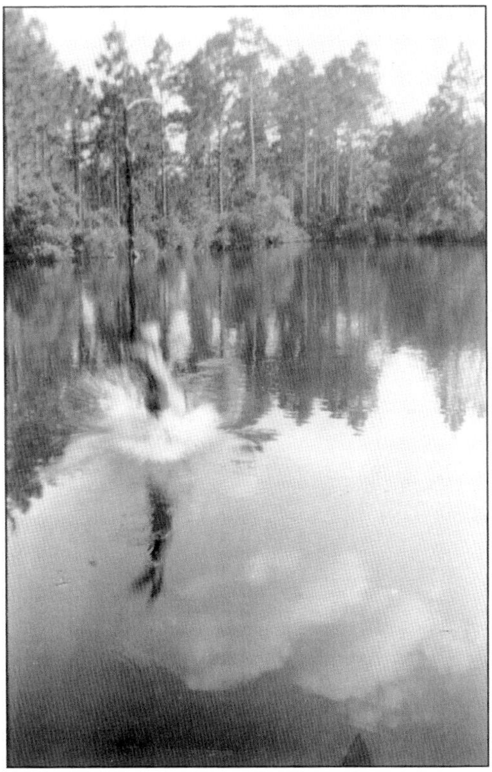

One day in February 1954, people thought a young fisherman had been drinking too much when he announced that Blue Sink outside of Jennings had fallen. No one believed him, but upon their arrival at the sink, they saw the water was indeed gone. It was a gaping hole 100 feet deep and nearly 300 feet wide. The water never returned, and the area has grown up with brush and trees. (Contributor.)

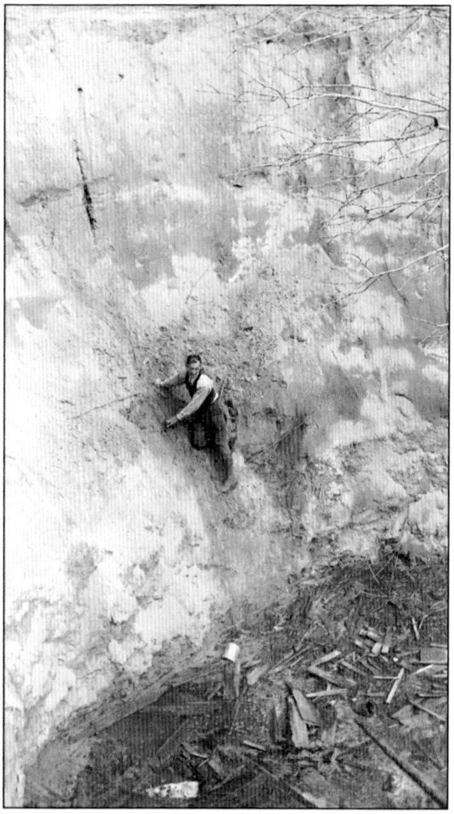

Steve Byrd awoke to the rumblings of the ground collapsing on February 9, 1936, when this "sink" formed on his farm, 5 miles west of Jasper. A shelter, two Model T Ford trucks, some lumber, and a tree were lost in the hole, but a relatively new Chevrolet truck was saved. The sink was about 90 feet deep and 40 feet in diameter. Since it was only about 20 feet from the house, the family home was moved farther away from the unstable ground. Byrd charged 10¢ admission per person to see the hole, which he used to help cover the expense of moving his home. Water half-filled the hole and receded again to reveal a cave. Louis Bembry and his brother, John, entered the cave to try to find the cause of the sink. (Both Florida Photographic Collection, State Archives of Florida.)

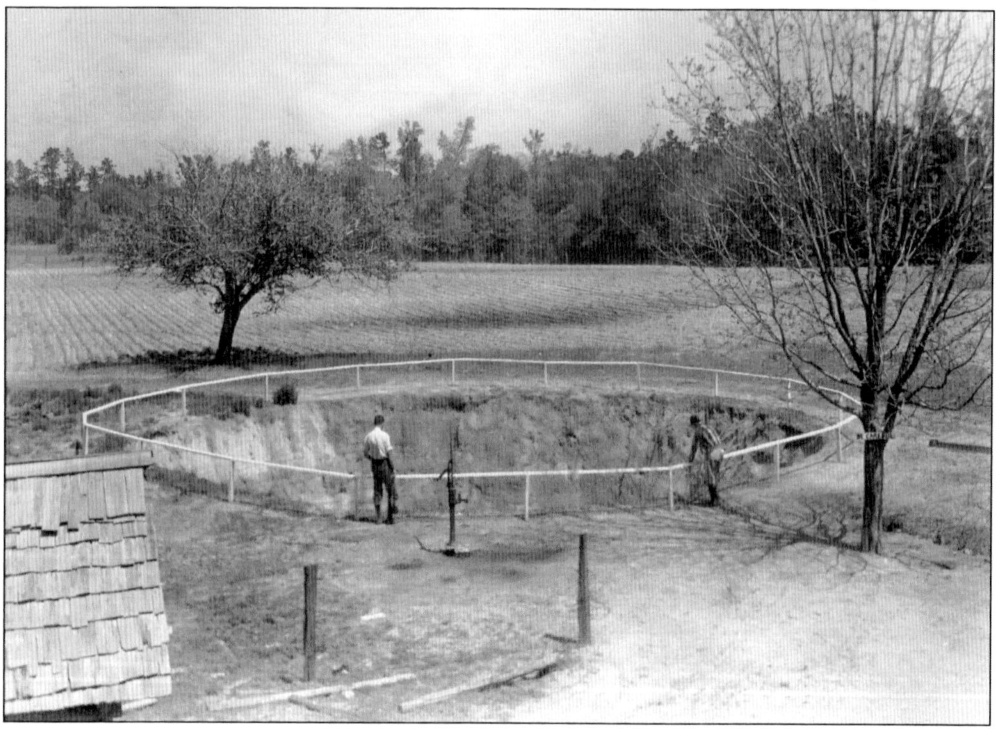

Two

Agriculture

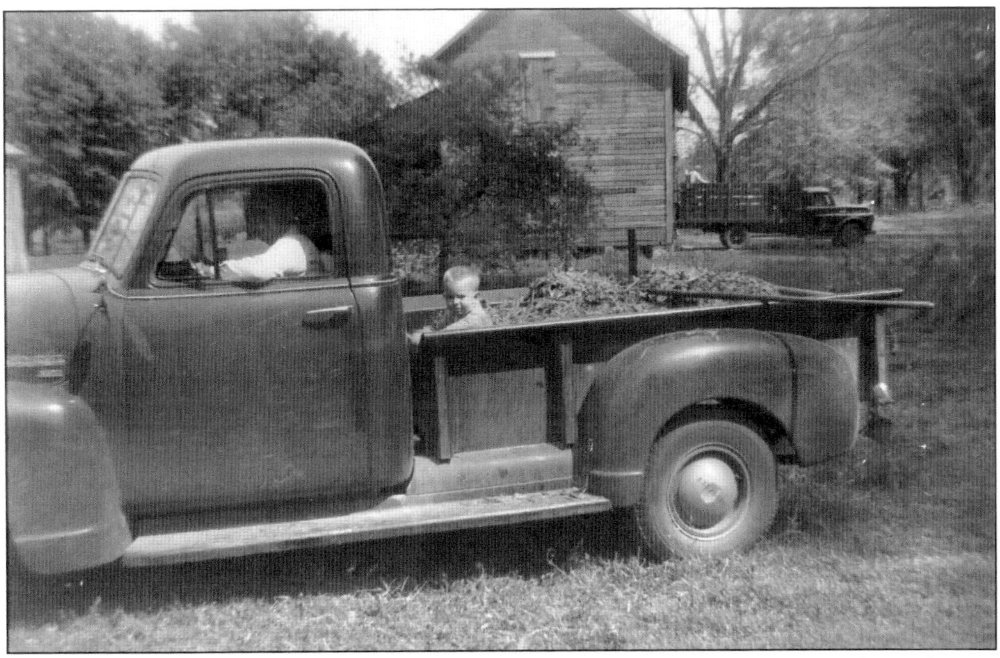

This 1950s photograph shows the Adams Farm, located on the old Adams Farm Road, now known as County Road 249. Robert Stanley Adams Jr. is seen driving the truck, and his son, Robert Stanley Adams III, is in the back of the truck. The day was clearly perfect for work—a rake and yard clippings fill the back of the truck. In the background of the photograph, a worker can be seen loading tobacco from the barn into the back of another truck. (Cliff Adams.)

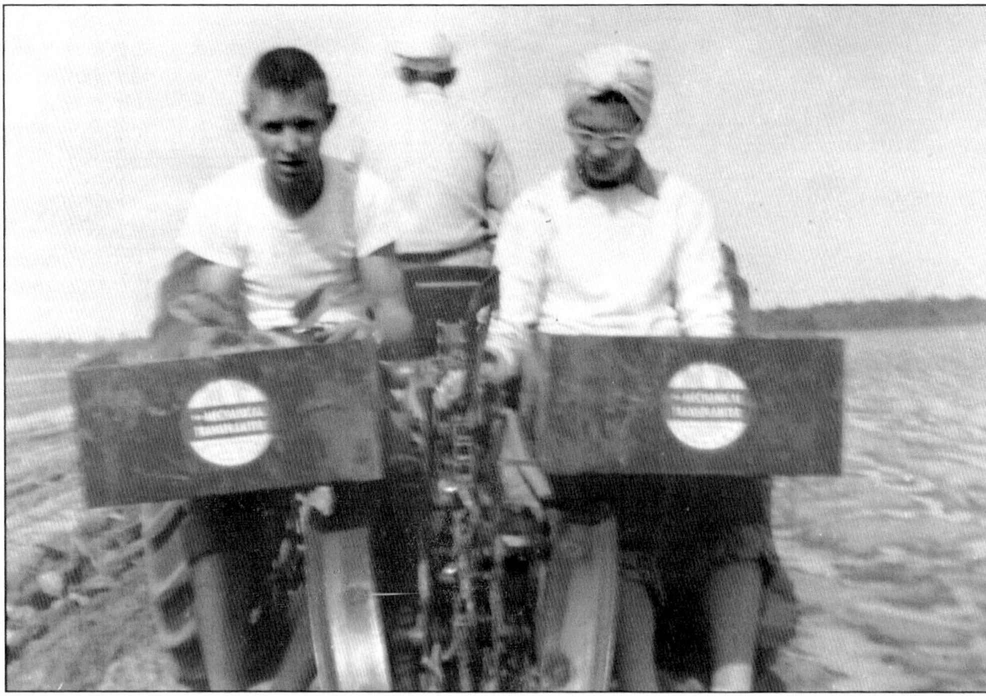

This 1959 photograph (above) shows citizens of Hamilton County planting tobacco in a local field. Joda William Newsome is driving the tractor, and Randolph King and Joann Newsome Knight are shown operating the seed dispensers. The photograph below shows Raymond Fields of Bellville pulling tobacco from the fields with a pair of mules in 1947. A sled of tobacco was pulled behind the mules, Teabo and Dolly, to the barns to be dried and cured. A sled was often constructed of a wooden plank with skids attached instead of wheels, so it would not bog down and become stuck in fields that did not drain well. The farmer would pull the sled between the rows of tobacco, harvesting the leaves as he went along. (Above, Florida Photographic Collection, State Archives of Florida; below, Evelyn Singletary.)

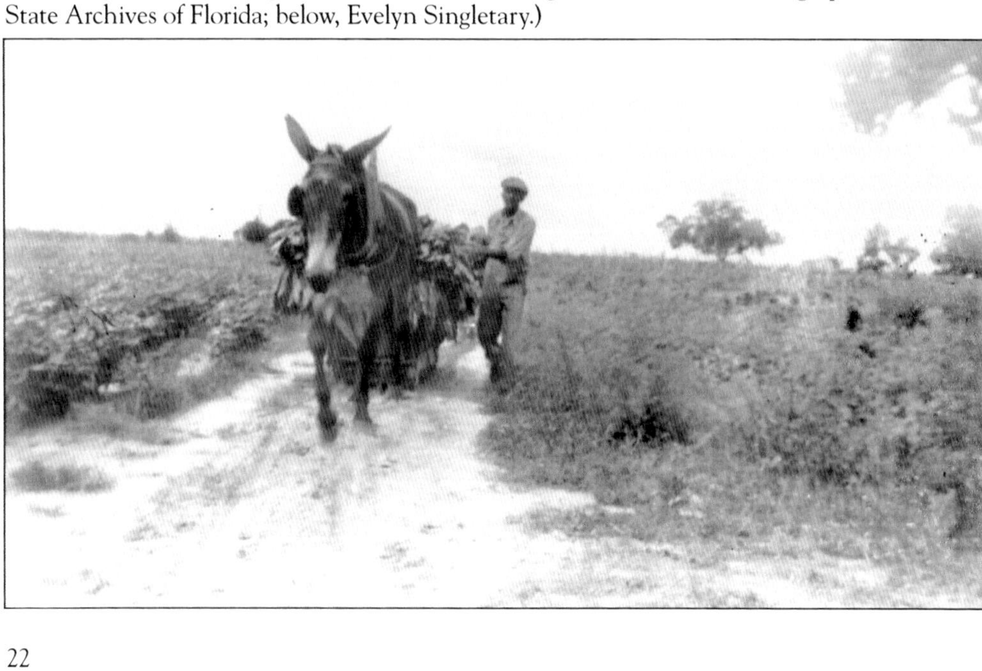

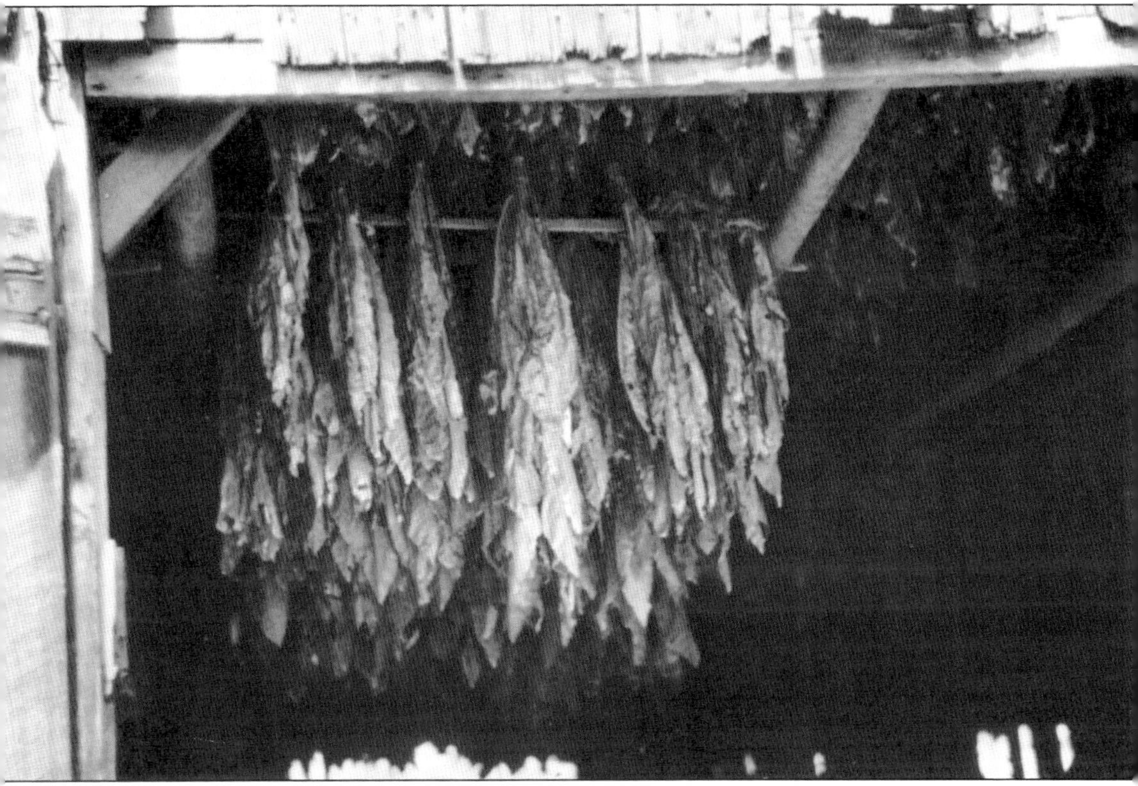

This 1960s postcard depicts hung tobacco drying in a stick barn. Although not located in Hamilton County, it is representative of the tobacco and barns in this area. It is said John Bradshaw should be given the credit for planting the first tobacco in Hamilton County in the early 1900s. The sandy loam soil found in much of the county is crucial for the growing of tobacco. An unusual bright-colored tobacco is produced when plants are grown here and is then sold for a premium price at markets. In 1947, more than 3,000 acres in Hamilton County were planted with tobacco, and it was estimated that more than three million pounds of tobacco leaf would be produced and sent to market. (Author's collection.)

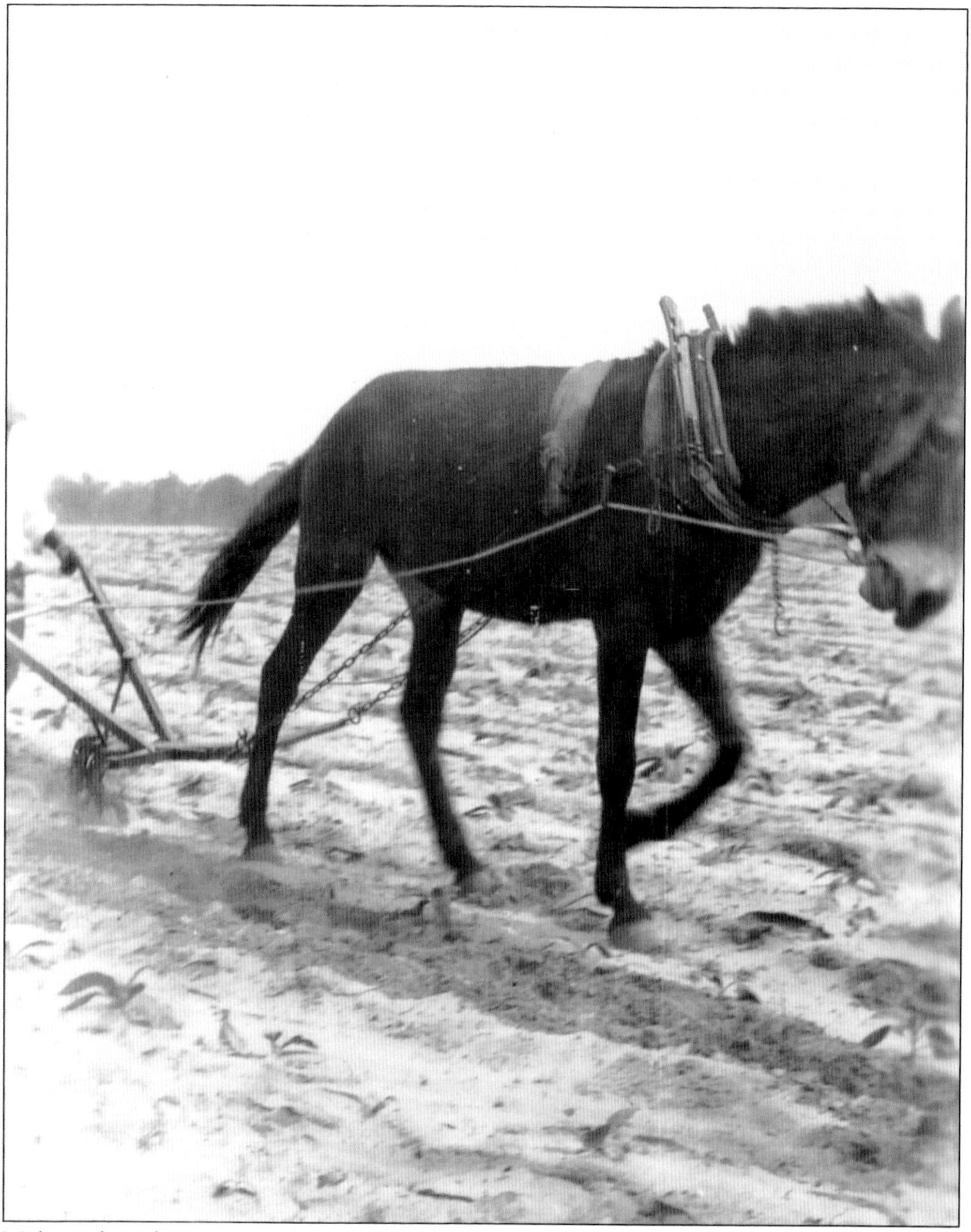

Mules such as this one owned by Stanley Adams Sr. were often utilized to help prepare fields for planting. In this mid-1940s photograph, an unidentified person is holding a plow as the mule pulls it. In order for the rows to be straight, one must walk behind the mule holding the farming implements in place. Although many mules had names, the name of this one has been lost to history. (Cliff Adams.)

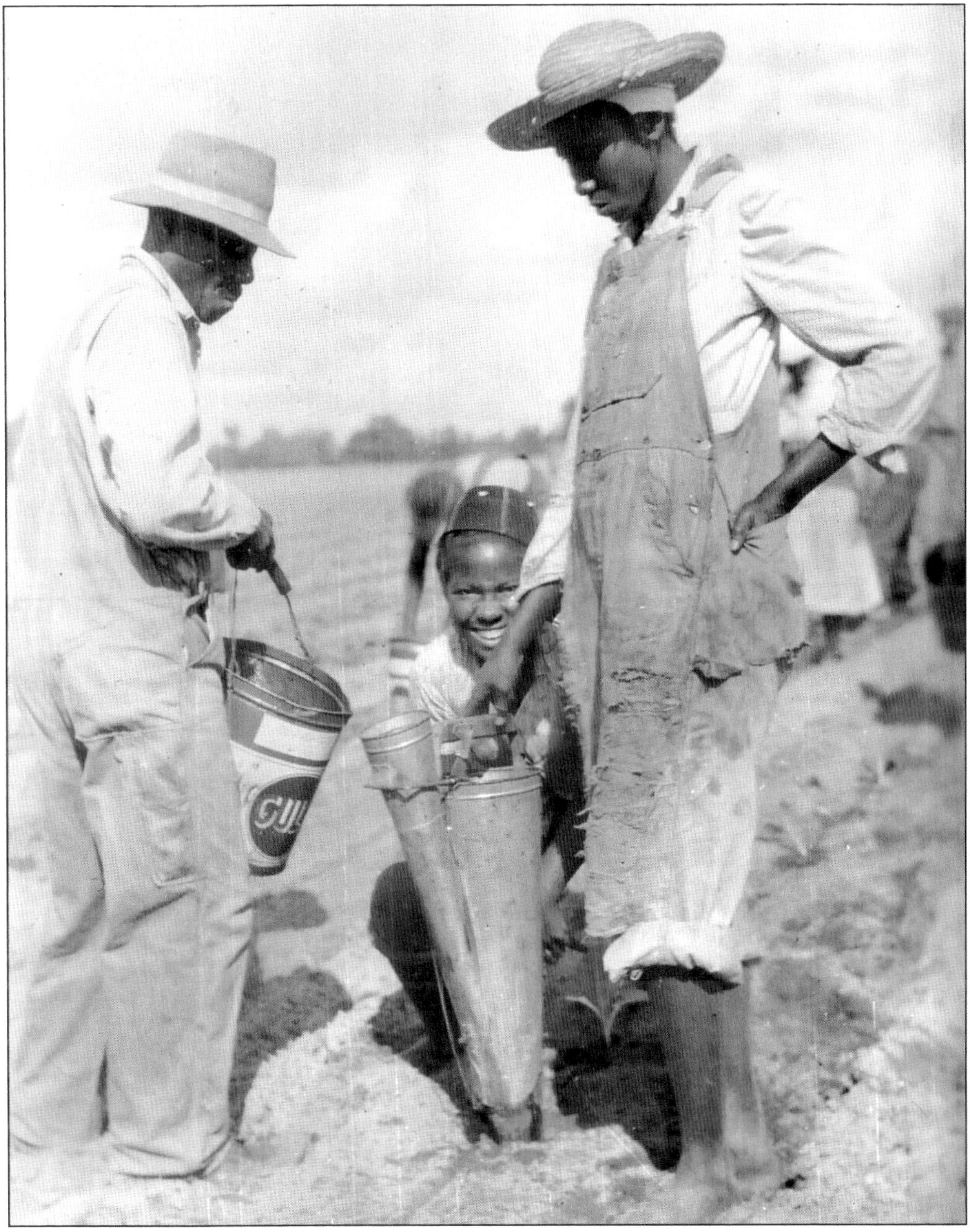

Dorsey Bell Walker (right), a sharecropper on the Adams Farm in the mid-1940s, and two assistants work with a tobacco plant transplanter. This device was used to transplant small tobacco plants from the growth bed to the field, where they would complete the growing cycle and be harvested. (Cliff Adams.)

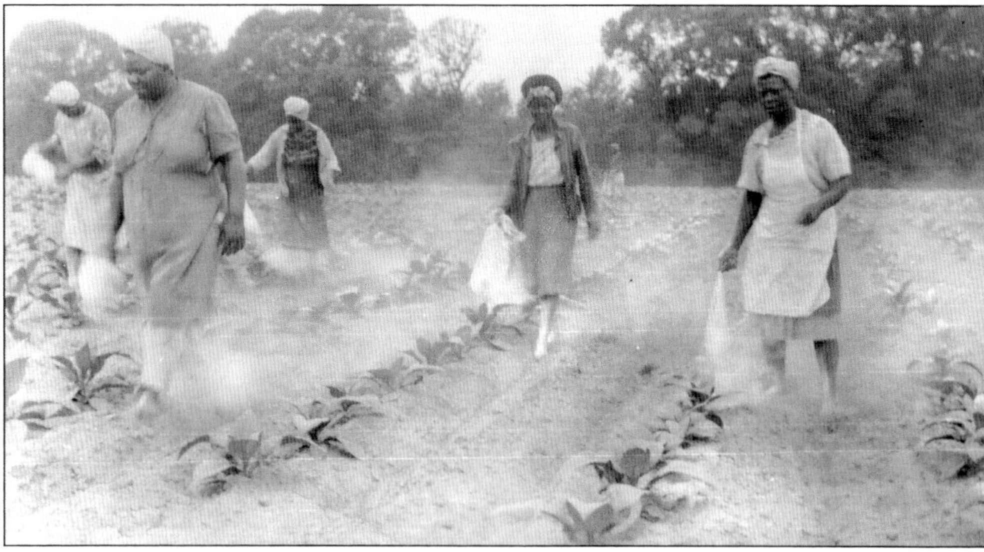

Because of the large number of insects that would attack tobacco, it was necessary to dust the tobacco regularly. Mixed powdered poisons were placed in the middle of squares of tobacco bed cloth, and the corners were pulled up to make small pouches. Shown here are several women dusting the tobacco plants. In the 1940s and 1950s, little was known about the effects poison might have on a person's health. (Cliff Adams.)

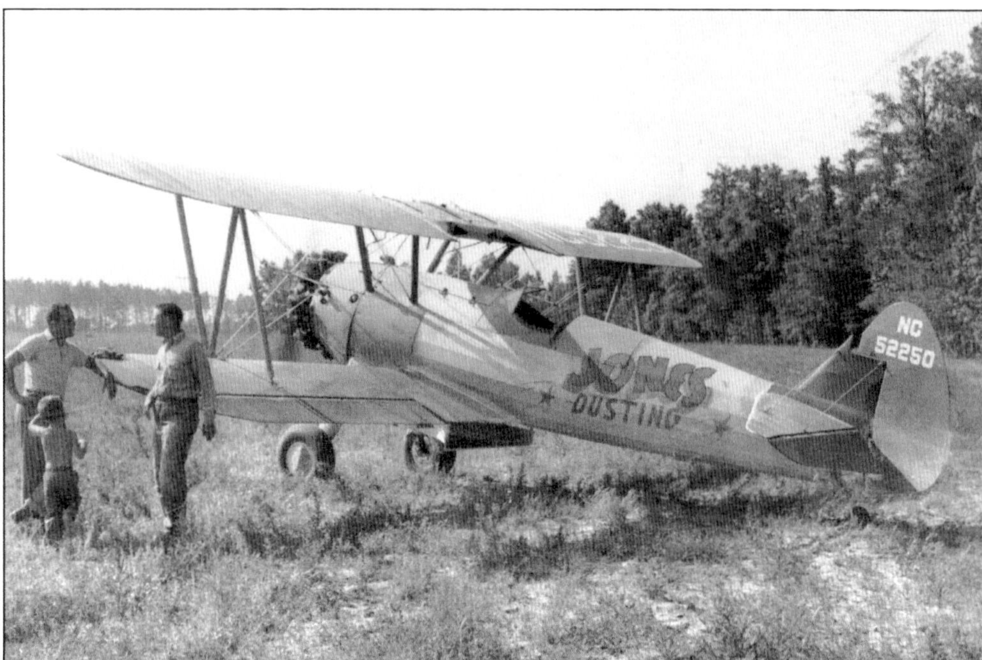

Crop-dusting planes were often used by farmers with large fields to treat. A few niche pilots would complete the job for a fee. Crop dusters needed a safe place to land the plane in order to refill with pesticides. In this 1950s photograph, Cliff Adams is shown looking at the plane while his father, Stanley Adams Jr. (left), and the pilot discuss matters. (Cliff Adams.)

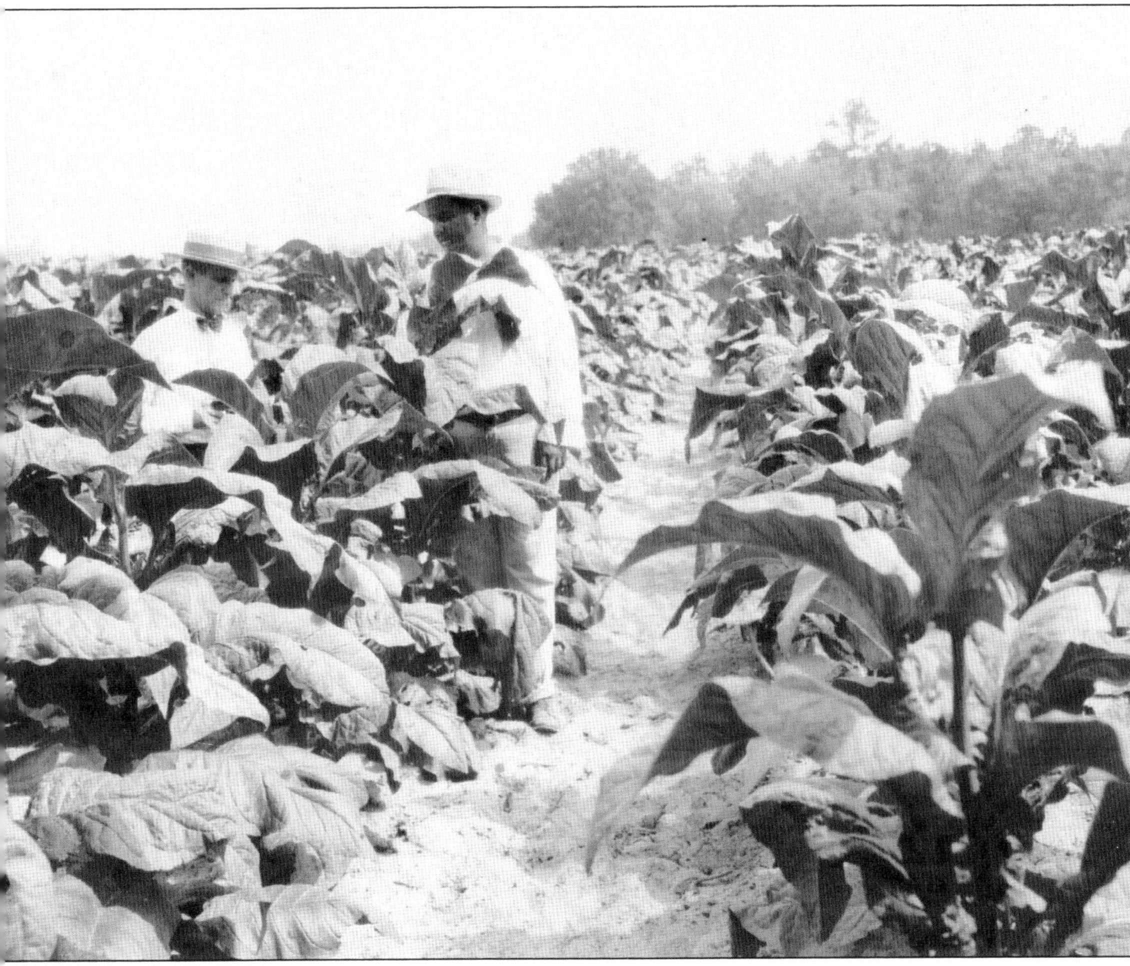

Tobacco must be cropped at precisely the right time in order to be curable and therefore usable. The two men shown here are inspecting the tobacco leaves for maturity, health issues, and insects. On the right is Robert Stanley Adams Sr., a prominent farmer in Hamilton County, but the man on the left is unidentified. (Cliff Adams.)

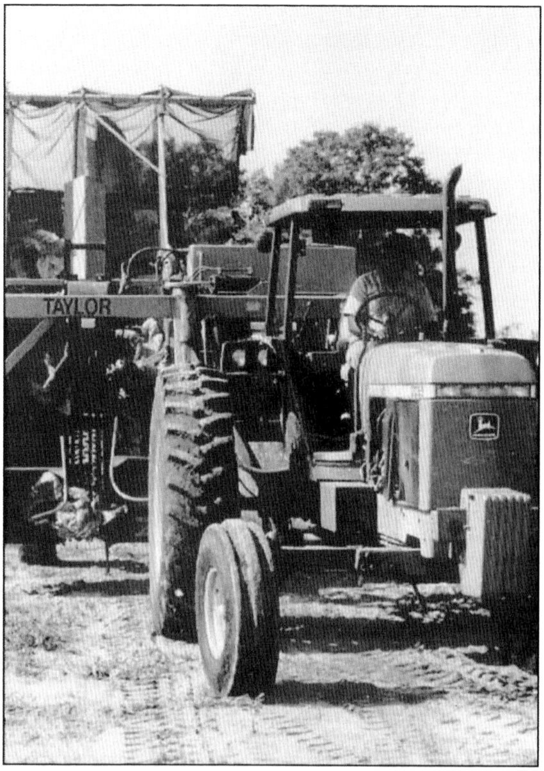

The four photographs from 1985 on these pages show some of the important steps in processing tobacco. The harvester, a sophisticated piece of farming equipment, is driven to the field to harvest the tobacco. Rather than dozens of farm workers harvesting the tobacco by hand, a harvester can accomplish in a single day what would otherwise have taken days. The man on the harvester is Willie Lee, a hand on the locally owned Deas Farm. (Marian Deas.)

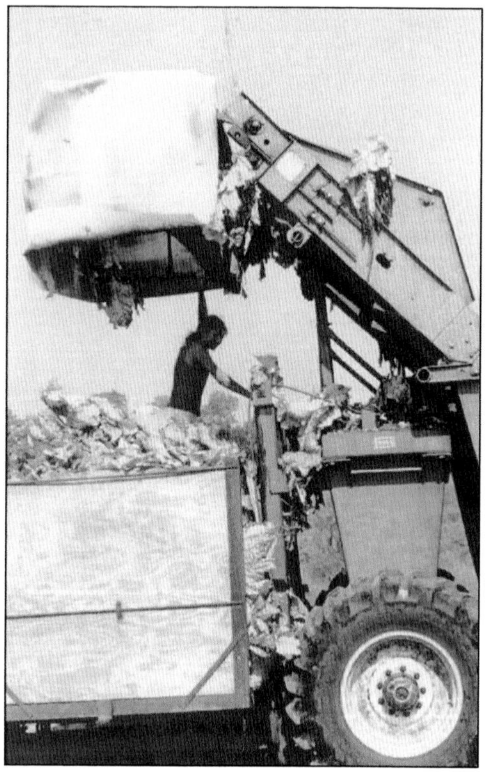

Once in the tobacco field, the harvester is adjusted to cut the proper number of leaves from the tobacco plant. The leaves are then transferred to a trailer to be transported to the tobacco barn. Shown here is Stacey Wynn, keeping the tobacco leaves straight as they go into the trailer to facilitate easier unloading at the barn. (Marian Deas.)

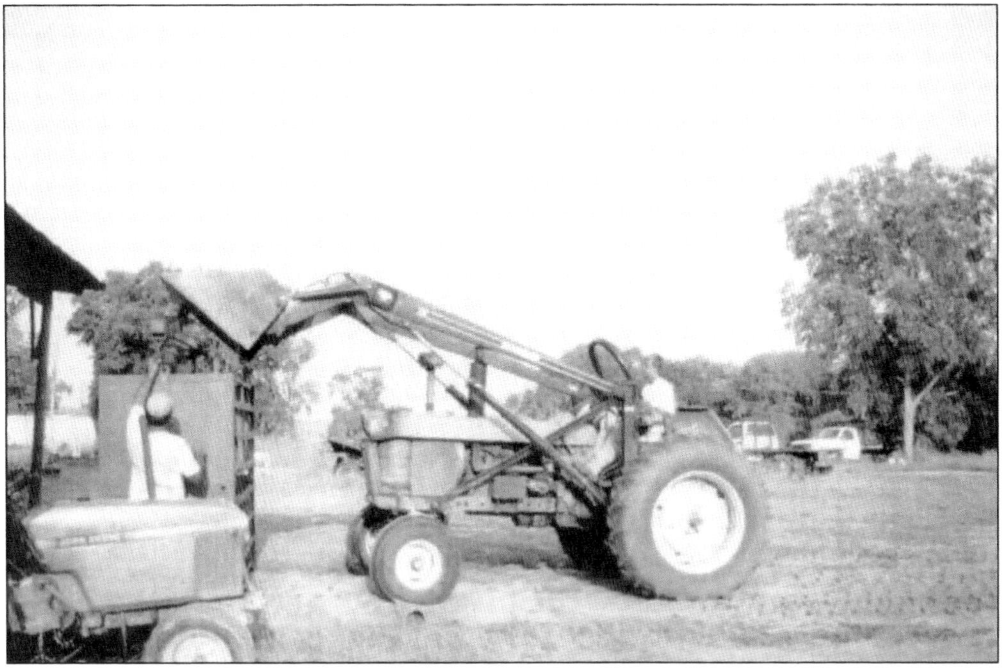

Dusty Cone uses a tractor to carry tobacco to the barn for curing, which can make or break the ability of tobacco to sell. Fire-cured tobacco is hung in barns where hardwood fires smolder continuously for three days to 10 weeks to produce tobacco low in sugar and high in nicotine for pipe tobacco, chewing tobacco, and snuff. Flue-cured tobacco is hung in barns with external fire boxes that allow heat into the barn but no smoke. It takes about a week to produce tobacco low in sugar and medium to high in nicotine for cigarettes. (Marian Deas.)

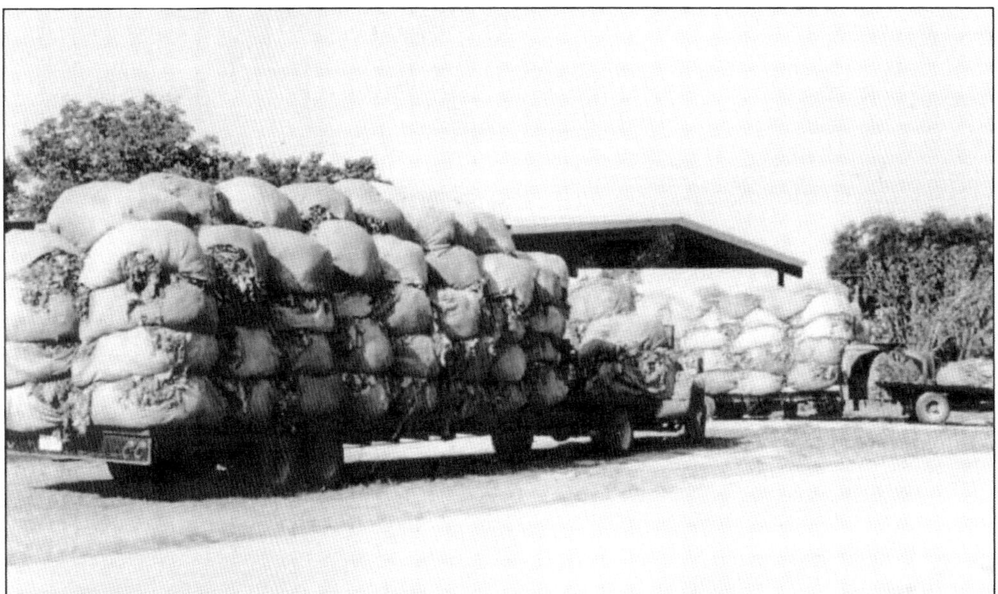

A good year of tobacco cultivation is always evident in the amount of tobacco being hauled to the market sales. These trucks at the Deas Farm are loaded and ready for market, where the bundles will go home with the highest bidder. (Marian Deas.)

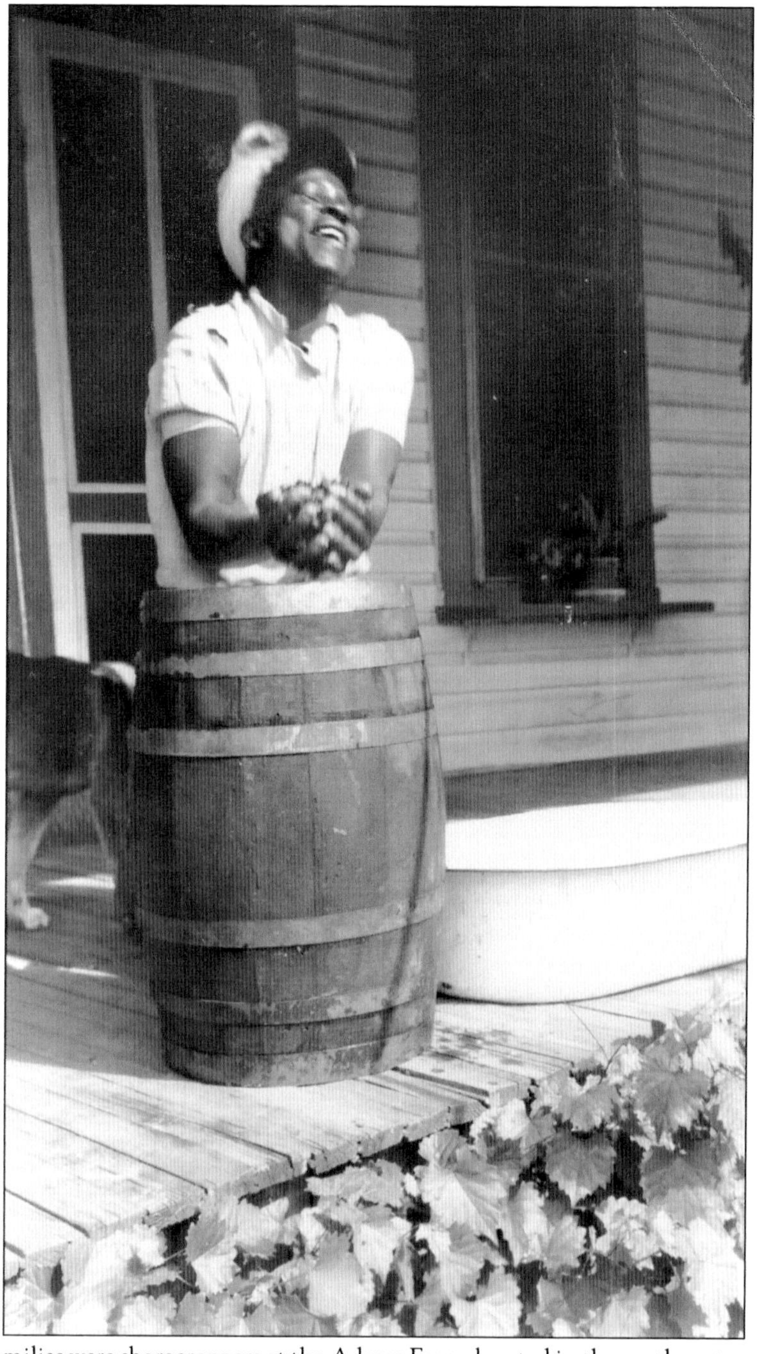

Nearly 40 families were sharecroppers at the Adams Farm, located in the southwestern area of the county, living on the farm that consisted of hundreds of acres. Robert Stanley Adams Sr. provided a pleasant community for the sharecroppers who helped him tend his land. A commissary and housing were provided for them. Throughout the years, sharecropping has diminished, and the farm is run solely by members of the family. Shown here is a member of one of the sharecropping families, Rachael, taking a break after working in the fields all day. Her last name is unknown. (Cliff Adams.)

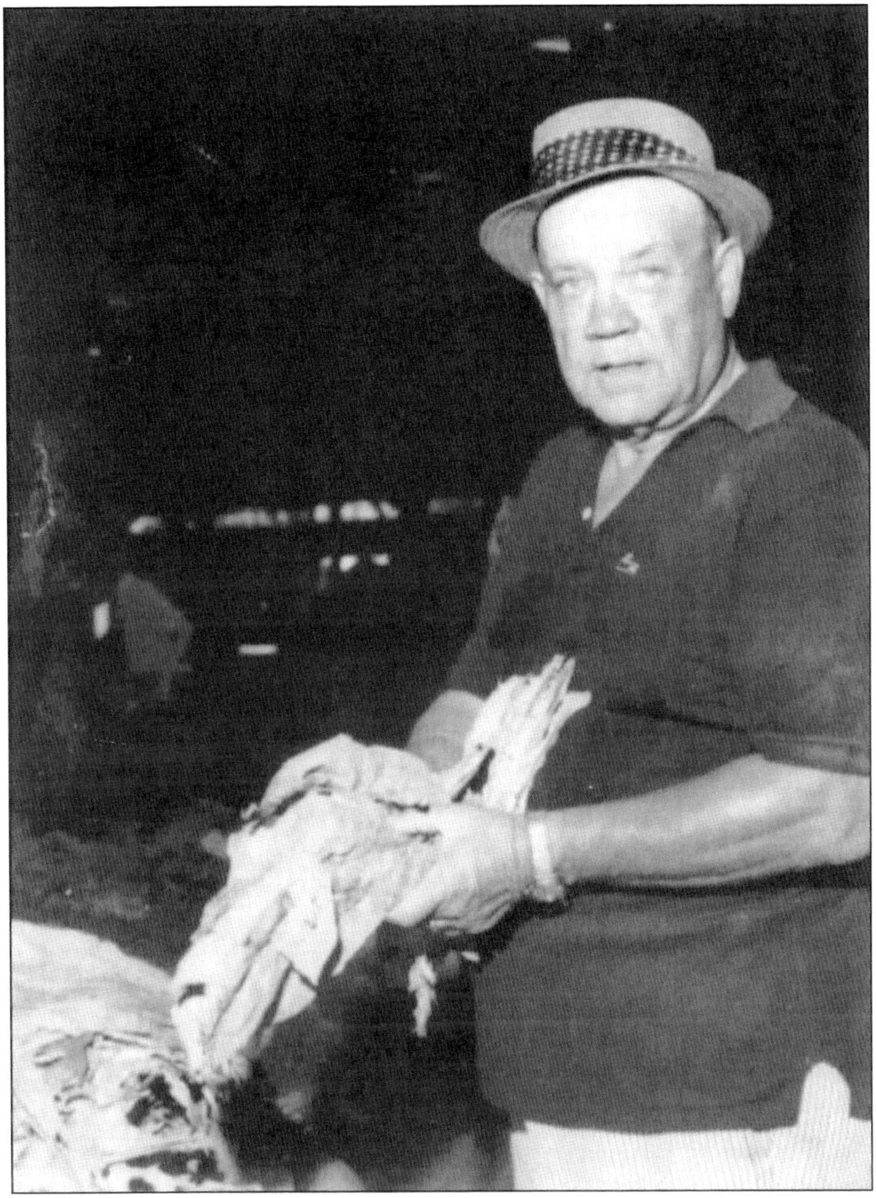

Ernest Stamps "Butch" Chandler Sr. and his brothers became experts in the planting, growing, curing, and selling of tobacco in North Carolina. In 1929, some enterprising folks in Hamilton County thought the area could benefit from the growth of tobacco but had no idea how to go about the process. Ponce de Leon Sandlin, president of the Hamilton County Bank, heard of the Chandler boys and their knowledge of tobacco. He arranged for Kenneth Chandler to come to town in 1929 as a "demonstrator," and Butch followed in 1932. For years, the brothers worked as demonstrators. Later Butch Chandler became an auctioneer. In the 1940s, he was instrumental in establishing the Hamilton County Farmers Co-Operative Tobacco Market, and in 1947, he helped build two of the warehouses. When his health became questionable, after many years of growing tobacco on his own farm in Hamilton County, Chandler turned it over to his son, Stamps. Chandler married Virginia Bridges on June 8, 1940. He passed away two years after they celebrated their 50th anniversary. (William S. Mitchell IV.)

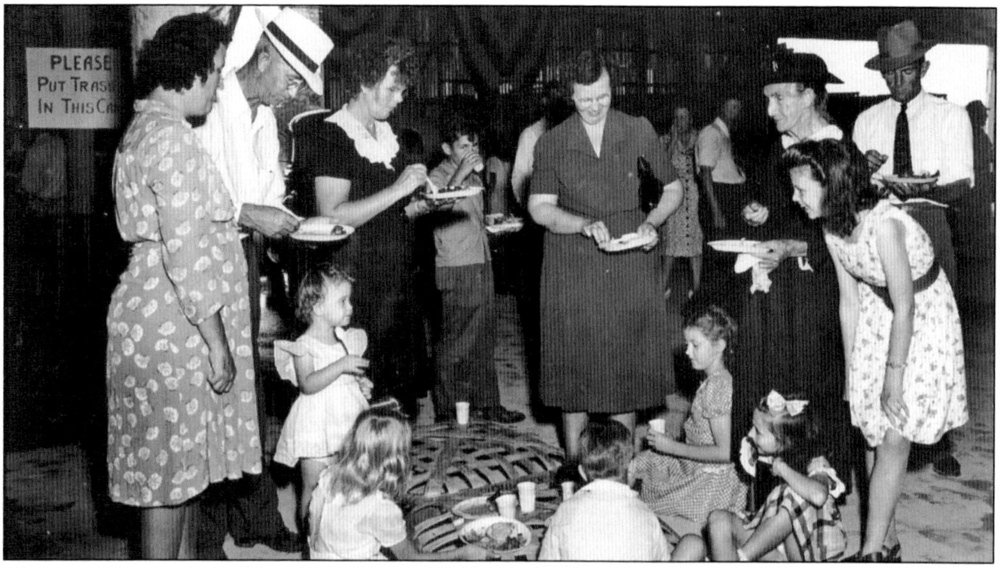

The warehouses of the Hamilton County Tobacco Corporation were dedicated on July 19, 1947. J. T. Bridges was chairman of the festivities, with Judge Hal W. Adams as master speaker of the ceremonies. A double-header baseball game was played after a barbeque meal served by the Ladies Auxiliary Club. In the evening, the VFW sponsored a dance in the warehouse. In the pictures, several citizens enjoy dinner and camaraderie (above), while eight-month-old Mary Odum finishes her meal on the floor of the warehouse (below). O. T. Hobgood and Joe Wilkins leased Warehouse No. 1, and Kenneth C. Chandler and Ernest Stamps "Butch" Chandler leased Warehouse No. 2. Butch Chandler auctioned his first pile of tobacco to Charlie Day of Asheville, North Carolina. He operated his warehouses for 38 years until 1984, when he sold them to Ray Doris, of Gallatin, Tennessee. Doris operated a window manufacturing plant, Energy Savings Products (ESP), in the warehouses until he moved to a larger location. (Both Florida Photographic Collection, State Archives of Florida.)

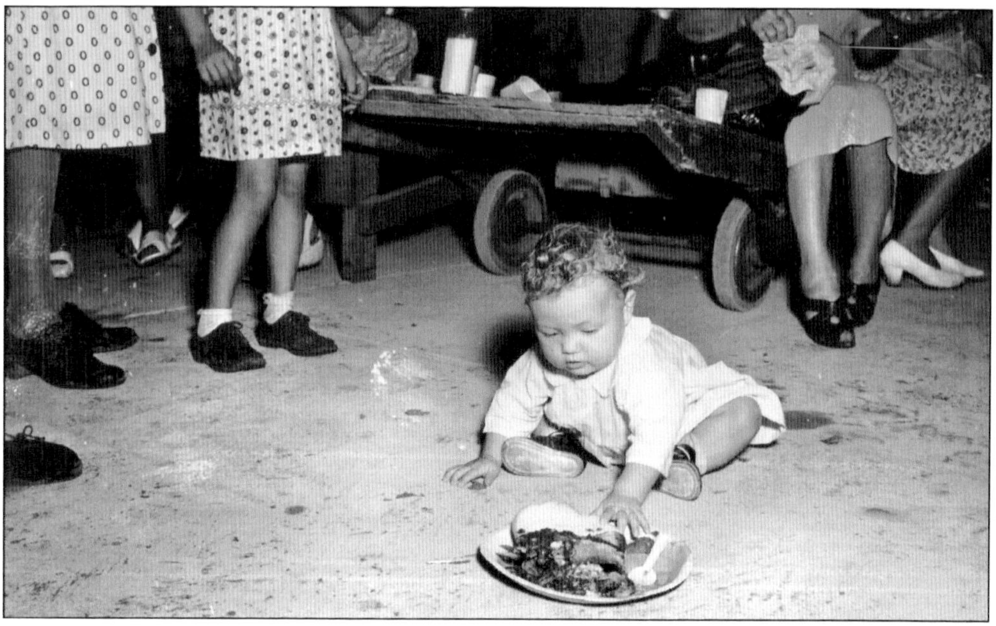

Marking the dedication of the new tobacco warehouses in 1947, a contest was held for the "Tobacco Queen" of the Hamilton Market. In the picture at right, Dorothy Ann Hay is holding some golden cigarette leaf tobacco after being crowned Tobacco Queen. She is fourth from the right in the lower picture of some of the 17 contestants. Her father, Ralph Hay, was a timber and turpentine contractor for the railroad and the Jacksonville Naval Air Station. Her mother, Lura Celeste Cone, taught school in Hamilton and Putnam County schools. The Hays were interred in Riverside Cemetery in White Springs—he in 1966, and she in 1971. Dorothy Ann and her husband, Hubert Buckley, live in Gainesville, Florida, and have two children. (Both Florida Photographic Collection, Florida State Archives.)

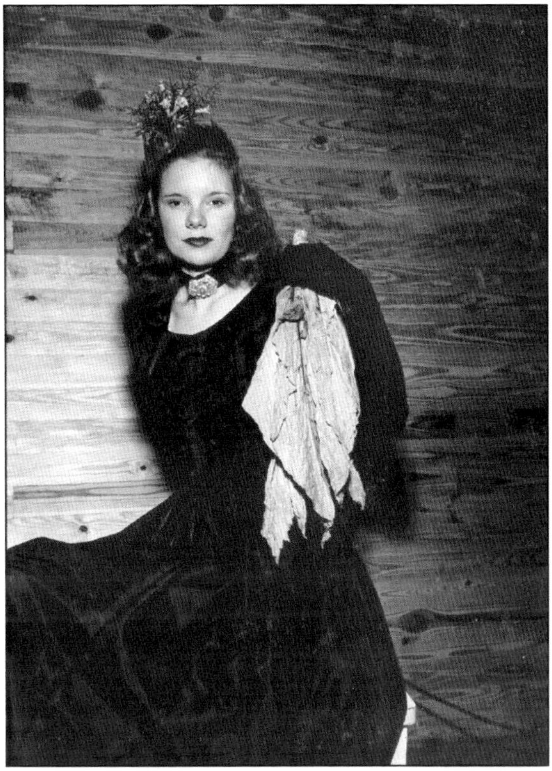

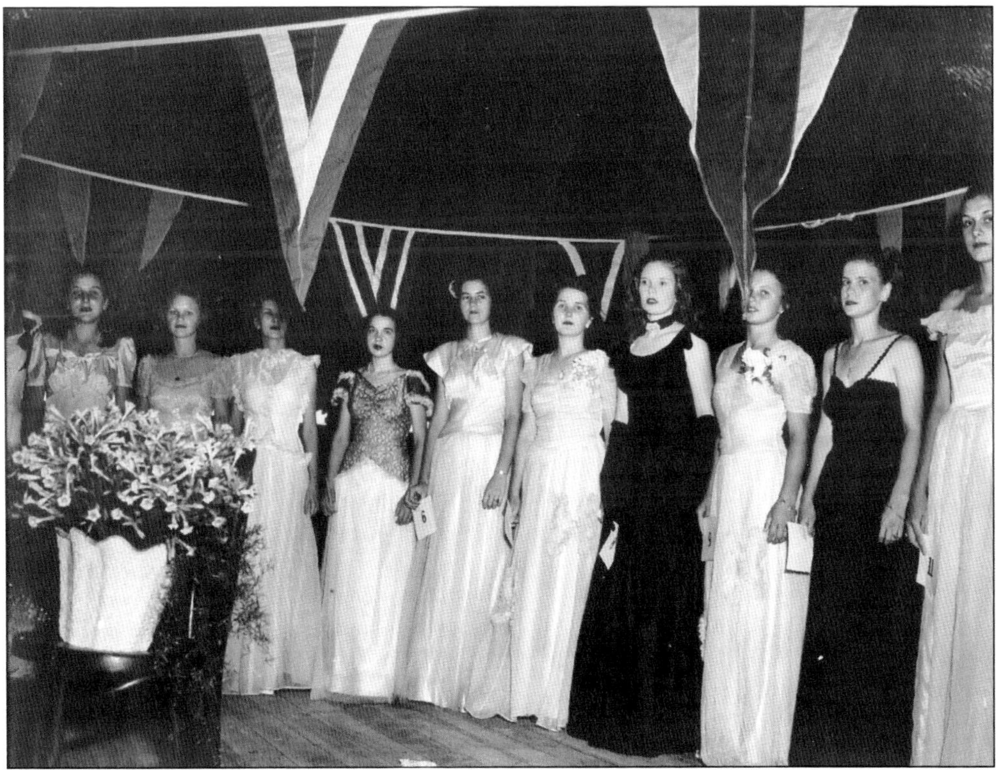

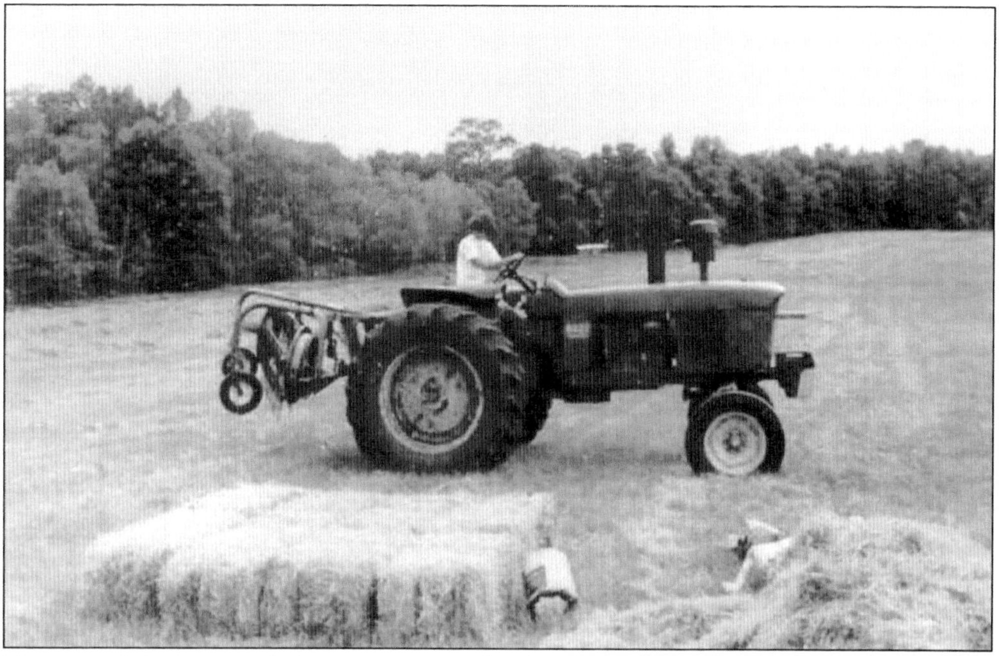

Hay can only be harvested when it is a certain height—typically 14 to 18 inches high. The time it takes for hay to reach the proper height depends on the amount of rain an area receives. Shown is Sylvia Deas Cone, daughter of James and Marian Deas, as a young girl working in a hay field. She married Gary Cone, and they have three children. (Marian Deas.)

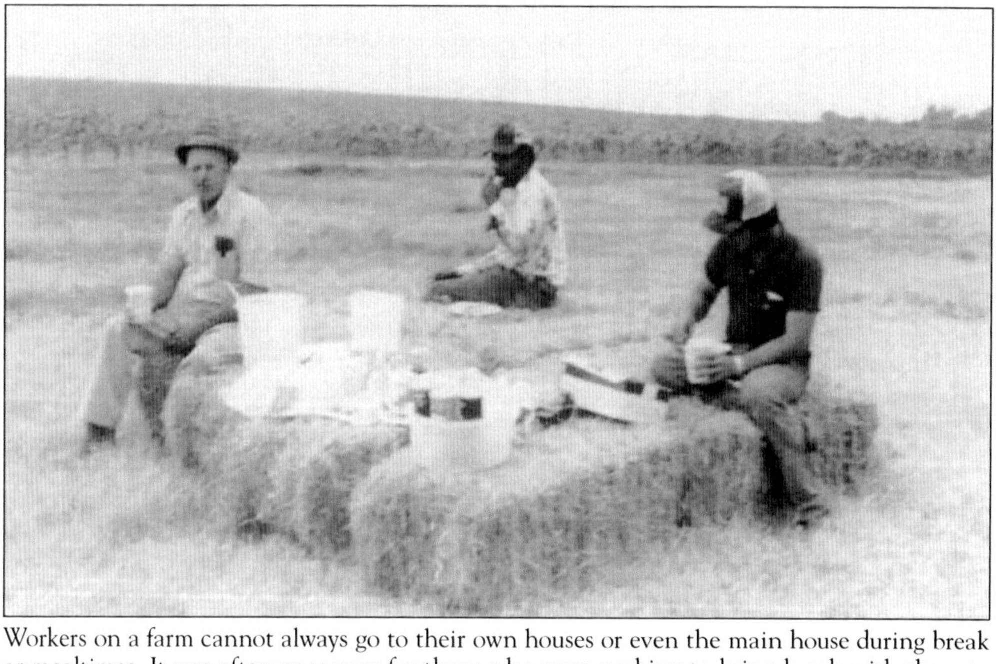

Workers on a farm cannot always go to their own houses or even the main house during break or mealtimes. It was often necessary for those who were working to bring lunch with them to the field. Lunches commonly consisted of leftovers from dinner the night before or sandwiches. Shown in this late-1970s photograph are, from left to right, James Deas, Bill Graham, and Gary Cone enjoying their lunch. (Marian Deas.)

In the 1930s, Charlie B. Harrison and M. A. V. Kennedy of Ware County, Georgia, purchased the turpentine operation and still east of Jasper. C. H. Coulter managed Kennedy Still until 1946, when John Davis, also from Ware County, became manager. In the 1940s, Harrison sold his share to Kennedy. Later his son, Cecil A. Kennedy, was designated the owner. It is now a planted pine tree farm and leased hunting preserve under the management of Waldo Kennedy, son of Cecil and Pauline Kennedy. (Florida Photographic Collection, Florida State Archives.)

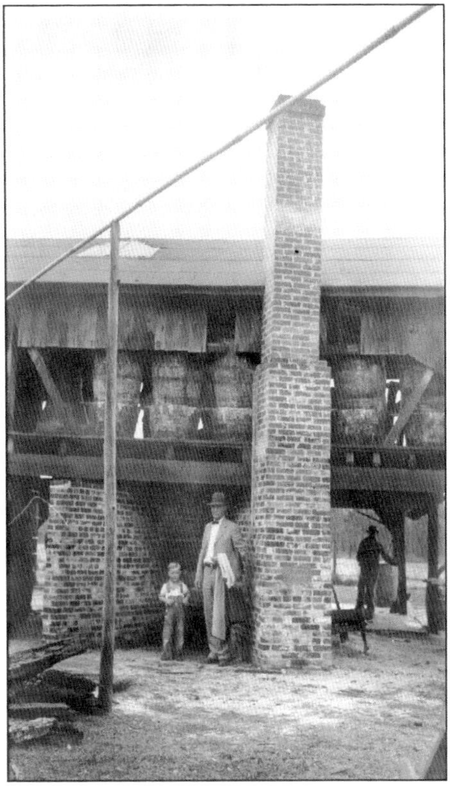

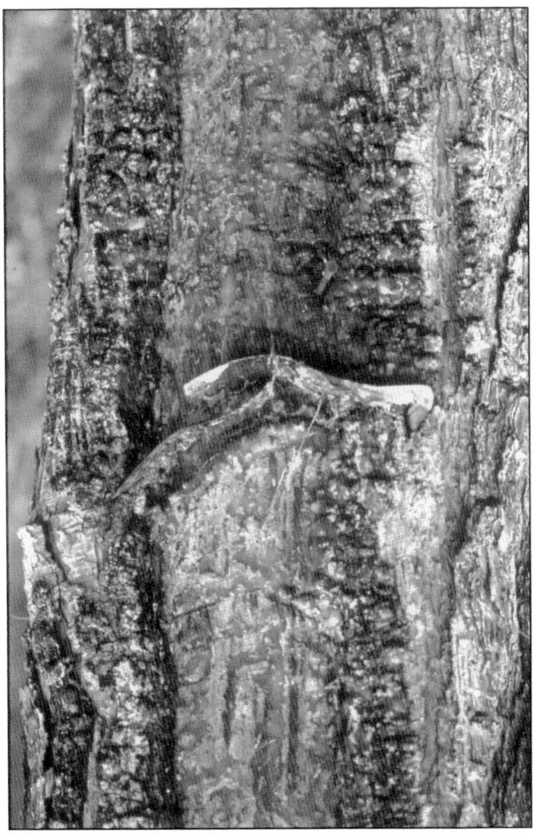

The turpentine or naval stores industry was important to Hamilton County in the 1920s and 1930s. Workers poured turpentine from cups fastened to trees into buckets, carried them back to the main still area, and poured the turpentine into large barrels for shipping. This 1981 photograph shows a tree that has been cut for a turpentine operation on Oliver Hunter's property. (Florida Photographic Collection, Florida State Archives.)

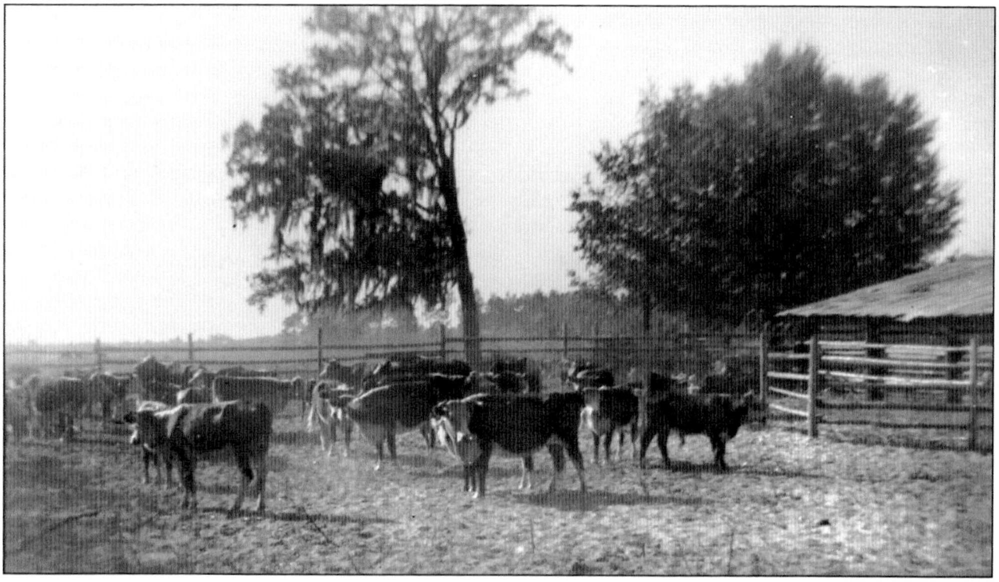

In 1846, the majority of agriculture in Hamilton County was cotton. By 1918–1919, due to rising prices of cultivation, the crop was replaced by tobacco. In 1975, county extension agent Rance Andrews determined Hamilton County had the highest market average of tobacco in Florida. The value of cattle in the county, such as these owned by Stanley Adams Jr., pictured in the early 1950s, was estimated to be nearly $1 million. (Cliff Adams.)

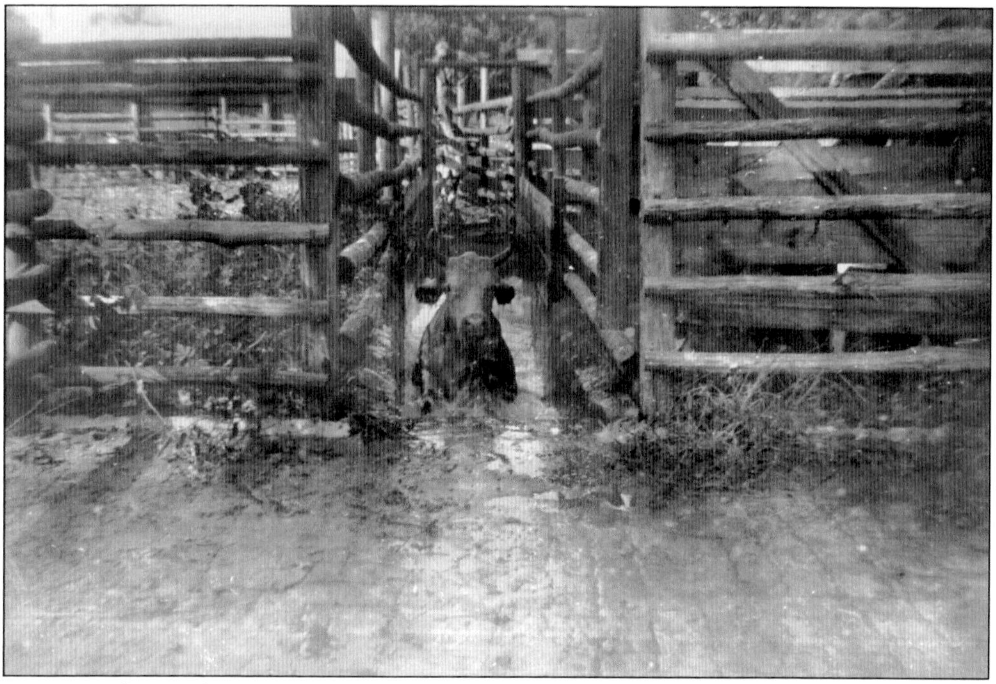

Numerous fleas, ticks, or mites on a cow could make the animal sick and useless. The county mandated that all cattle be dipped in pesticide. If a person's cattle were not dipped by the deadline, the cattle were confiscated, dipped in the county vat, and held on county property until the owner paid a fine and retrieved them. (Cliff Adams.)

The Adams Farm encompassed several hundred acres near County Road 249 in the southwestern area of the county. They grew tobacco and raised cattle and horses. Stanley Adams Jr. was born to Robert Stanley and Priscilla B. Bronston Adams, one of their three children. Here Stanley Adams Jr. is shown on the family farm with his favorite horse. (Cliff Adams.)

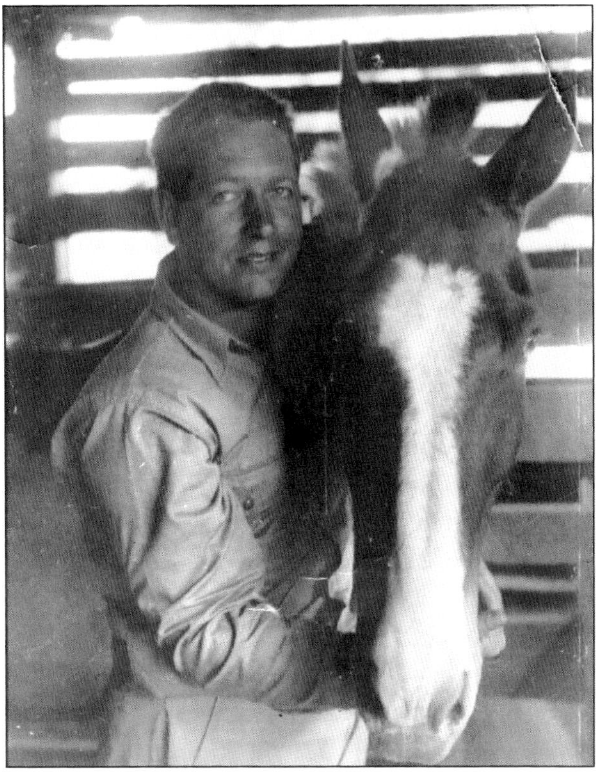

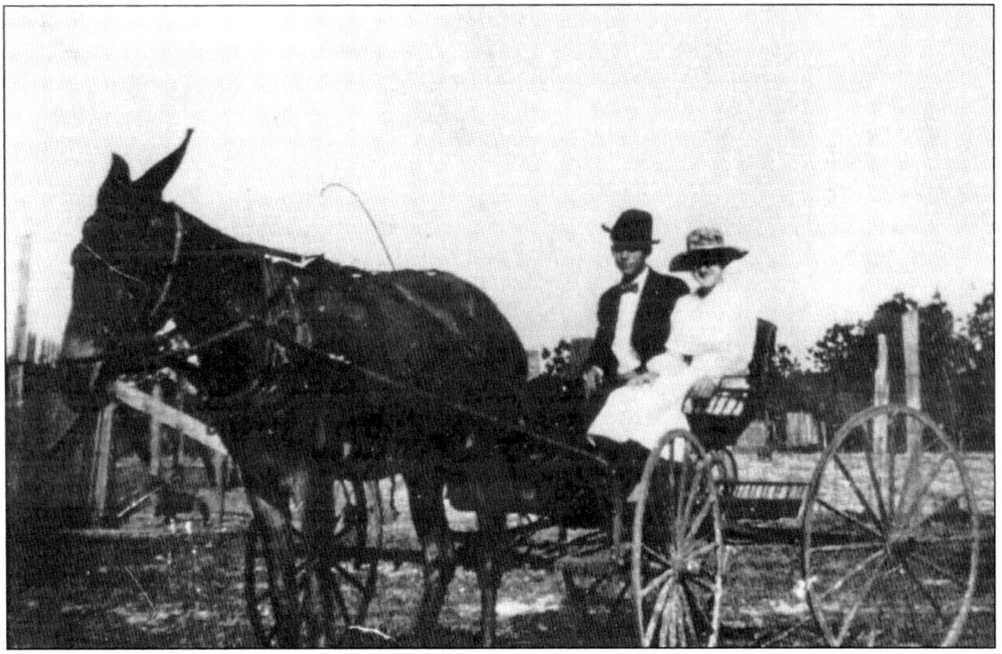

John Hall and Mellie Alderman Deas were married for 44 years before he died in 1960. For over half of their married life, they owned the same mule, Emma. With Emma, Deas planted and harvested 31 crops and raised all of his seven children. As can be seen, Emma enjoyed good health, only becoming ill three times during her lifetime. (Marian Deas.)

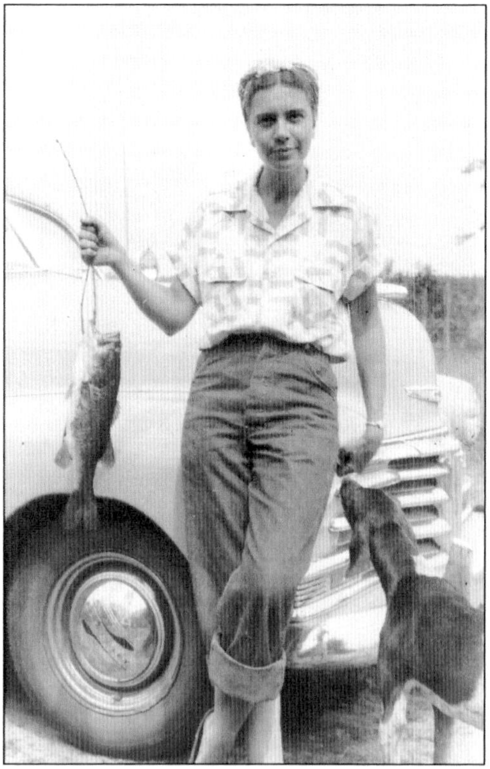

Women who live in the country are familiar with those activities that provide food and security for their families. Some women enjoy it; others simply perform the activities for the well-being of their families. In this 1950s photograph, Bette Wisenbaker Adams shows off a trophy catch from her day of fishing. (Cliff Adams.)

Hunting has always been a popular activity in Hamilton County. In 1911, a total of 35 structures in White Springs were destroyed because most of the white men were gone hunting when the fire began. The town was saved by the efforts of the black men who lived there. Here one can see that hunting was not limited to men only. Likely taken on the Adams Farm, this photograph shows Bette Adams (left) and Ms. Quattlebaum (right) hunting for quail with their pencil-tailed bird dogs. (Cliff Adams.)

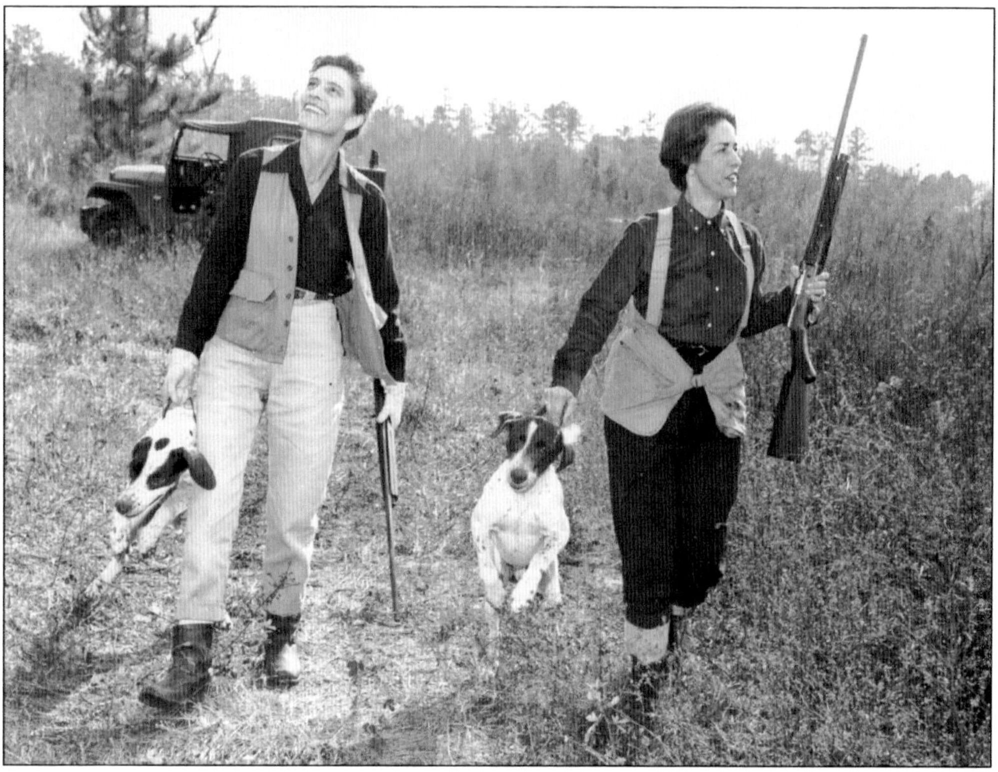

Three

Schools

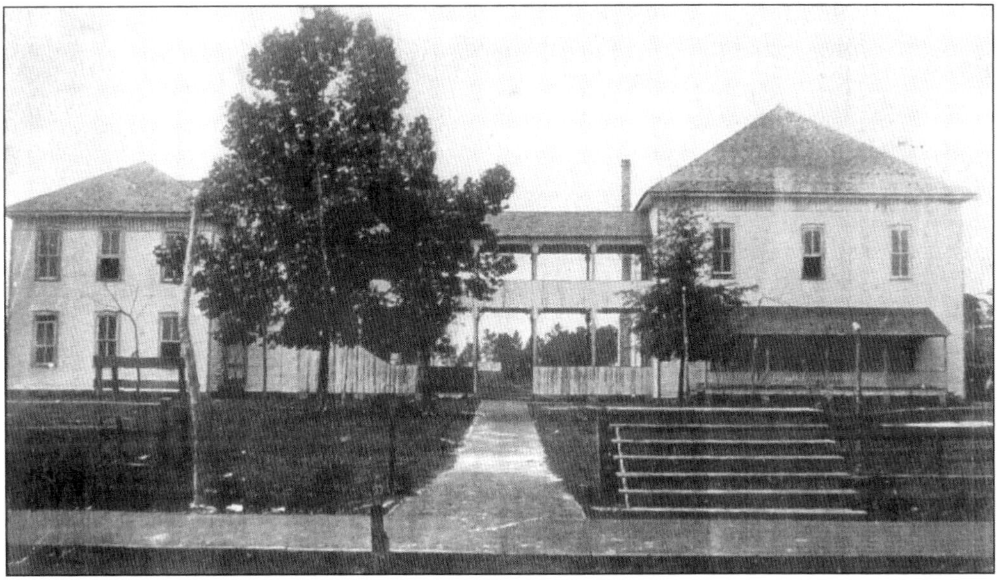

John Milton Guilliams founded the Jasper Normal Institute in 1890 on the site where the Woman's Club currently stands: 403 North West Sixth Avenue. Almost immediately upon its founding, the Jasper Normal Institute boasted a "large patronage" of students, having 55 graduates in 1896. Around 1898, the school was approved to provide "teacher education" to white students. By 1899, the school was in prime shape. The campus consisted of two "large, comfortable, two-story buildings" on 3 acres. Housed in the buildings were about 15 rooms, a library consisting of "several hundred useful volumes," a main chapel that would seat approximately 400 people, and a laboratory filled with a "liberal amount of physical and chemical apparatus." Guilliams had established a wide range of classes for students to attend, the highest being the Scientific Course and the Teachers' Course. Others included bookkeeping, shorthand, typewriting, telegraphy, commercial law, penmanship, and other courses "necessary to commercial work." There was also a music department with new pianos and classes in vocal music and elocution. The Jasper Normal Institute burned in 1925. (Marion Turner.)

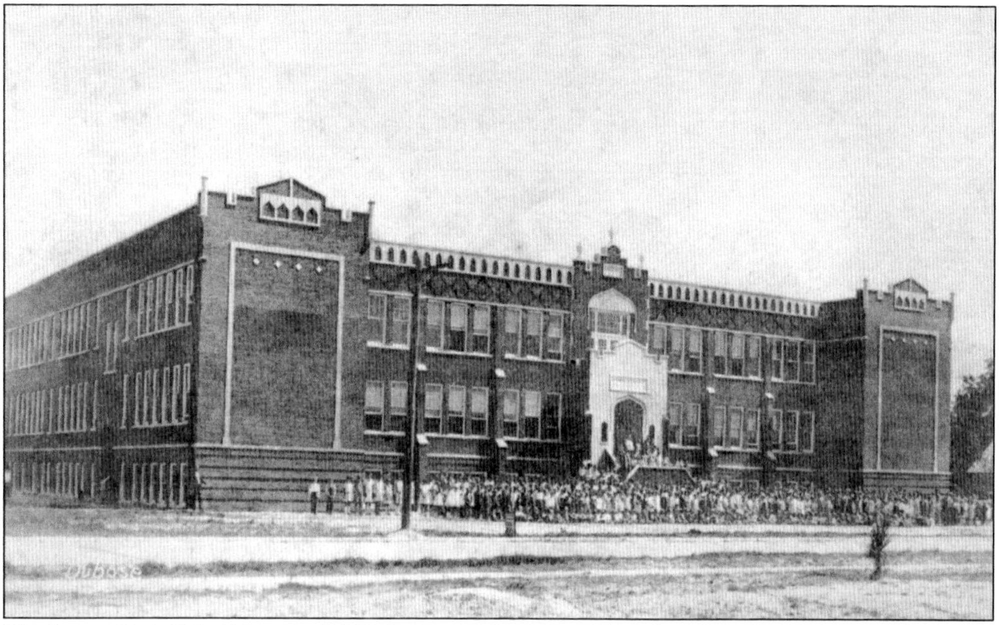

The Jasper High School was established about 1903 and combined with the Jasper Normal Institute. The institute prepared students to begin teaching immediately after graduating, while the high school was for college preparation. Jasper Normal Institute was discontinued about 1915. Ten years later, the high school burned, and classes were held anywhere possible until the completion of a new school at the corner of Northeast Second Avenue and Hatley Street. (Marion Turner.)

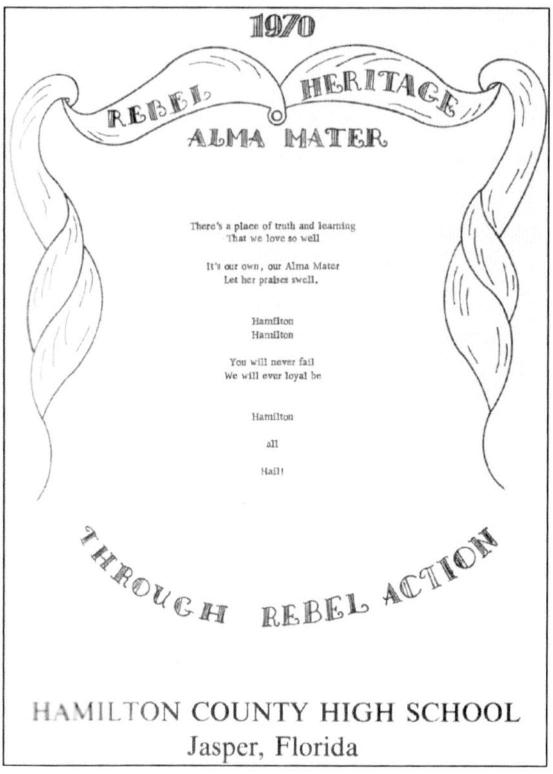

The Hamilton County High School, where the Rebels were the school mascot, was established in 1966 at the current location of the Hamilton County Annex Offices. Prior to that, it was Jasper High School, located where Bank of America is today. In 1970, the school changed the mascot from the Rebels to the Trojans. (Hamilton County High School.)

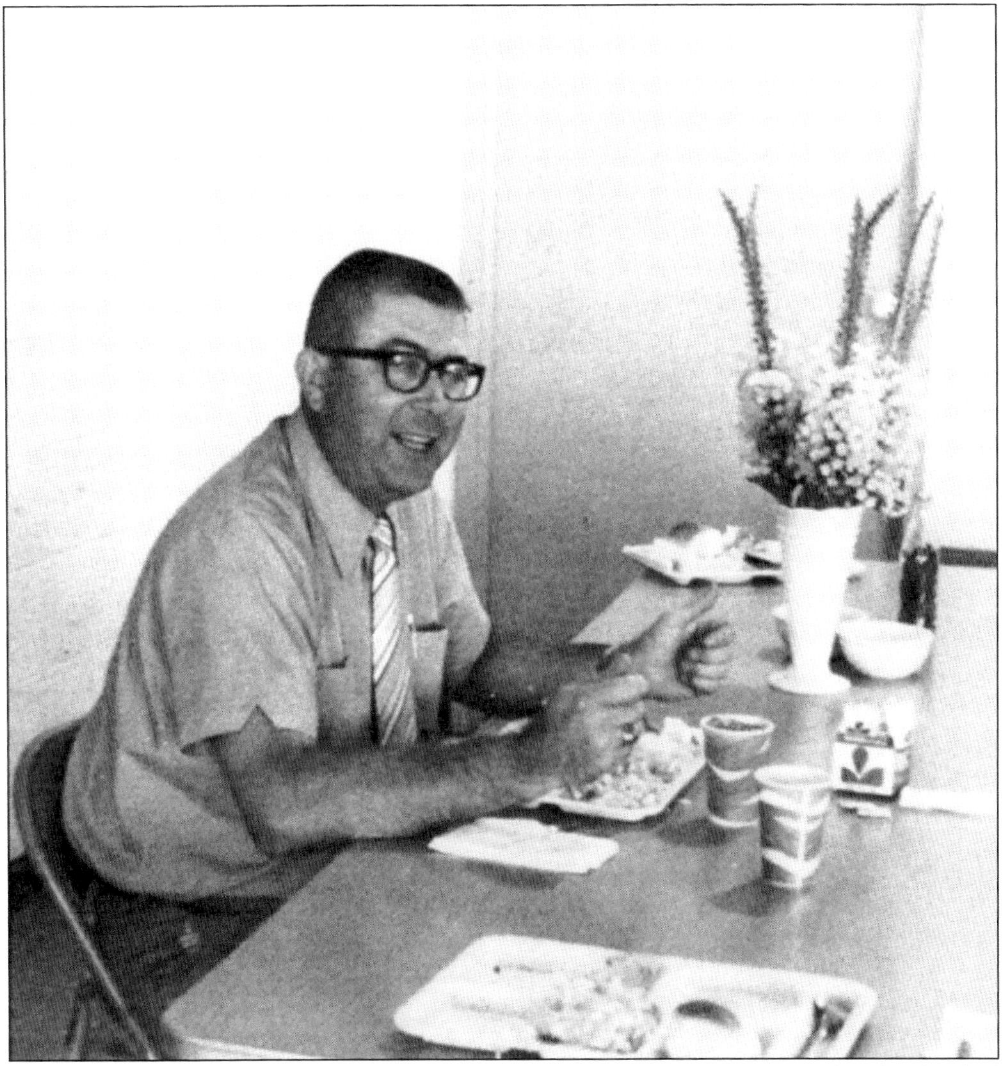

James "Jim" Coe and his wife, Jo, were active members in the Jasper Presbyterian Church. They had two children, Jamey and Nancy Jane. However, much of Coe's life was focused around the school system, as he felt education was very important. He served as a teacher, a guidance counselor, and a coach in the Hamilton County schools. During his educational career, he served in the U.S. Army during the Korean War. In the community, he was the president of the Lions Club. This 1974 photograph shows him eating lunch at Hamilton County High School. (Hamilton County High School.)

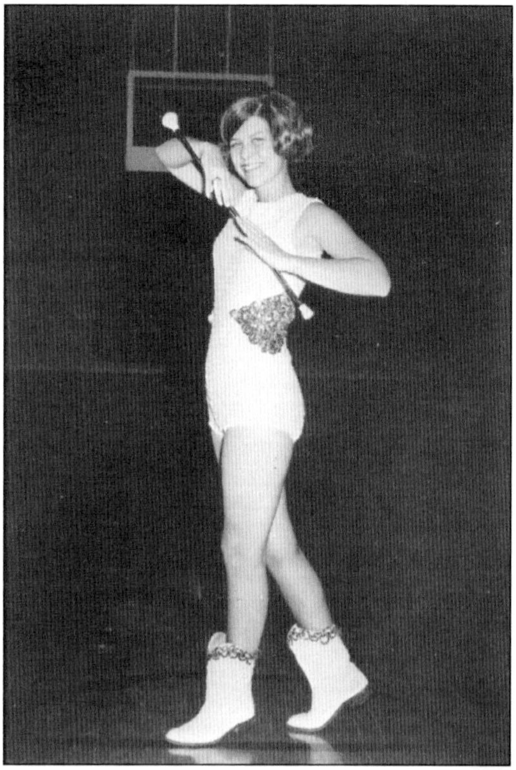

Margaret Ann Sapp (left) and Brenda Levin (below) were two of Hamilton County High School's majorettes in 1966. Sapp's father owned a lumber mill just outside the city limits of Jasper; he died when she was a young girl. Levin was the daughter of Charlie and Sylvia Levin, who owned Levin's Clothing Store. Both women moved away from the area after completing high school. (Hamilton County High School.)

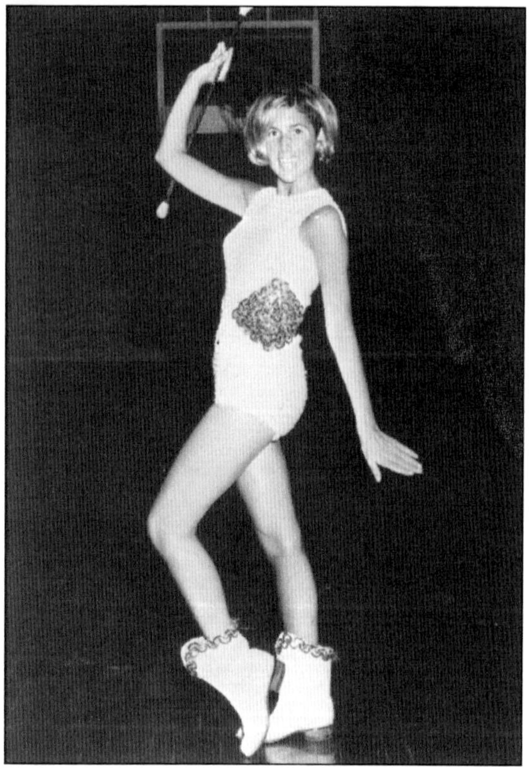

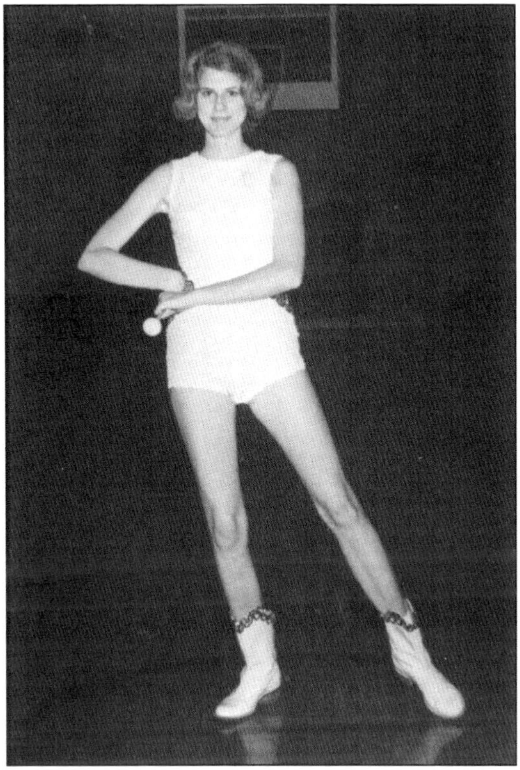

The other two majorettes in 1966 for the Hamilton County High School were Kathy Dedge (right) and Jan Tuten (below). Dedge married Danny Smith, and they have two children. She is currently a teacher at Central Hamilton Elementary School. The family remains in the county. Tuten was the daughter of Kenneth Tuten, longtime property appraiser in Hamilton County. He retired in 1989, when David Goolsby was elected. Jan Tuten has moved away from the area. (Both Hamilton County High School.)

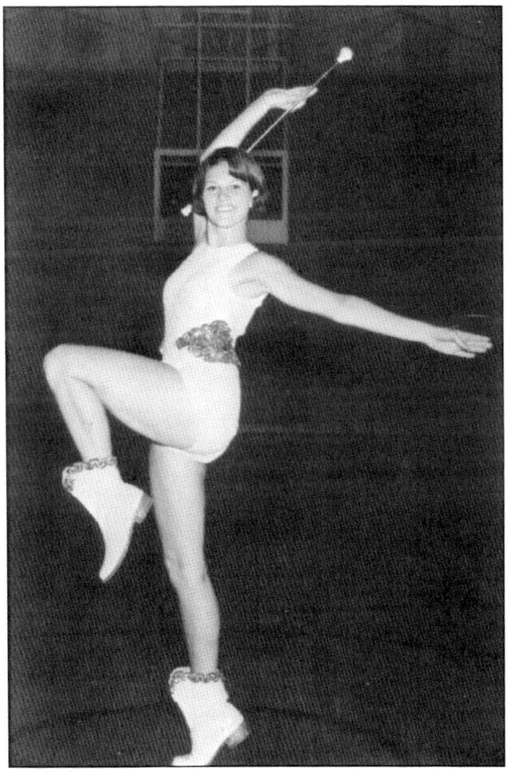

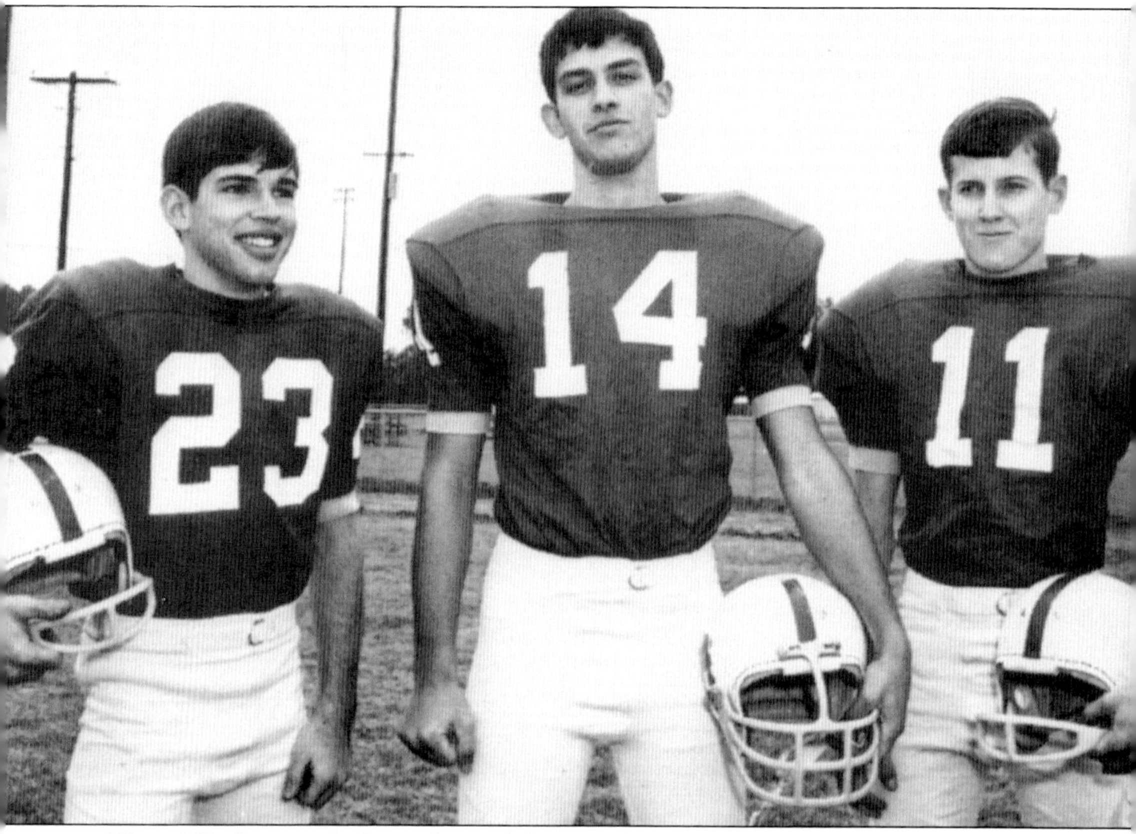

This 1968 photograph shows three of the star players of the Hamilton County High School Rebels football team. Shown are, from left to right, David Wilson, Greg Pittman, and Trammel Deas. Wilson married Margaret Ann Sapp, and they moved away from the area. Pittman moved to Lake City, Florida, and recently died of cancer. Deas married Laura Young, daughter of Aubra and Joanne Young, and together they have two children. (Hamilton County High School.)

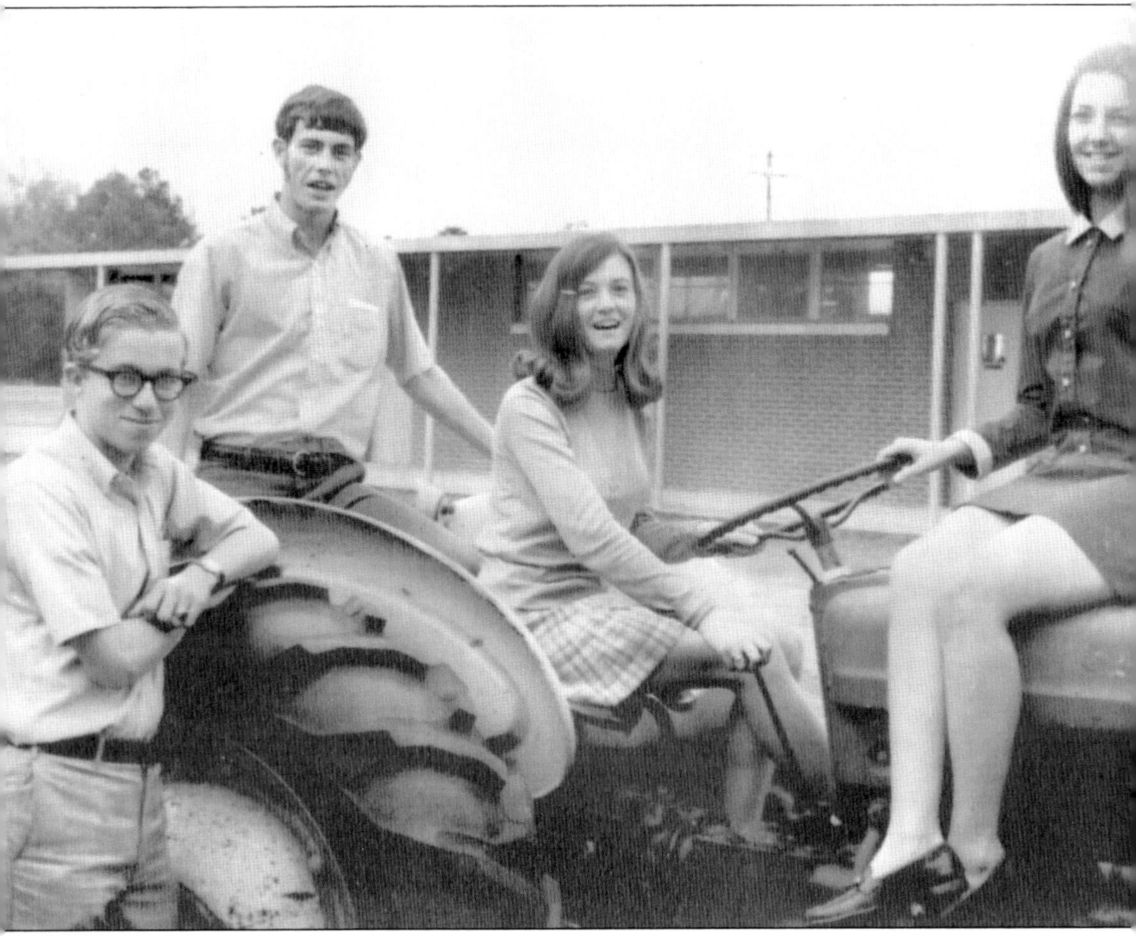

The class officers of the 1970 senior class were, from left to right, Arnold Avriett (reporter), Mike Mann (vice president), Kay Payne (president), and Amelia Hunter (secretary and treasurer). Avriett married Cathy Skinner, from Live Oak, Florida, and they have one daughter. Mann currently works for the Hamilton Correctional Institution. Payne was the daughter of Clyde and Billie Payne. Hunter worked for several years as the administrator of Hamilton County Hospital. She is currently married to Jim Tompkins and has one child. (Hamilton County High School.)

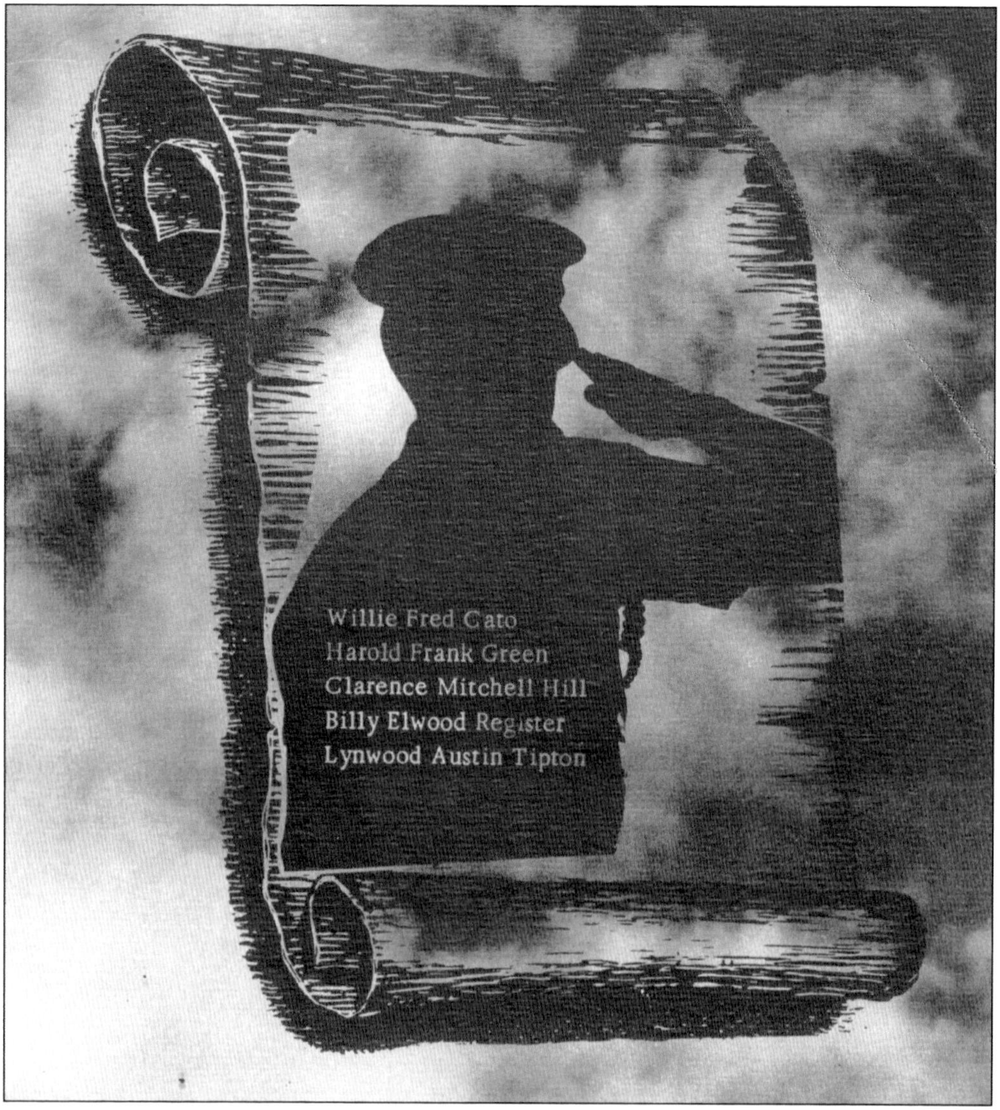

In 1970, the yearbook staff commemorated those young men fighting in the Vietnamese conflict. It was the intention of the yearbook staff to convey their thanks to these gentlemen for allowing them—the students—to remain here in the United States and participate in academic and extracurricular activities, sports, and dance events and to live with the happiness, freedom, and hope for the future that the soldiers provided for them. Willie Fred Cato was a native of White Springs, born on December 15, 1945. He fought in South Vietnam and died there on October 13, 1969. Billy Elwood Register was also a native of White Springs. He was born on August 26, 1942, and died in South Vietnam on March 22, 1967. Lynwood Austin Tipton was born on August 17, 1947, and died in a bombing in South Vietnam on March 6, 1967, days within his arrival. No information is known about Harold Frank Green or Clarence Mitchell Hill. (Hamilton County High School.)

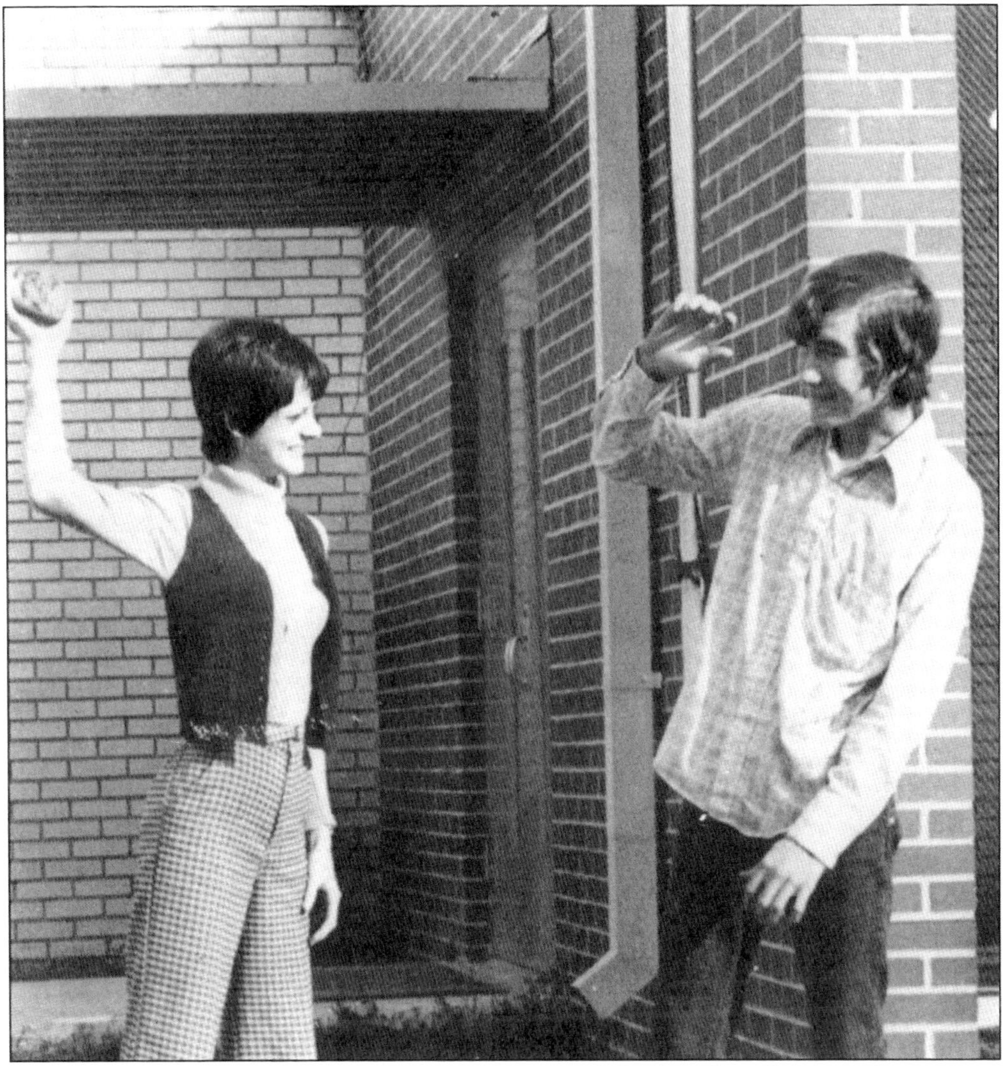

Debbie Mosely and Kenneth "Sonny" Scaff were voted the friendliest by their class in 1974. Although little is known about Mosely, Scaff is a prominent member of Hamilton County society. He graduated from Valdosta State College in 1977 with a degree in political science and history and went on to Mercer College, in Macon, Georgia, for his law degree, which he completed in 1984. From that point until 2007, Scaff worked for a local attorney, John McCormick. In 2007, he was elected as the county judge, the position he currently holds. He married Kathy Altman, daughter of Estes and Francis Altman, and together they have two children. (Hamilton County High School.)

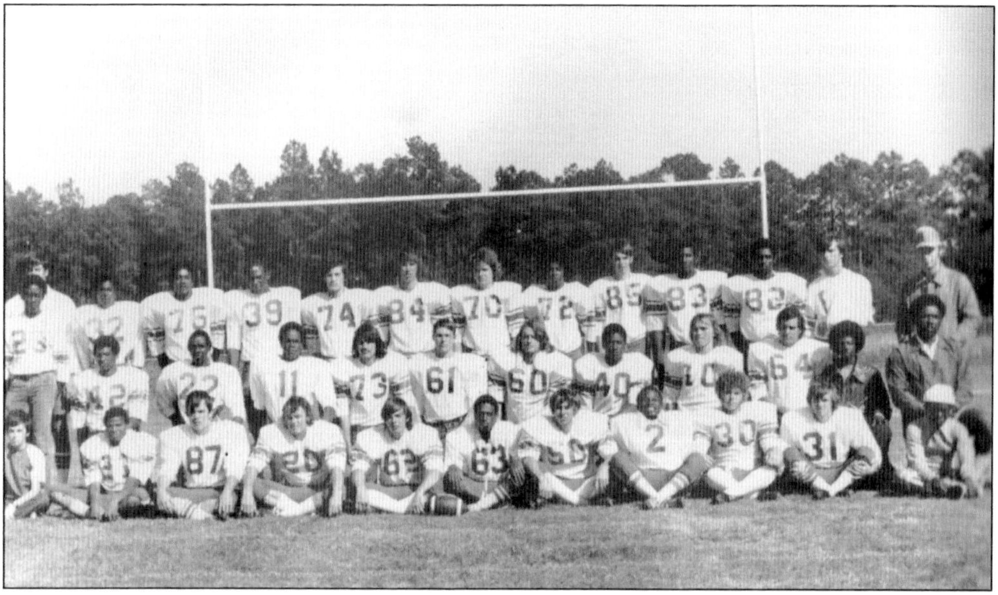

The 1975 Trojans football team was, from left to right, the following: (first row) manager Benjy Norris, Oscar Gibbons, Louis Edenfield, Kenneth Altman, Wyndell Mathis, Kenneth Dyke, Malcolm Tomlinson, Fred Claridy, Ross Henderson, David Shaw, and unidentified; (second row) Kevin Andersen, Carl Trotman, John Simmon, Anthony Allen, Tim Brearley, Kevin Morgan, Clyde McGhin, Willie Ingram, Alan Deas, Stanley Rhoden, manager Leroy Ford, and coach John Brown; (third row) coach John Westmoreland, Mathis Jones, Paul Bell, Harold Oliver, Alan Morgan, David Goolsby, David Schellenger, James Howell, Rex Mitchell, John Paul, Leroy Raiford, Roger Tomlinson, and coach Coy Whitener. (Hamilton County High School.)

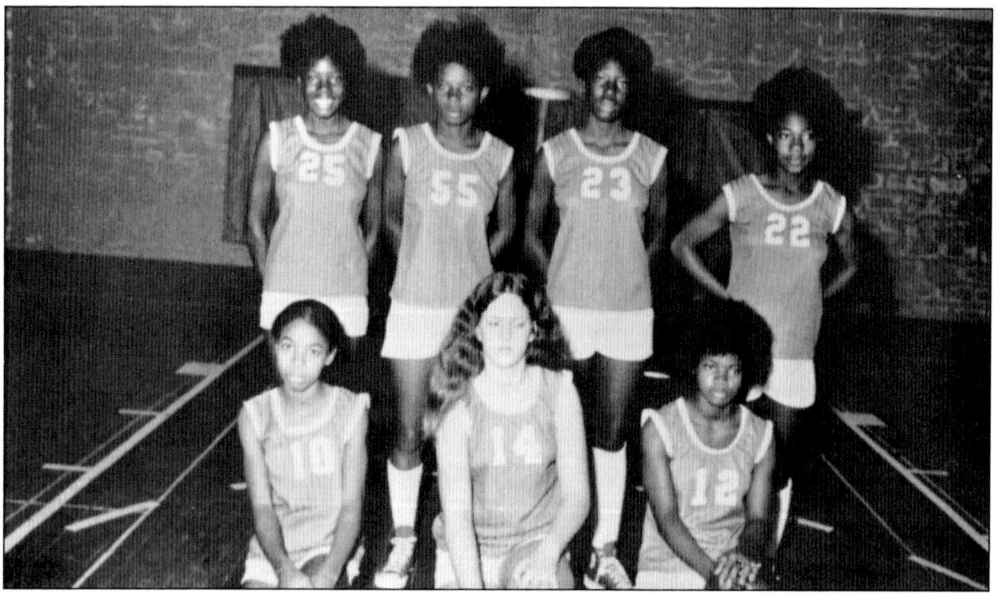

The 1975 Hamilton County junior varsity Trojanettes basketball team was, from left to right, (kneeling) Linnie Byrant, Susan Clay, and Thomasene Townsend; (standing) Anith Dye, Beverly Humphries, Jainth Dye, and Judy McCloud. (Hamilton County High School.)

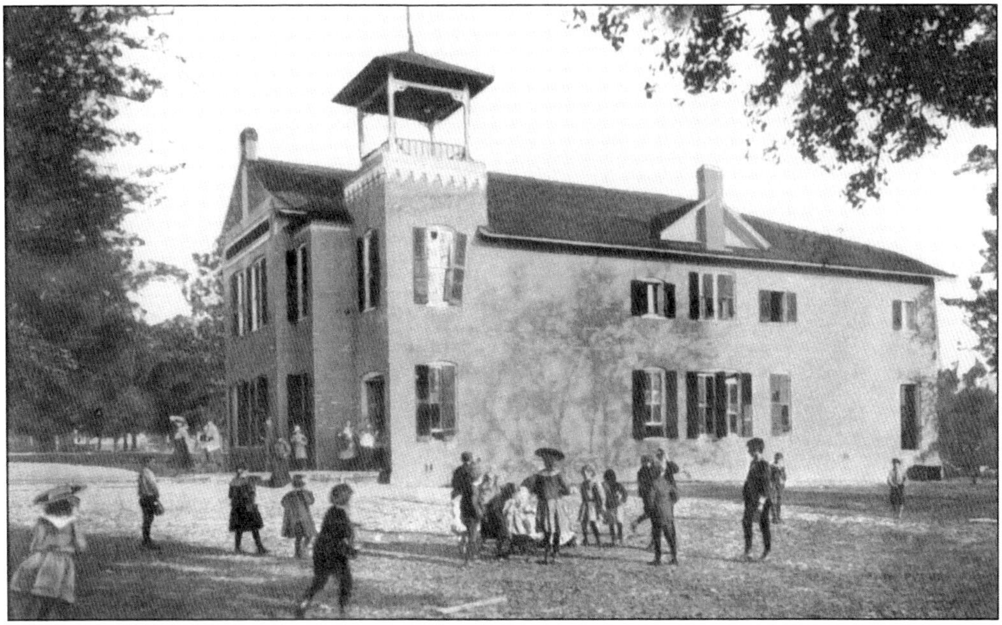

In 1887, the Florida Normal School and Business Institute at White Springs was established by C. F. Cone, G. A. Wright, R. M. Kendrick, William Roberts, Francis Adams, O. K. Paxton, and John L. Morgan. They were allowed to have up to 20 acres and the buildings, but it is unclear how much land they actually utilized. Normal schools were initially founded to teach high school graduates the essentials of teaching students. (Alan Fouraker.)

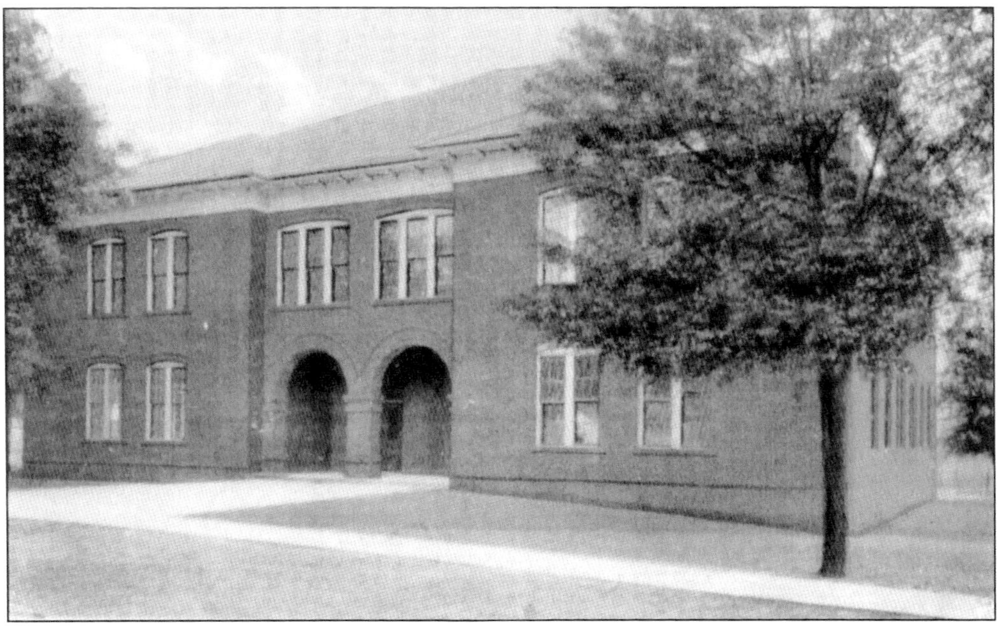

The Old White Springs School on College Street (now River Street) was closed because of water damage to the building's foundation. Even after another school was built in 1940, the students continued to eat lunch at the old school. In 1965, the upper grades in the county were consolidated into the Hamilton County High School in Jasper. The school in White Springs continued teaching the first through eighth grades. (William S. Mitchell IV.)

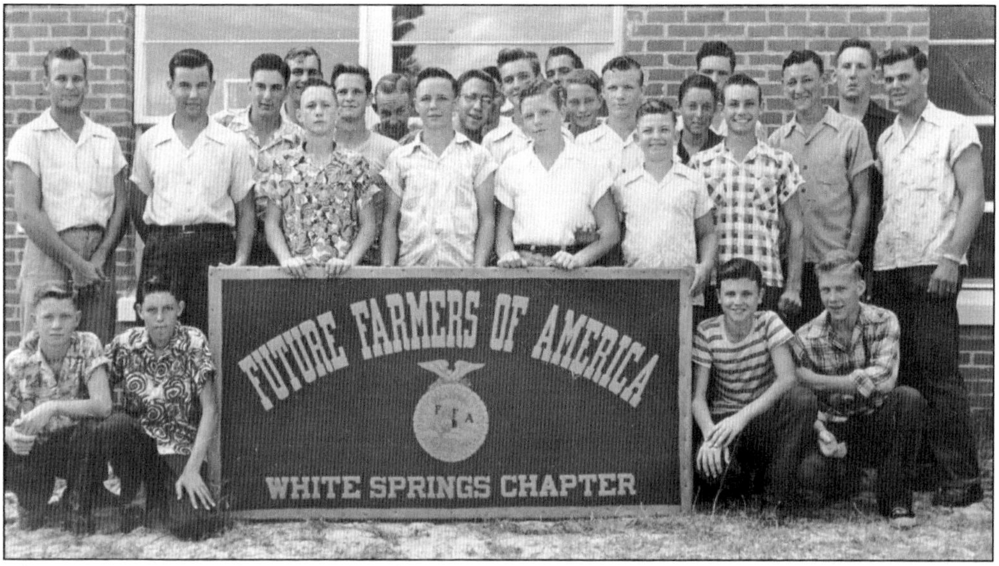

The Future Farmers of America (FFA), White Springs Chapter, in 1953 included, from left to right, (first row) Eddie Tomlinson, Donald Lee, Bobby Walker, and Bobby Ray Sistrunk; (second row) Vincent Jones (teacher), Melvin Ginn, Johnny Williams, David Shaw, Billy Clark, Bobby Ginn, Nathan Morgan, J. M. Morgan, and Malcolm Greene; (third row) John Wiggins, Leon Bryan, Jorry Beauchamp, Donald Conner, Leonard Conner, Willie Frank Stormant, Willie Ray Bryan, Clynn L. Lyons, Wayne Tomlinson, Wade Harris, Lonnie Lee, Willie James Crews, and Jerry Barnett. (Malcolm Greene.)

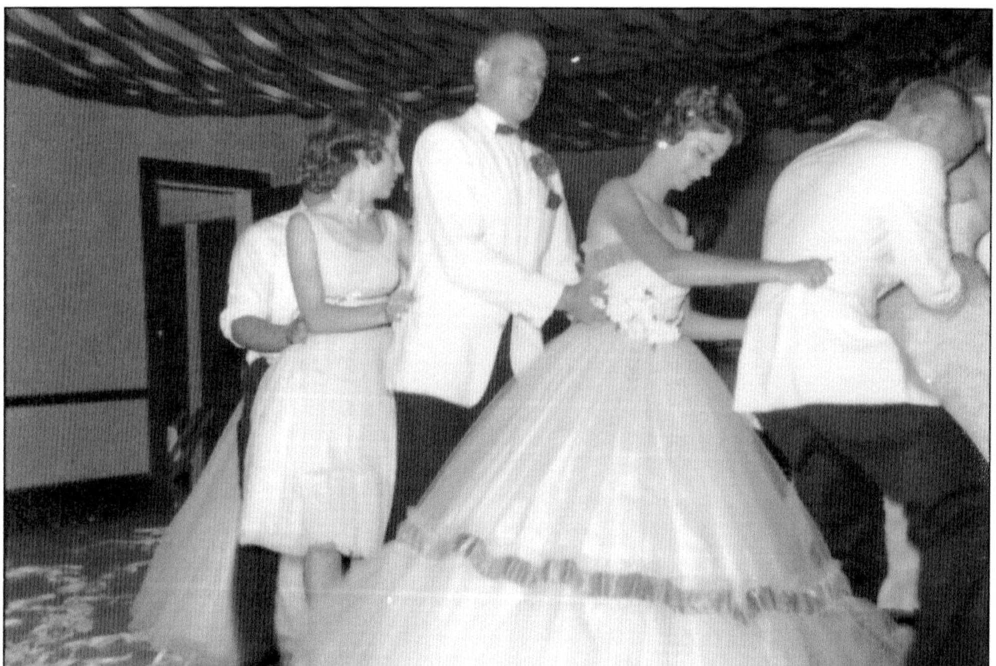

From left to right, Florence Connor, Buddy Ogburn, Patsy Lee Whitaker, and James Lovett enjoyed a night of dancing and fun at their junior-senior prom in 1961. In the same year, young Whitaker was crowned as the first "Junior Jeanie with the Light Brown Hair." (Phyllis Whitaker.)

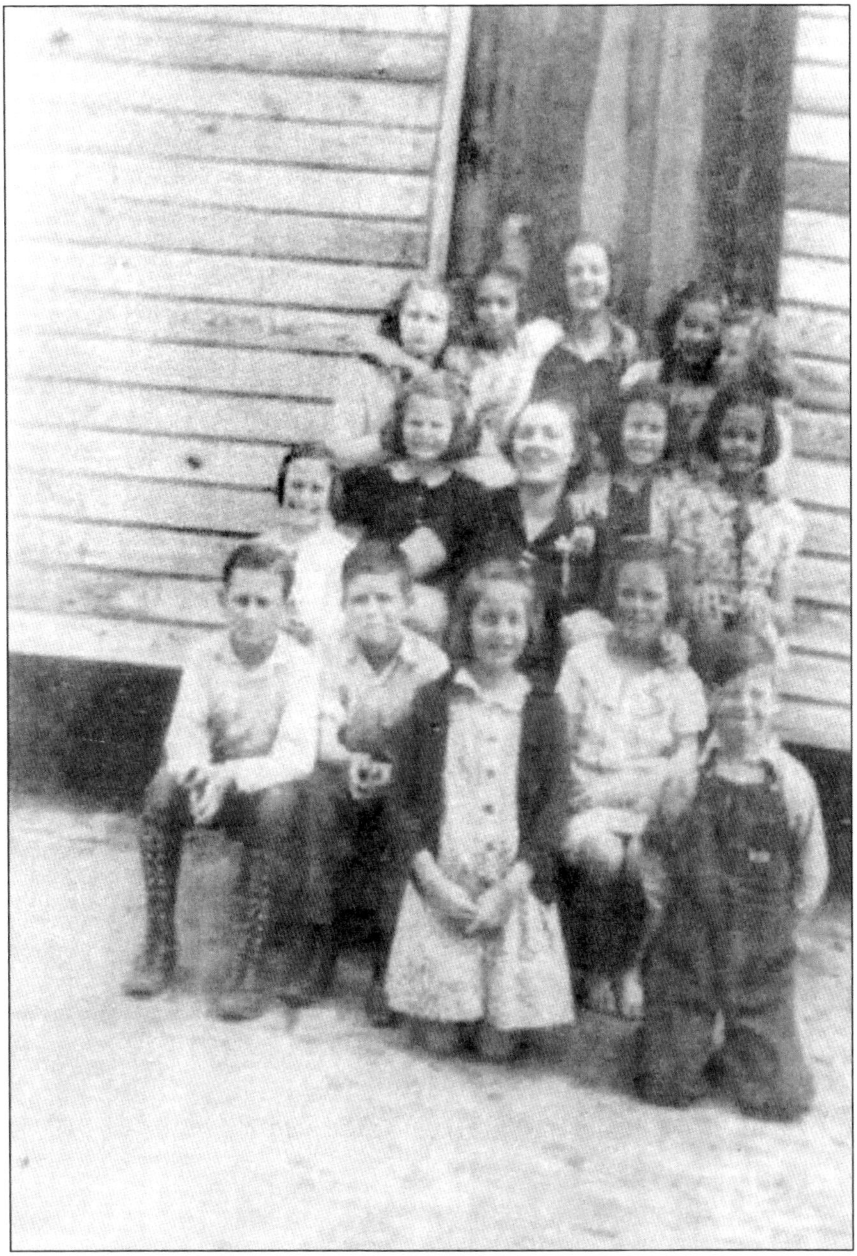

In the late 1800s and early 1900s, many "local" schools were in Hamilton County. These were schools where neighborhood children, many of them related to one another, lived within walking distance of the school. One teacher commonly taught all of the subjects, including reading, writing, and arithmetic, to all of the students. School terms often ran for two to four months, twice a year. Shown in this early-1900s photograph are grades five through eight of Burnham School, located on County Road 146, about a half mile from Burnham Christian Church. Pictured from left to right are (first row) James Deas, G. W. Alderman, Geree Deas, Pauline Knighton, and unidentified; (second row) Dick Deas, Rubye Deas, ? Bryan (teacher), Inez Alderman, and Veda Hurst; (third row) Hazel Deas, Geraldine Deas, Eunice Hurst, Loucile Burnham, and Lanora Deas. (Marian Deas.)

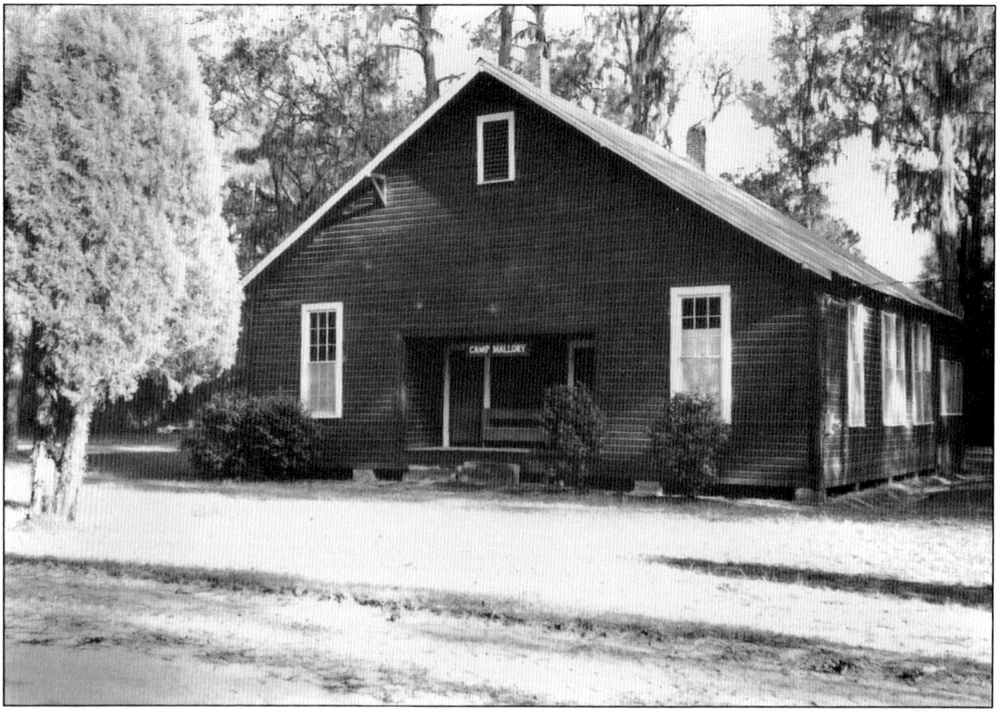

This photograph from 1999 shows Belmont School, about 12 miles east of Jasper off County Road 135 (Woodpecker Route). In 1936, Roy Burnett was the principal and one of the teachers was Lottie Mae Deas. Charlie and Russell Rhoden, Joe Hogan, Clyde Hunter, and L. A. Edenfield are some of the students who attended Belmont School. Now called Camp Mallory, the building is used to house hunters during the season. (Malcolm Greene.)

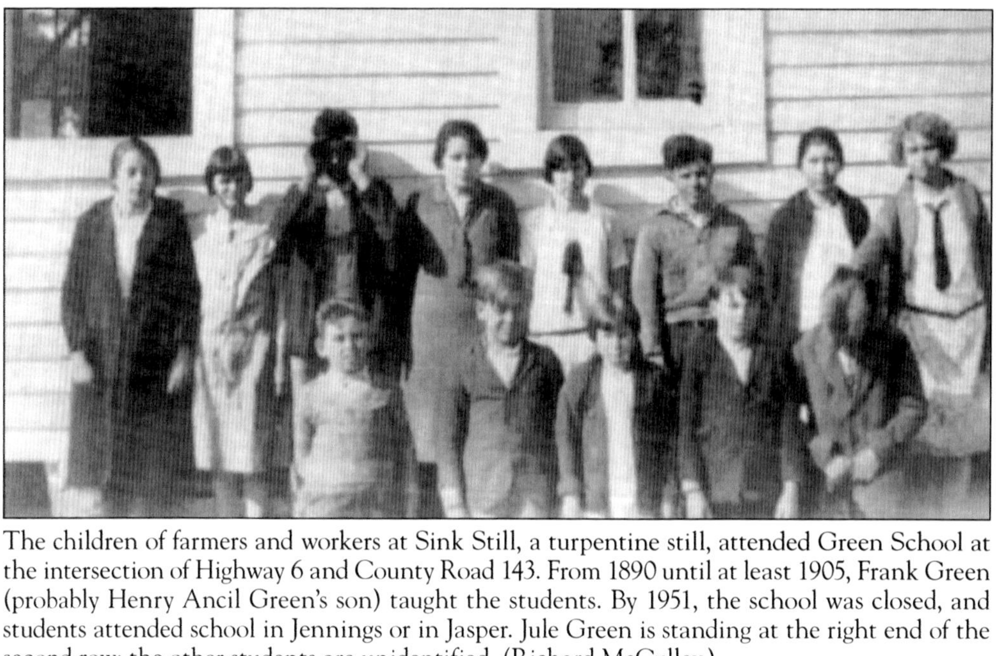

The children of farmers and workers at Sink Still, a turpentine still, attended Green School at the intersection of Highway 6 and County Road 143. From 1890 until at least 1905, Frank Green (probably Henry Ancil Green's son) taught the students. By 1951, the school was closed, and students attended school in Jennings or in Jasper. Jule Green is standing at the right end of the second row; the other students are unidentified. (Richard McCulley.)

Four

HOUSES AND CHURCHES

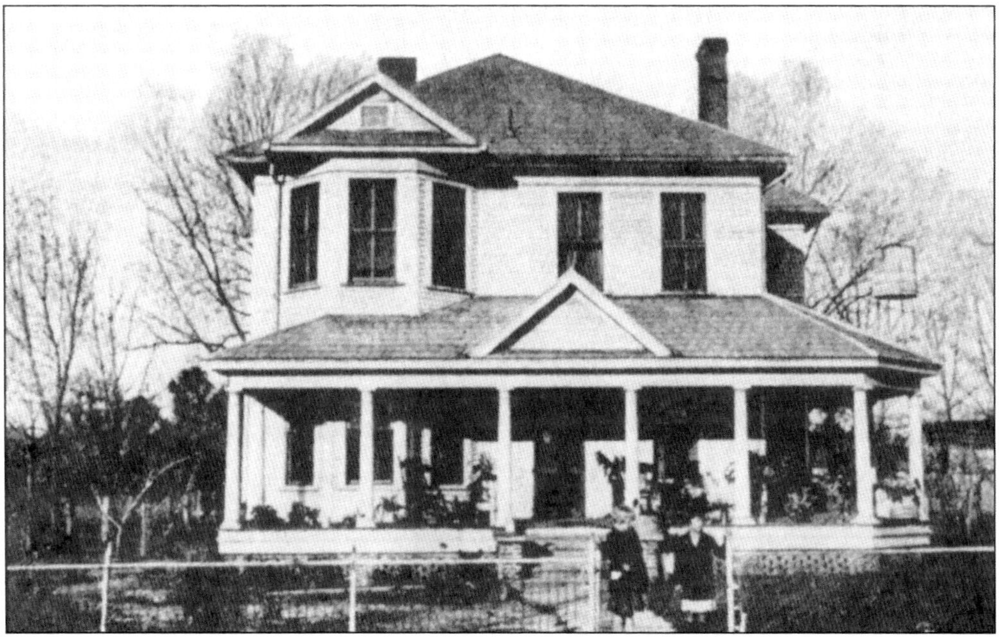

The A. L. Wise house was built about 1912 by Dr. William Marvin O'Cain. Dr. O'Cain and his wife, Maggie Knowles O'Cain, barely finished the construction of the home on South West Central Avenue before the birth of their second child, William Marvin O'Cain Jr. However, she was never satisfied with any of her homes—if it was time to repaint or make repairs, it was time to either move to a new home or build a new one. Hence, after several years, the home was sold to Wise, who owned Wise's Drug Store on the corner of Central Avenue and Hately Street. Opened in 1911, Wise operated the pharmacy until William Jackson purchased it. (William S. Mitchell IV.)

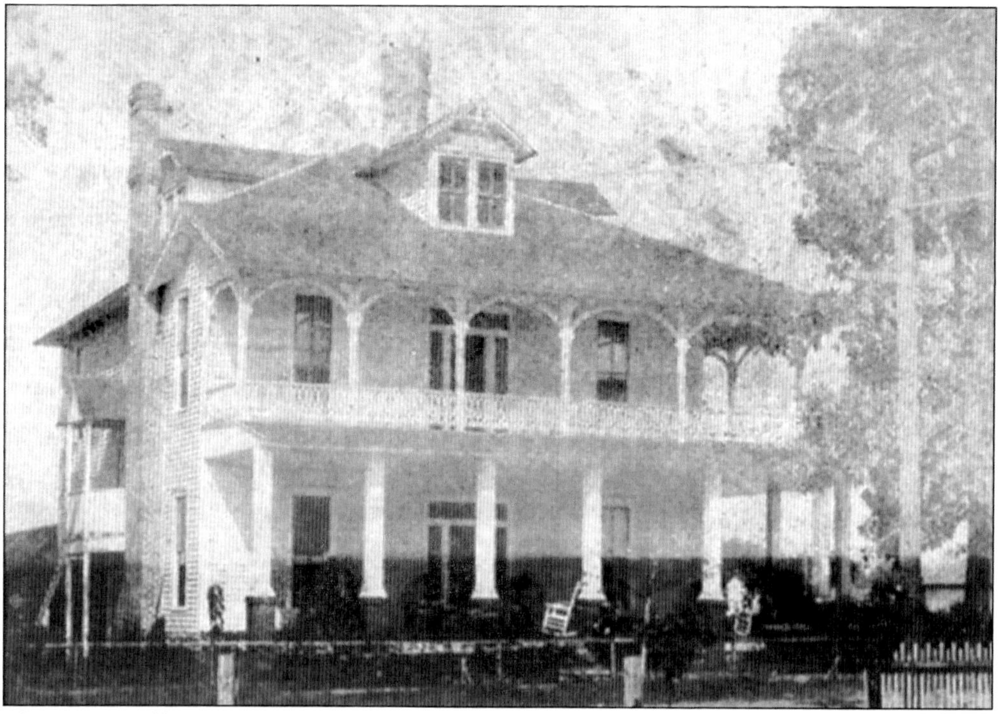

The Press Sandlin House (Kirby L. Sandlin House) on Southwest First Avenue was built in 1895, using yellow-heart growth pine from John High's mill at a cost of almost $4,500. Family members lived in the home until the 1980s, when it was sold to non-family residents. Several teachers from Jasper Normal Institute boarded with the Sandlin family, including John M. Guilliams, the principal, and his wife, Fannie. (Marion Turner.)

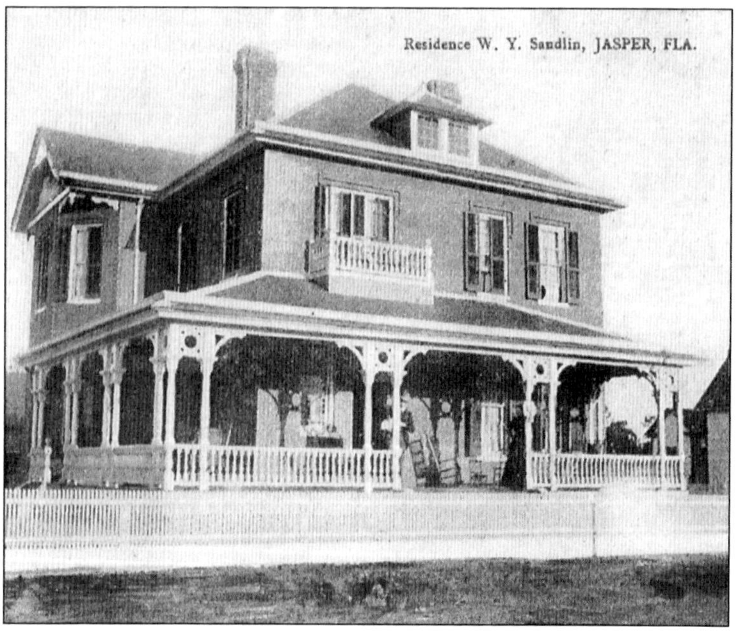

William Yulee Sandlin was born at Blount's Ferry, Columbia County, on May 23, 1851. He married Frances L. Bryan, and they had four children: Addie Eulalia, John Robert, Ponce de Leon, and Fred M. Sandlin, who died shortly after birth. This home, located one block from Central Avenue, was built in 1885 but later burned. A small brick apartment house was located on the lot in early 2009. (Paul Marion.)

'mel House in "Exceptional" category in state of Florida

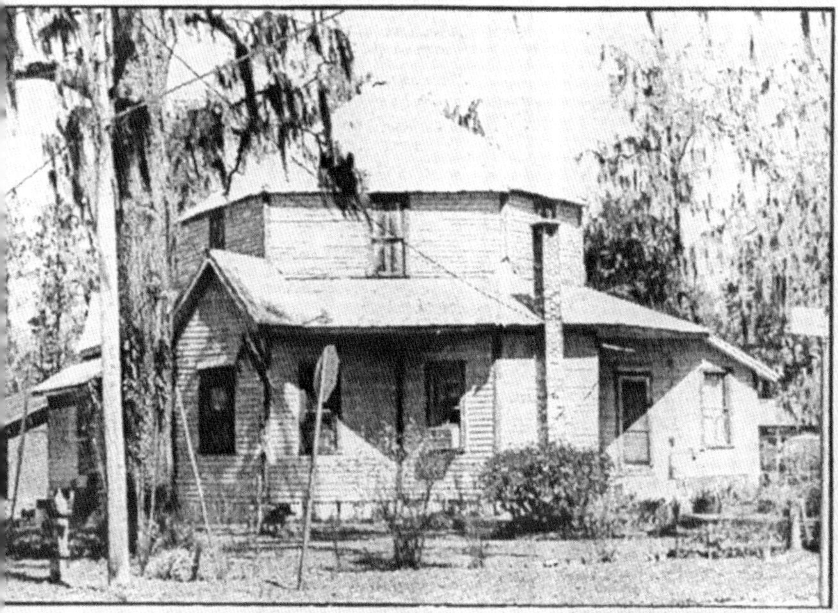

The old Tompkins-Plyme House was built around 1895 by Dr. Dean R. Tompkins and is considered to be unique in character. The two-story house is hexagonal in shape. All of the rooms have five to seven sides. The second floor is basically one large room with six irregular sides that form a hexagon. Orginally the second floor functioned only as a light well and was not living quarters. A balustraded walkway ran around its perimeter. Its unusual plan places it in the "Exceptional" category for it is one-of-a-kind in Jasper and probably in the region, if not in the state. In Melanie Barr's thesis, a preservation plan for Jasper, she said that it was doubtful that any town would be able to produce a residence as bizarre or unique as the Tompkins-Plymel house in Jasper, 311 SW Fifth Avenue.

Dr. Dean R. Tompkins built a unique house about 1895, located on Southwest Fifth Avenue in Jasper. In the hexagonal, two-story building, all of the rooms inside have five to seven walls. The upper floor is a single large room with six sides. Originally, the area was not considered living quarters, as it was a light well with a balustrade walkway encircling it. The house has recently become vacant. (Marion Turner.)

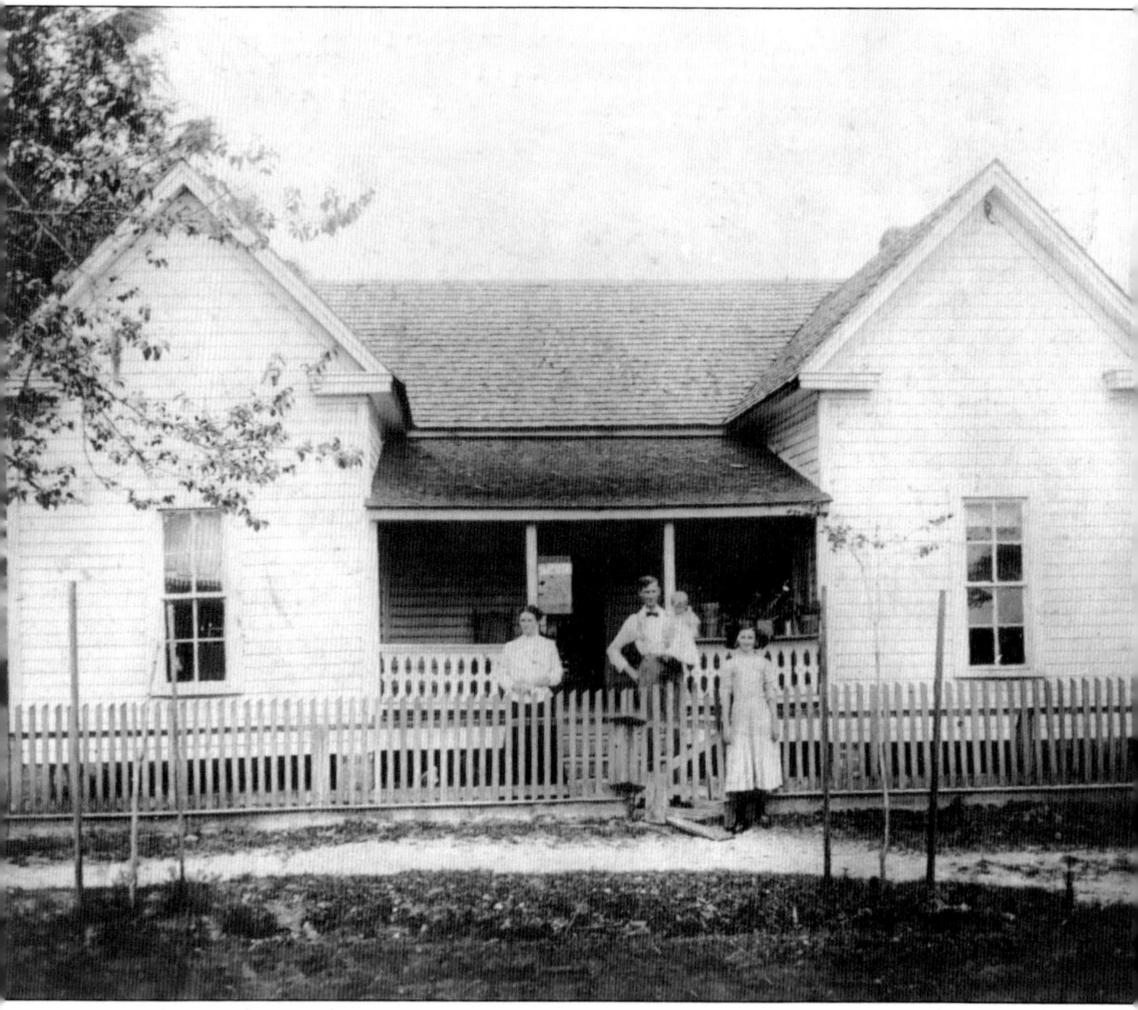

Matthew Walter Wetherington was born in Echols County, Georgia, on February 22, 1877, to parents John and Jane Wetherington. He married Georgia Johnson of Suwannee County, and they had two children: Charles and Mildred. Wetherington was a member of the city council in Jasper for eight years, from 1924 to 1932. Immediately following his term on city council, he was elected as the tax collector of Hamilton County. He held the office for only a short time before illness forced him to retire. Mildred Wetherington Sapp, his daughter, finished his term for him but did not run for reelection in 1934. Kirby L. Sandlin filled the position at that time. Wetherington died on July 16, 1945, and was buried in Evergreen Cemetery, as was his wife, who died in 1981. (Alan Fouraker.)

This was the original farmhouse on the Adams Farm, built by Frank Adams. Because there was no heat or electricity, there was a fireplace in every room. In the late 1940s, when Stanley Adams Jr. married Bette Wisenbaker Adams, there was still no electricity. The young couple lived in the house for a short time until they were able to move into a home of their own. Kept in fair condition throughout the years, the house burned down in the early 1960s. (Cliff Adams.)

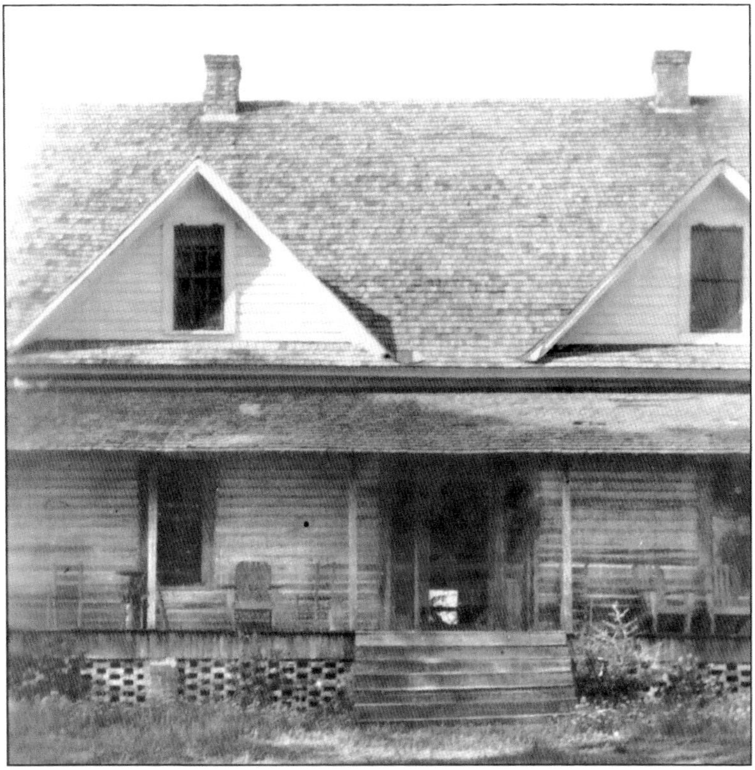

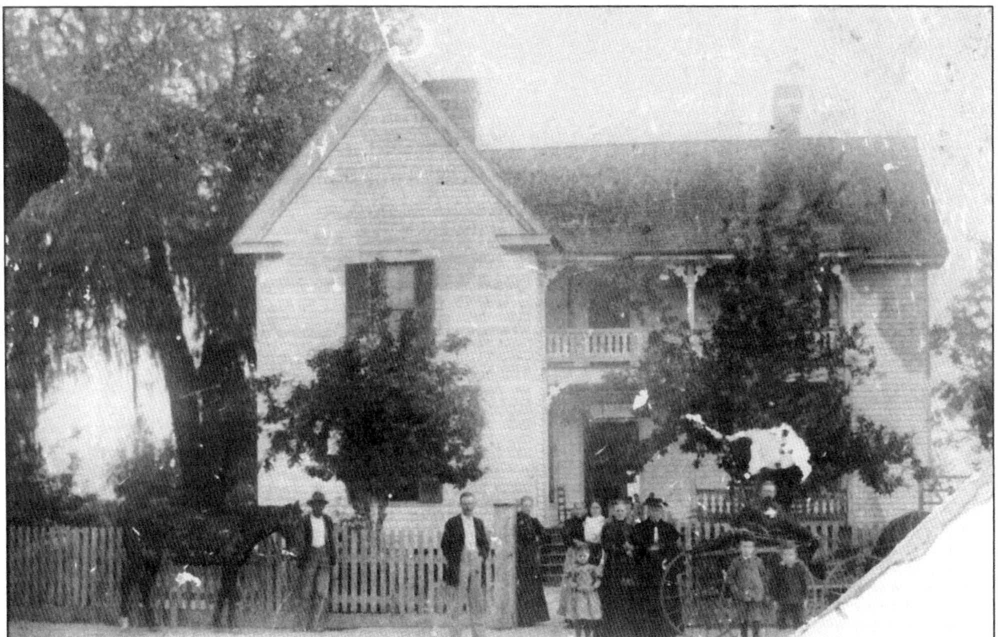

This cabinet card photograph from the 1890s was found in an old photo album belonging to the Marion family. Although the individuals and the house in the photograph are unidentified, they were surely members of Hamilton County society. It is very likely they were relatives of Nathaniel Peter Marion. (Paul Marion.)

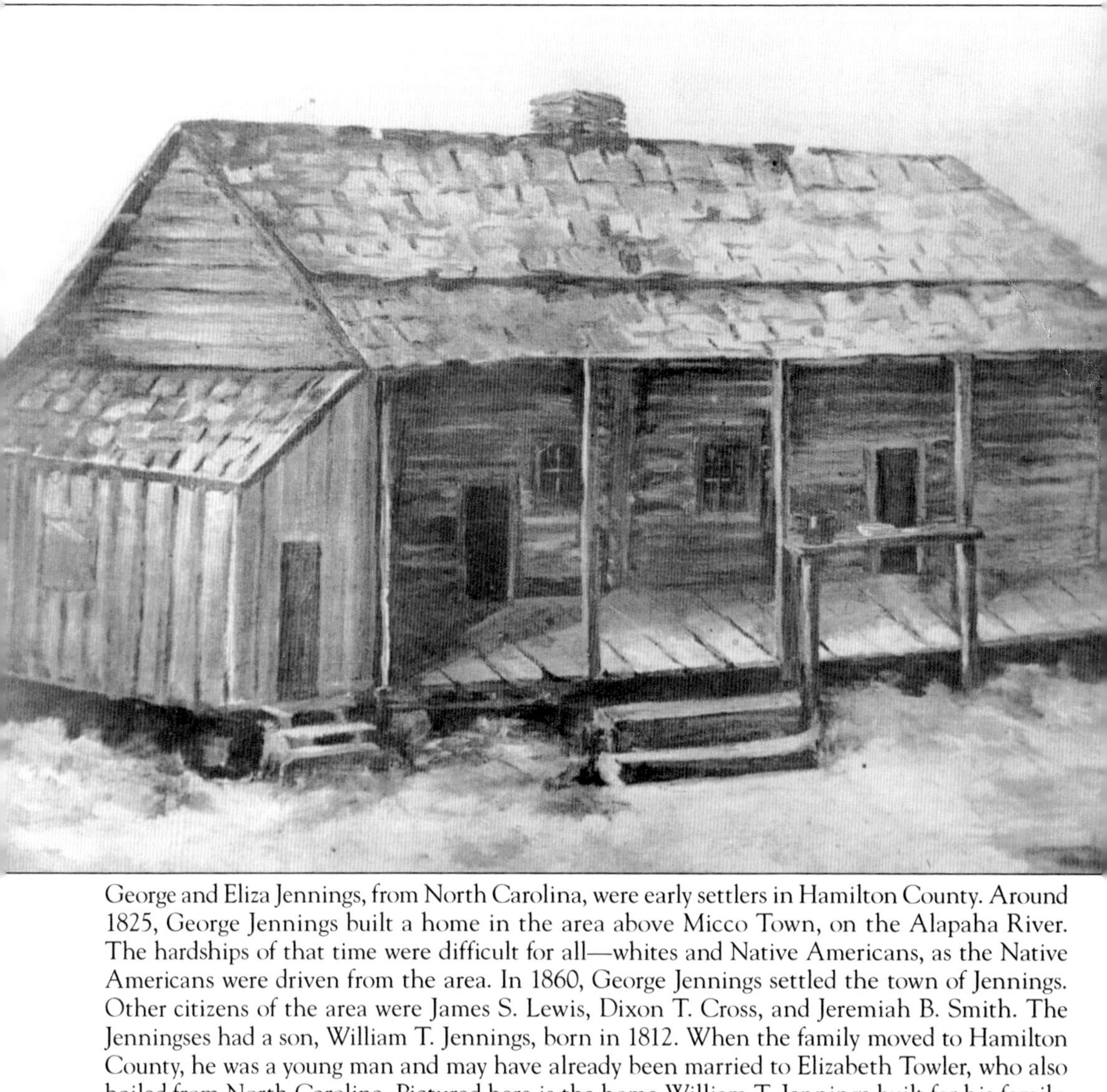

George and Eliza Jennings, from North Carolina, were early settlers in Hamilton County. Around 1825, George Jennings built a home in the area above Micco Town, on the Alapaha River. The hardships of that time were difficult for all—whites and Native Americans, as the Native Americans were driven from the area. In 1860, George Jennings settled the town of Jennings. Other citizens of the area were James S. Lewis, Dixon T. Cross, and Jeremiah B. Smith. The Jenningses had a son, William T. Jennings, born in 1812. When the family moved to Hamilton County, he was a young man and may have already been married to Elizabeth Towler, who also hailed from North Carolina. Pictured here is the home William T. Jennings built for his family, called the Jennings Homestead. He and Elizabeth had only one child, Sarah Jane Jennings, in 1839. Elizabeth Jennings died in 1859; William T. Jennings lived until 1891. The Jennings Homestead still stands on Jennings Bluff Road off Highway 41, although it is in disrepair. (Florida Photographic Collection, Florida State Archives.)

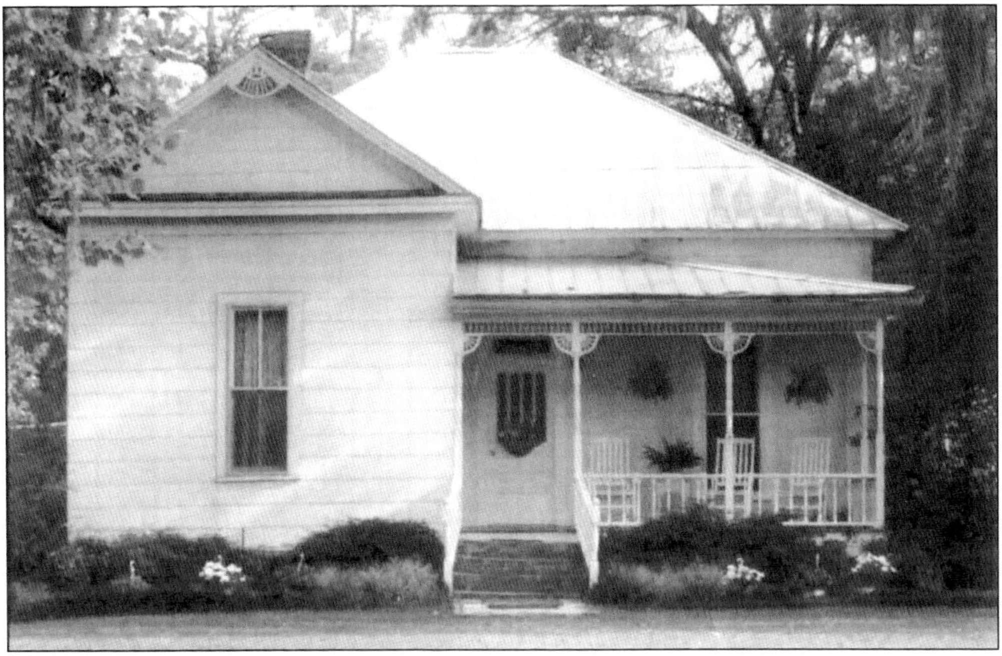

John Hall Sr. and Mellie Alderman Deas moved in 1928 to this home, located about 7 miles from Jennings. The family remained in the house for several years. Two of their children, Mandy and Wanda, were born in the home. Upon moving to the country from Jennings, John Hall Deas Sr. sold his grocery store to a local citizen and took up farming. (Marian Deas.)

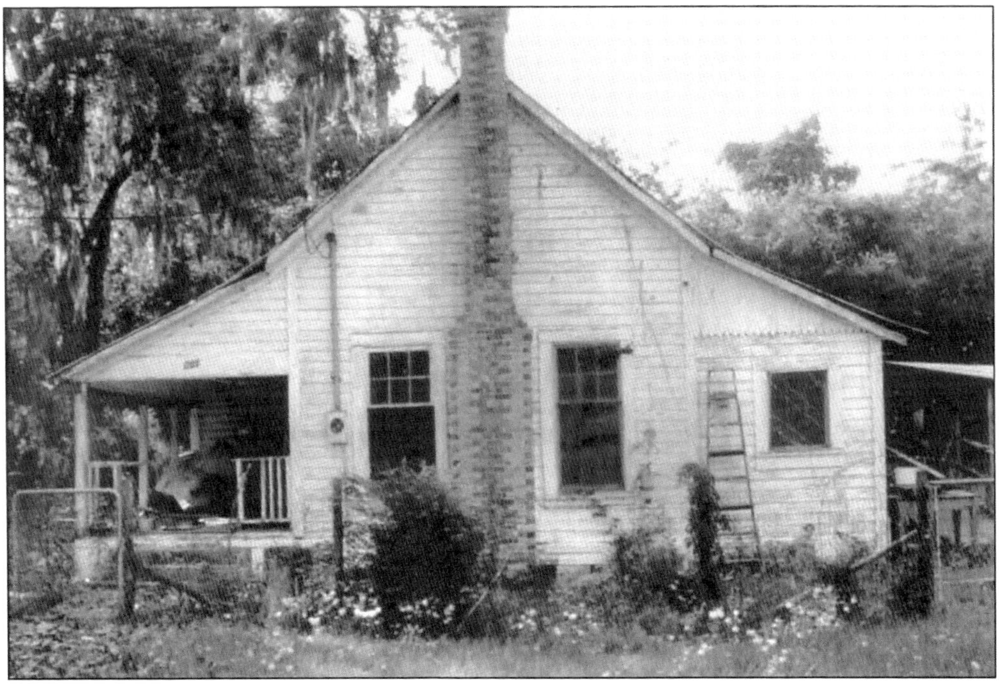

This house, located in Jennings, was built prior to 1926. James Deas, son of Mellie Alderman and John Hall Deas, was born while the family lived here. Although the house remained vacant for several years, it is now being remodeled and restored. (Marian Deas.)

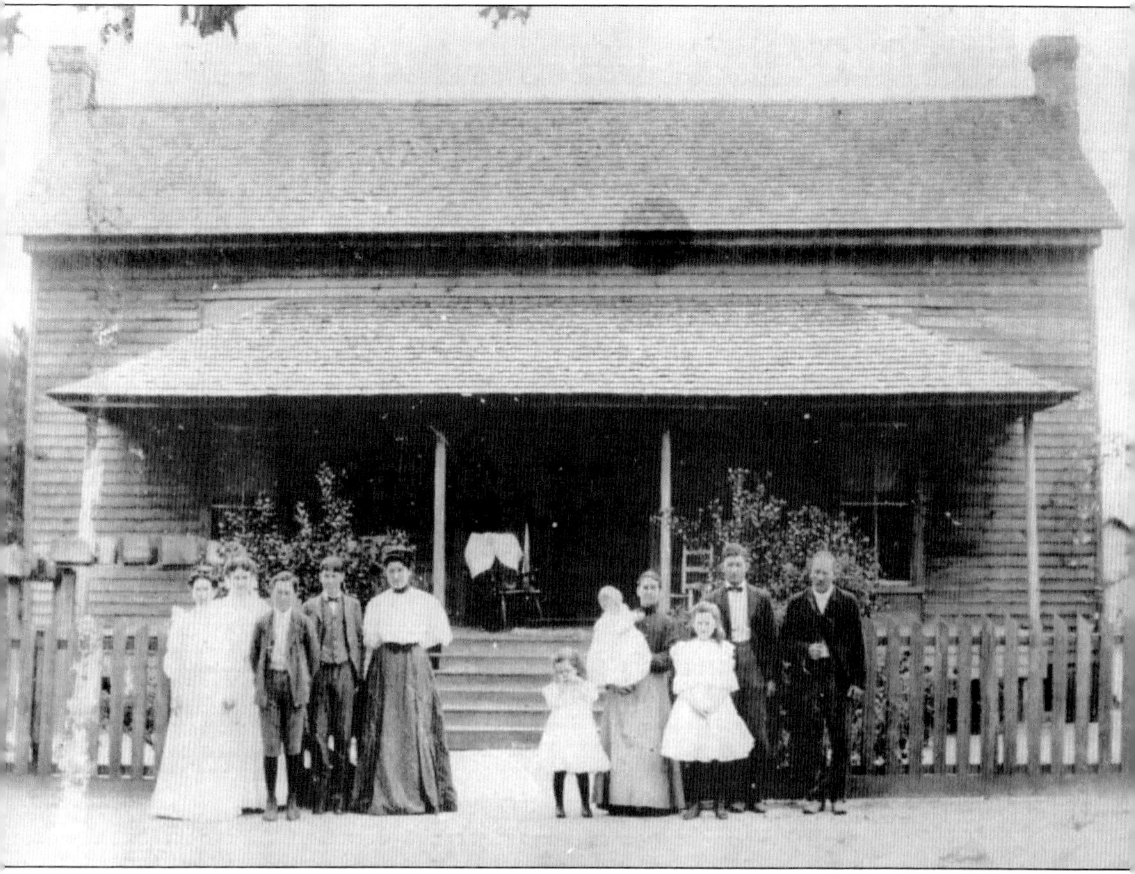

Built about 1900 by Barzilla and Amanda Cunningham Alderman, this house was located approximately 2 miles east of Jennings, in the area behind where the Jennings Outdoor Resort Campground is located now. The homestead has been gone since at least 1955; the exact date of its demise is unknown. Shown here in this 1907 photograph are, from left to right, Anna, Mamie, Jim, Gordon, Melissa, Lottie, Winfred, Amanda (mother), Mellie, Bert, and Barzilla Alderman (father). (Marian Deas.)

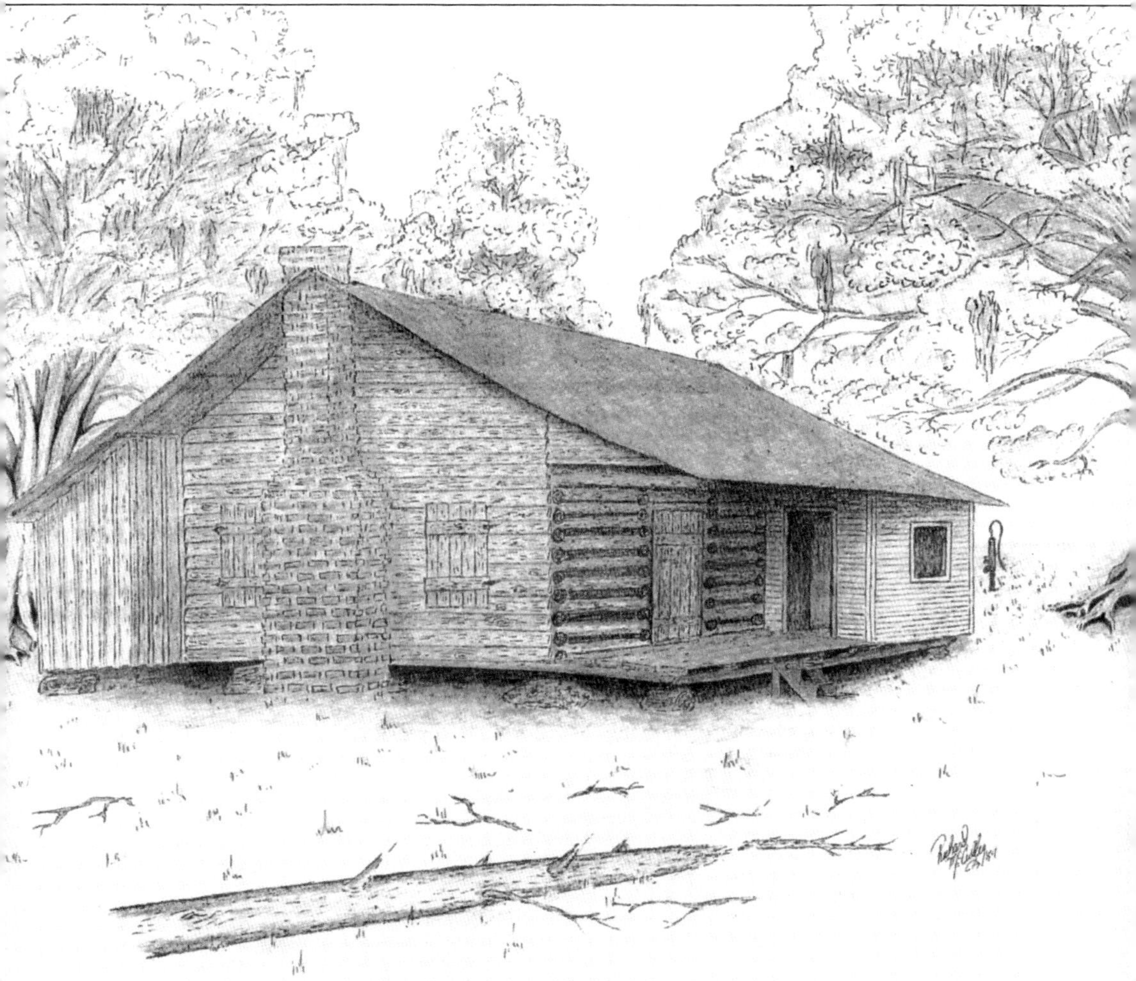

This drawing by Richard McCulley shows the Wells Cabin, located on County Road 143. Alexander G. Wells built the cabin around 1870. He lived there for nearly 50 years with his wife, Sarah, and raised 11 children. Wells worked the surrounding land, collecting turpentine from the yellow pine trees nearby. The Wells Cabin was sold to Dan Kirkland around 1920, and Wells moved to Madison County. Richard and Carol McCulley now own the property where the cabin is located and run a camping and trail ride operation, McCulley Farms. They began restoring the cabin in 1999 and completed the project after several years. Descendants of Alexander G. Wells donated some of the items that can be found in the cabin today. (Richard McCulley.)

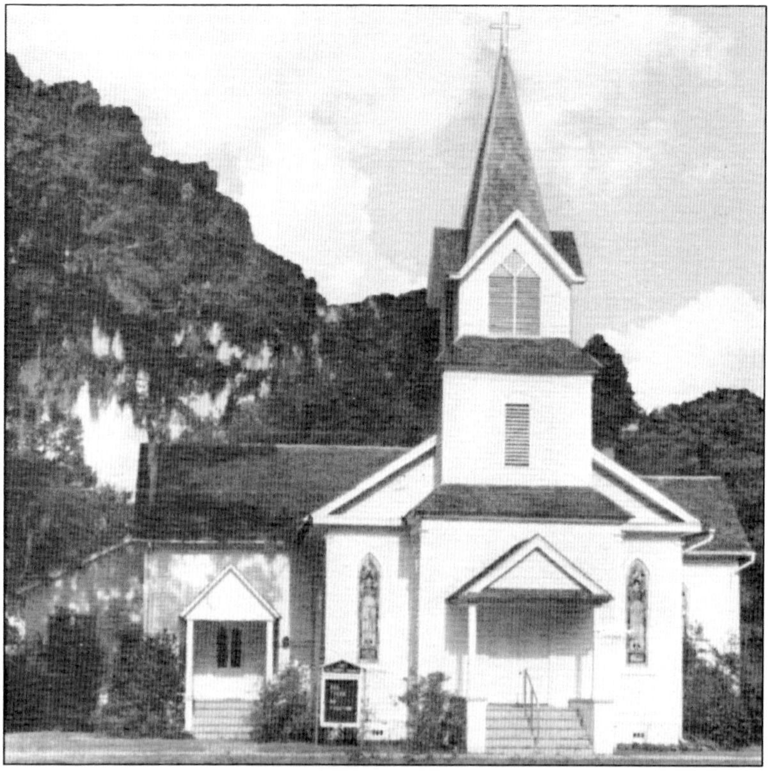

The First Methodist Church of Jasper was first located in the northwest part of Evergreen Cemetery, in a log cabin built in 1847 or 1848. About 10 years later, it was destroyed by a hurricane. Church members met in the Baptist sanctuary until a new building was completed on the corner of East Central Avenue and Fifth Street in 1878. The church was added to the National Register of Historic Places in 1978. (Mildred Shepherd.)

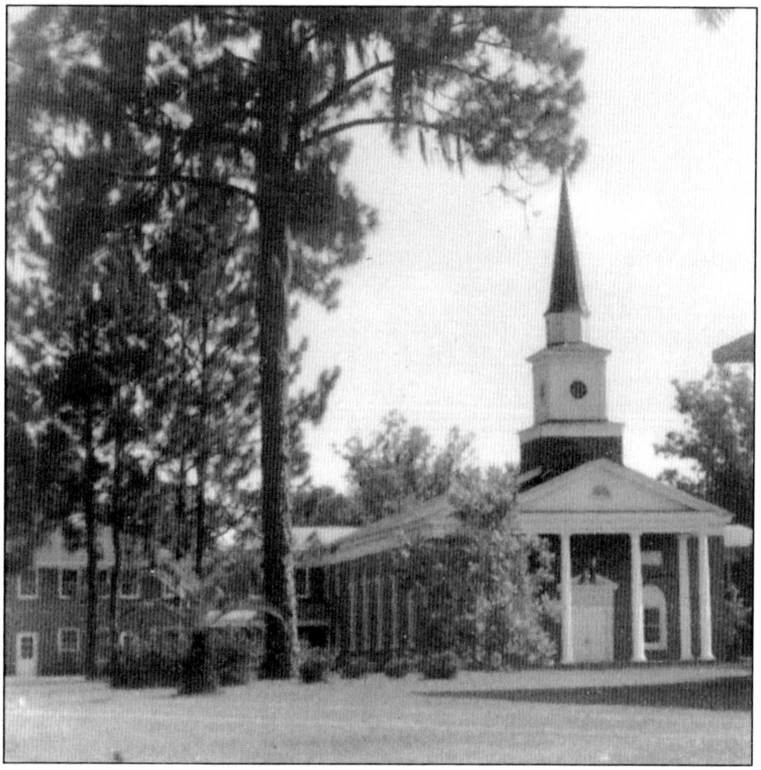

This early-1960s photograph of the First Baptist Church in Jasper shows the newest sanctuary and the educational building. In 1882, church members purchased the lot from Zenobia Hately and erected a wooden building on it. Another was constructed about 1911 and the present building in 1959. Early church members included J. R. Watson and his wife, Evan Morgan and his wife, Mary Rouse, Mary Hall, and James Ward and his wife. (Marion Turner.)

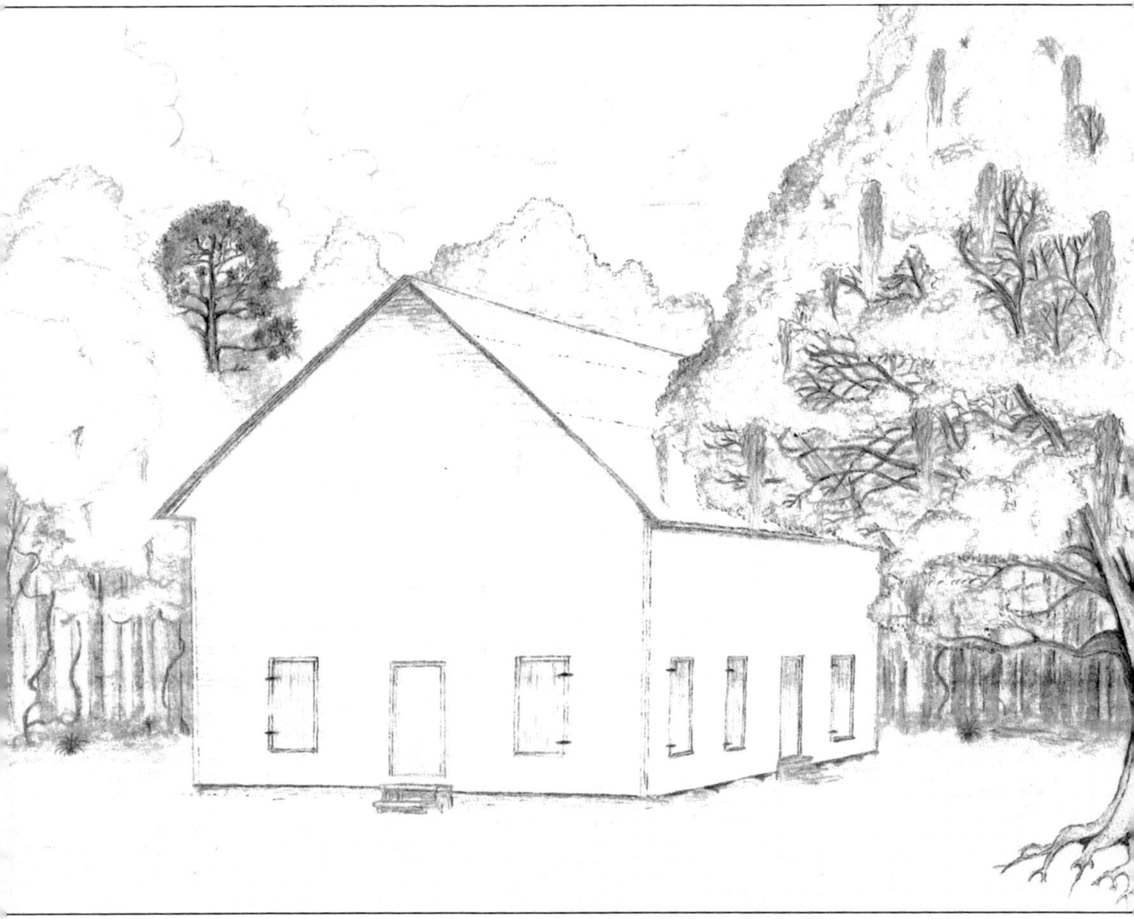

The Antioch Baptist Church, located near State Road 6, was built around 1903 with lumber donated by Eugene West, who owned West Lake Mill. Services were stopped at the church in 1933, although the building remained in good condition. Throughout the years, it has fallen into disrepair and has been looted several times. Some of the timber from the Antioch Church building was used to restore the Wells Cabin located at McCulley Farms. The earliest grave found on the Antioch Church property was from 1901, indicating that the area was populated before the church was established. Although the cemetery remains largely unused, some burials have occurred as late as the 1970s. (Richard McCulley.)

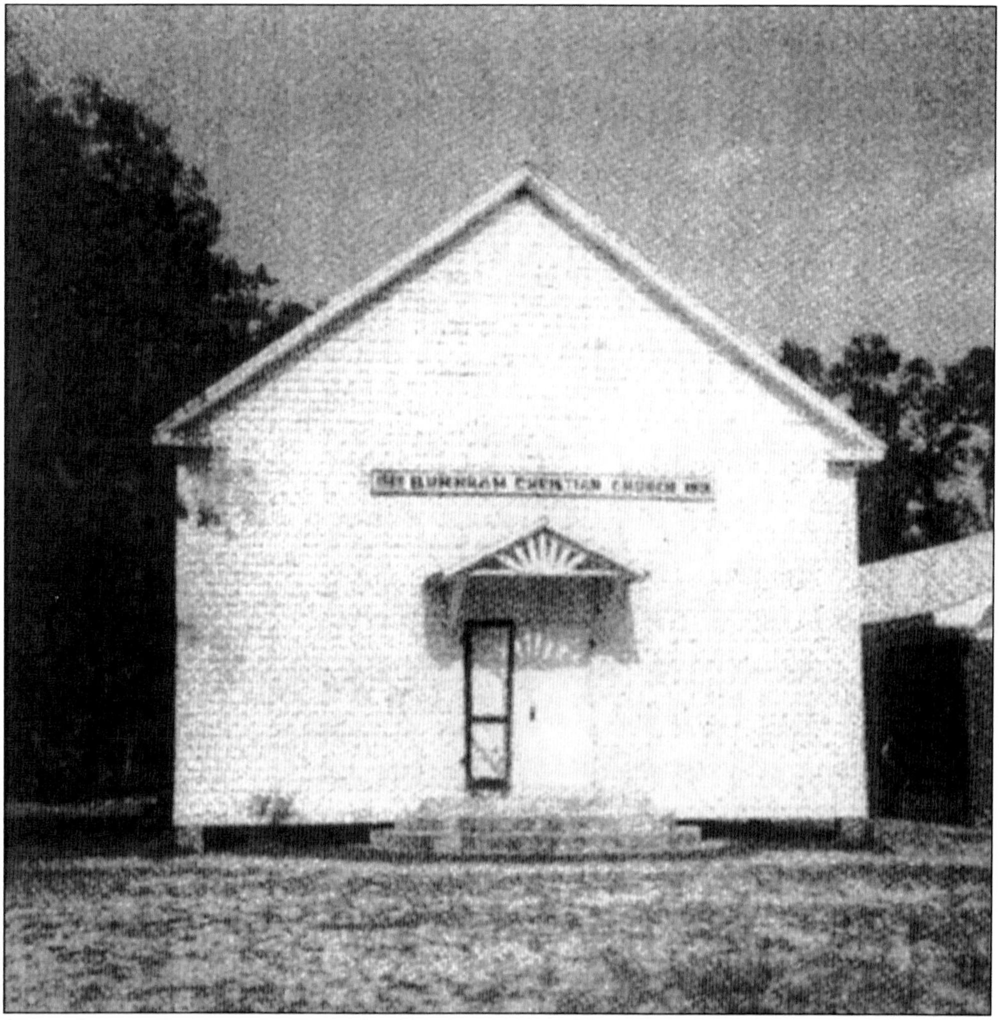

Shown here is the one-room frame building constructed by Perry Dixon and Bob Blair for use as the Burnham Christian Church sanctuary as it stood in the late 1890s. Used for several decades, the building was constructed sturdily—intended for long use. In 1936, an extension was added on the east end. Ten years later, an extension on the west end was added. This building was replaced by a brick structure in 1967. (Marian Deas.)

The first building for Burnham Christian Church was constructed about 1888, using lumber and material from Ellaville. This wood-frame building was used until 1967, when a new brick structure was completed. Ground-breaking for the new building occurred in 1966, however, and is shown in the photograph at right. Pictured from left to right are Albert Deas, James Deas, Joel Selph, Harlon Burnham, Doyle Morgan, Buddy Burnham, I. T. Carter (contractor), Edward Murphy, and Rev. Paul Nobles. The photograph below shows a group of churchgoers discussing the new church while gathered around bricks to be used in the new building. (Both Marian Deas.)

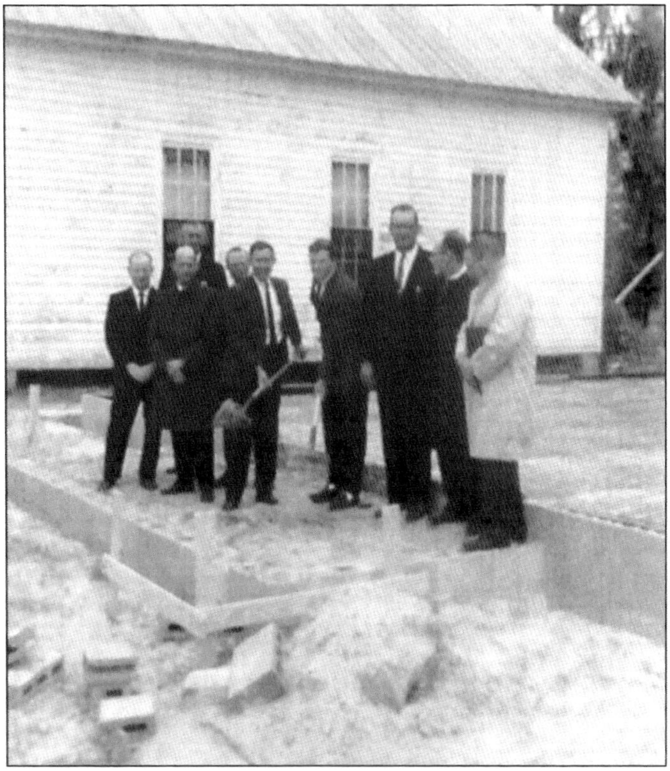

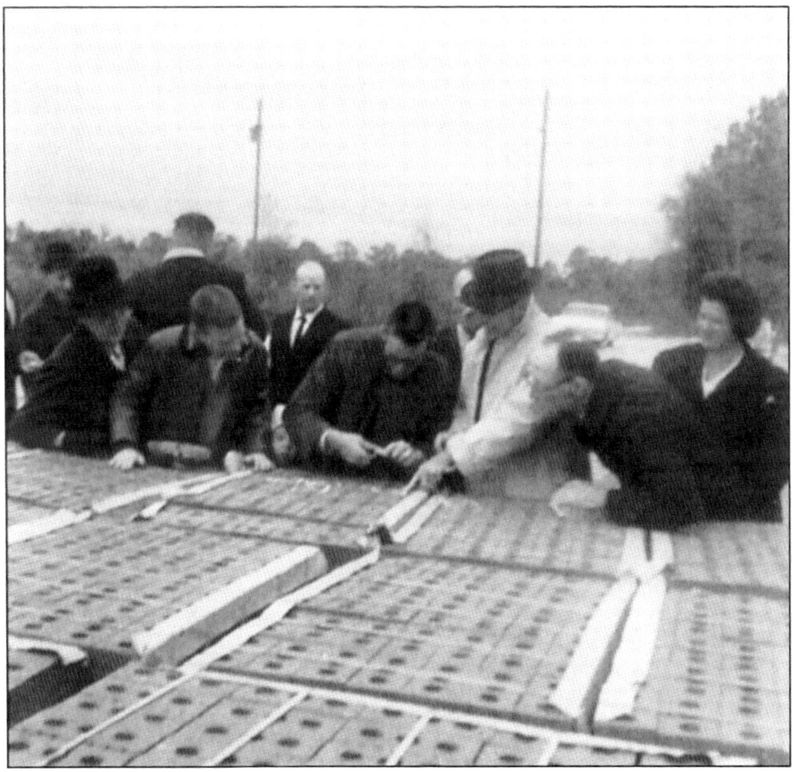

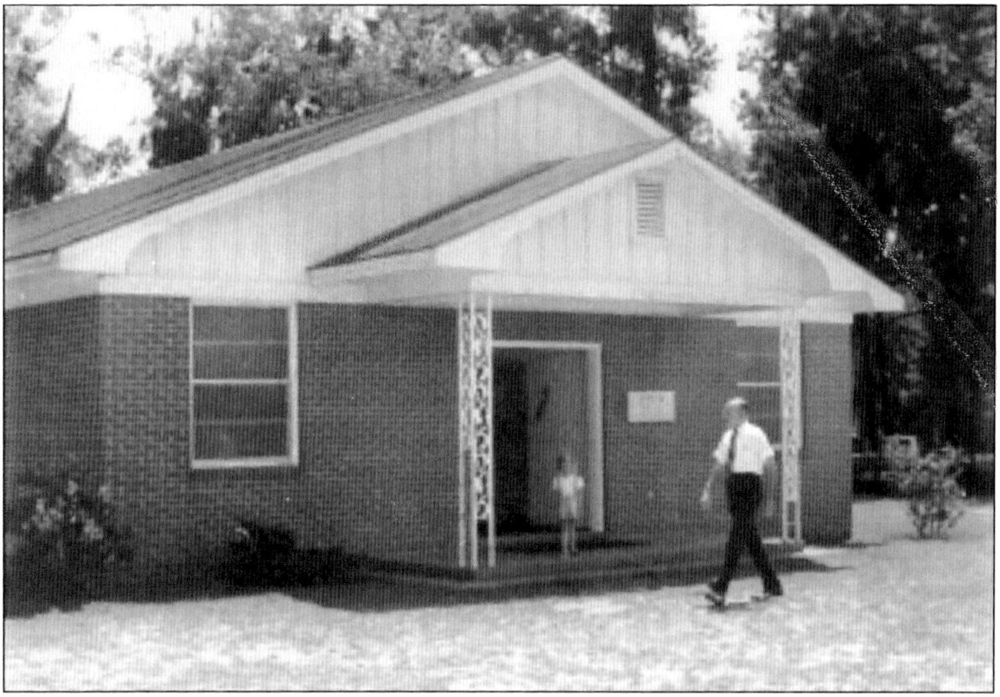

The above photograph shows Burnham Christian Church after its completion in 1967. Many church members were important in the planning, fund-raising, building, and completion of the church, making it a great source of pride for church members. New columns were added in 1976 to replace the wrought-iron uprights at the entrance. In 1985, members of the church installed a steeple to complete the image. The below photograph shows the church after several expansions in 1987 and 1991. (Marian Deas.)

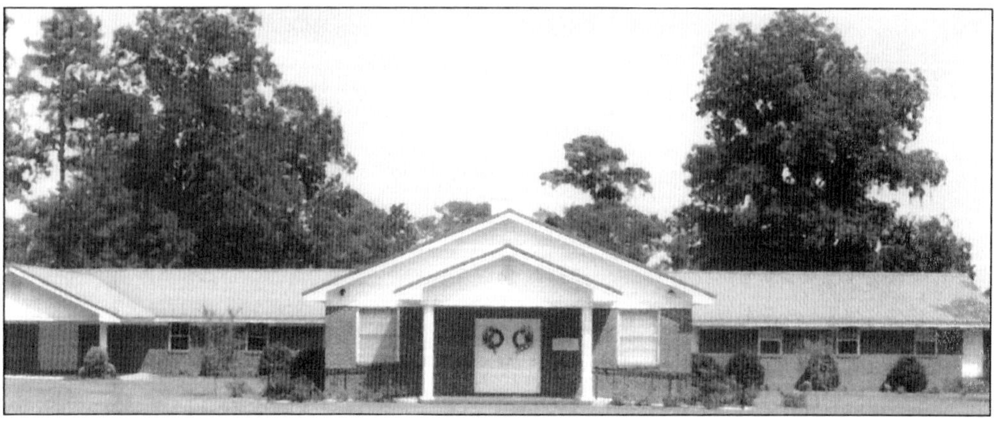

Five

JASPER

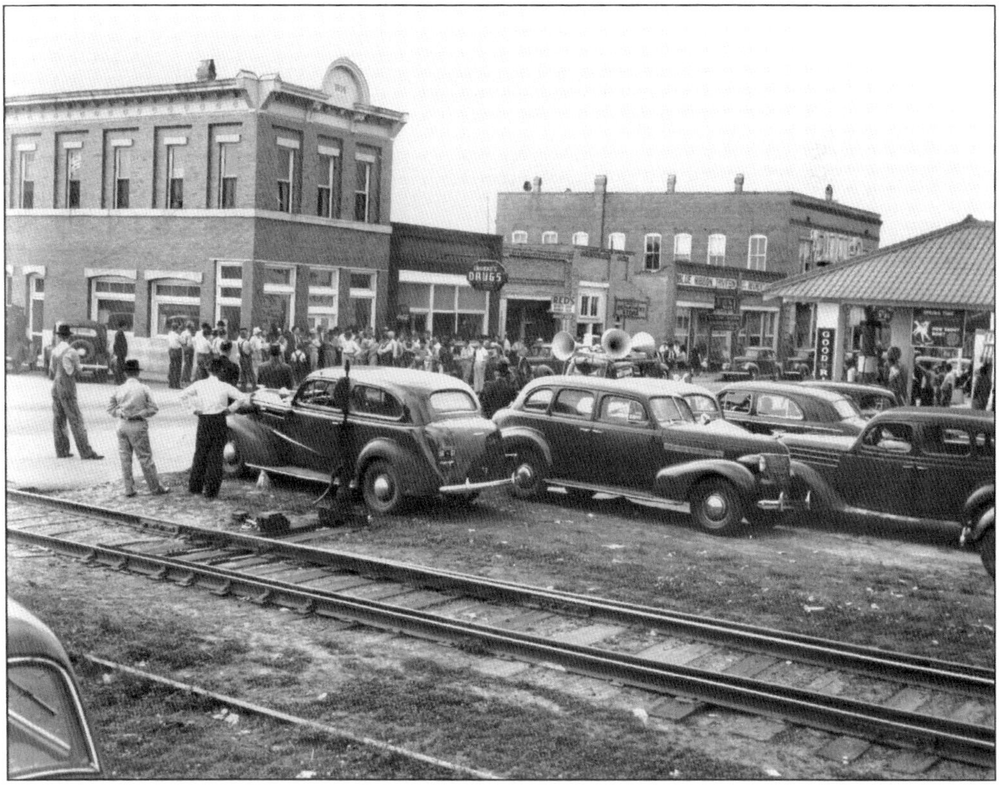

Francis P. Whitehair paid a visit to Jasper in 1940 with the hopes of gaining votes in the Florida governor election. He and Spessard Holland fought for the votes of rural, agricultural Florida by portraying themselves as common men. Whitehair was an attorney, businessman, and citrus grower from Deland, Florida. He lost the race to Holland and never held an elected office, although he did run the Department of the Navy under Pres. Harry Truman. On the left-hand side of the photograph is the First Commercial Bank, built in 1914. The bank operated for nearly 22 years before succumbing to the Depression in 1936. At that time, the bank and all properties that were owned by it were sold to the highest bidder in an effort to recoup its losses and hasten the return of the depositors' money. The building still stands today, and although it has been remodeled on the inside, the outside looks much the same as it did in 1940. (Florida Photographic Collection, State Archives of Florida.)

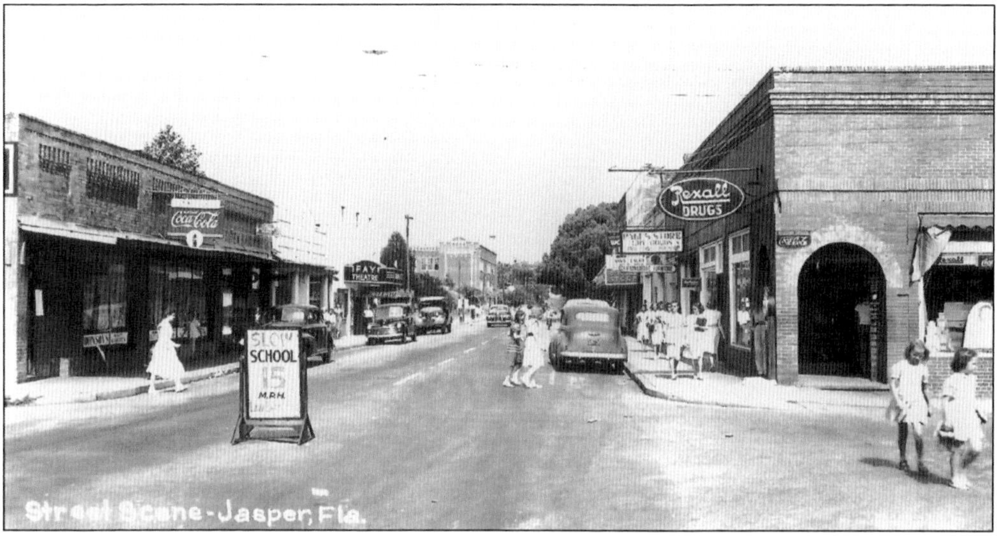

This mid-1950s photograph shows students leaving Jasper High School (the last brick building on the left side of the street). Many stopped in Rexall's Drug Store for a fountain drink and snack. The store was owned by Woodrow Wise, who operated it under the name Wise's Drug Store until he accepted a contract from Rexall in late 1939. Great excitement ensued when Wise hung the Rexall Drugs sign, replacing a worn Coca-Cola sign. (Paul Marion.)

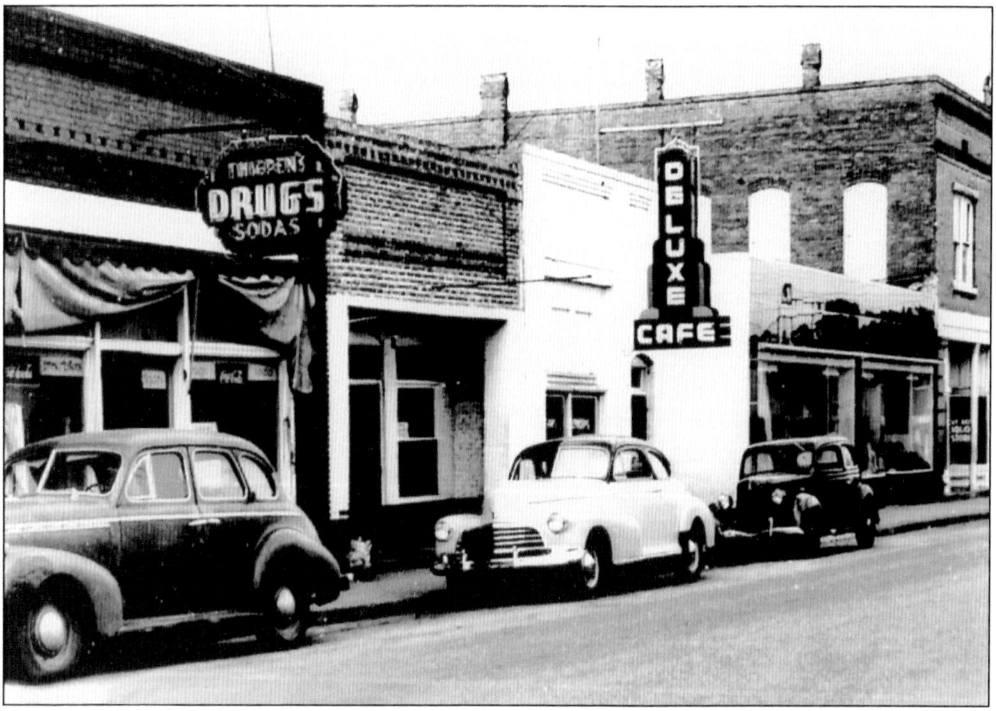

Adam's Drug Company, owned by Dr. Corbett, Dr. Bruce, and Math Wetherington, was sold in 1930 to W. W. Ingram, and he changed the name to Ingram's Drug Store. After almost 30 years, Ingram sold the shop to brothers Joe and John Thigpen. While John took care of the Thigpen Drug Company in Hamilton County, Joe operated their second pharmacy in Alachua. John married Annie Lee Cason of Jasper. (Paul Marion and Alan Fouraker.)

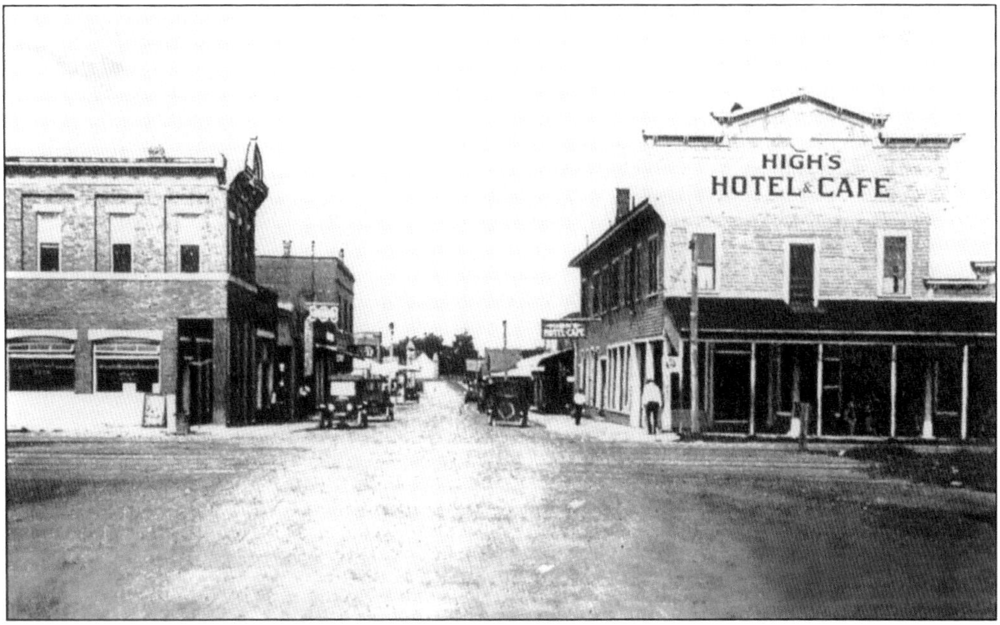

John Edward High worked for Ed Baker at his mill and eventually bought it and most of the surrounding land. In the early 1900s, he converted the Frank Adams building, at the corner of Hately Street and Central Avenue, into the High Hotel. A dinner cost 50¢ for locals and 75¢ for tourists. Hotel guests received three meals and a room for $1 a day. (Paul Marion and Alan Fouraker.)

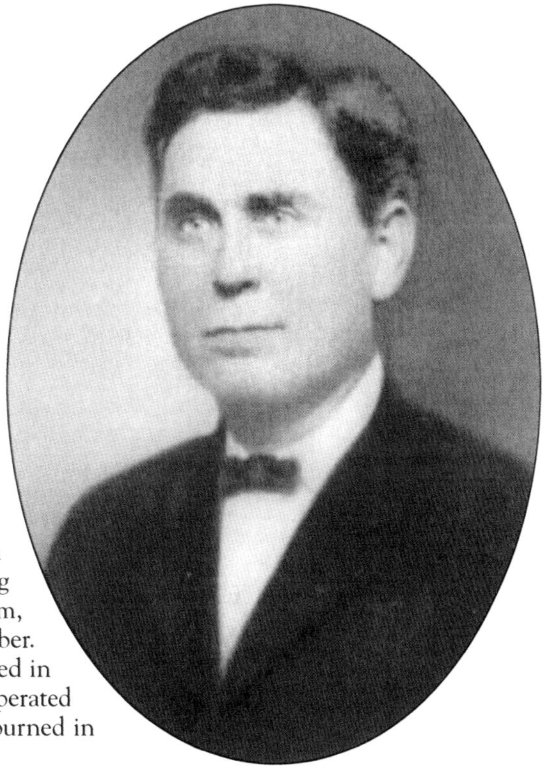

Prior to owning the High Hotel, High worked as a railroad engineer. Because he had to work on Sundays, he was expelled from Hardship Baptist Church. After achieving prosperity, he built a new church for them, although he was not allowed to be a member. High died in 1928, at age 72, and was buried in Evergreen Cemetery. The High Hotel was operated by his wife, Helen McTeer High, until it burned in the early 1930s. (William S. Mitchell IV.)

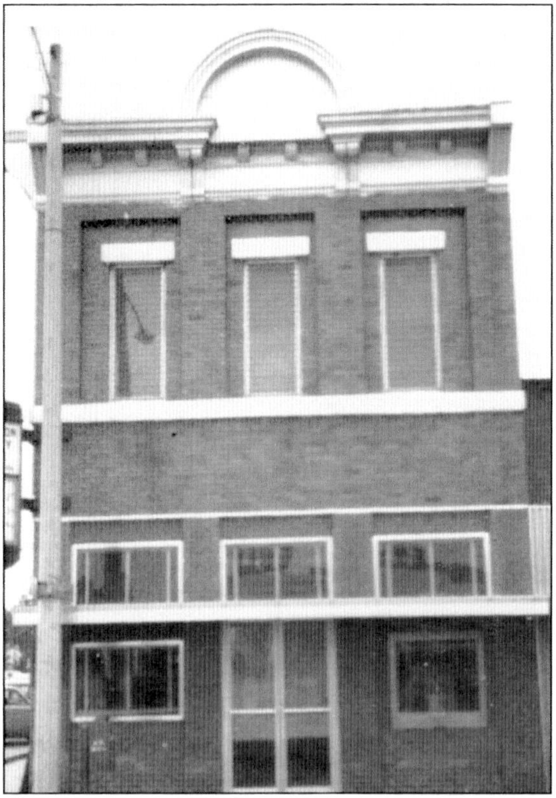

The Hamilton County Bank opened in June 1934 in the old Commercial Bank building (left photograph) on the corner of Hatley Street and Central Avenue. Directors T. T. Scott, Frank Bamberg Harrell, W. B. Lewis, J. A. Corbett, G. W. Harmony, and George Westmoreland worked diligently to convince people it was safe to deposit their money with the bank. Eugene Adicks Jr. began working at the Hamilton County Bank (below) in 1940. He served as vice president, executive vice president, and president. In the late 1960s, the bank relocated to the corner of Hately Street and Highway 41 (former location of Jasper High School). In 1987, Barnett Bank of Jacksonville purchased the bank, where Adicks remained as a consultant another two years before retiring. Although the first building is no longer a bank, the original vault, marble work, and teller window remain. The latter building is now owned by Bank of America. (Both Hamilton County High School.)

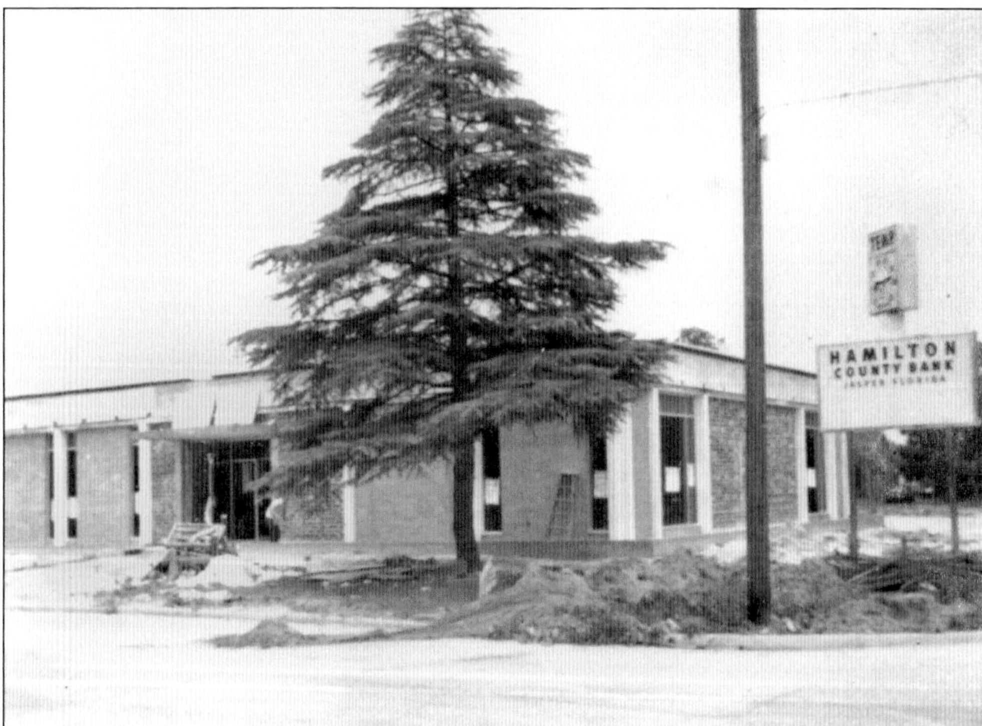

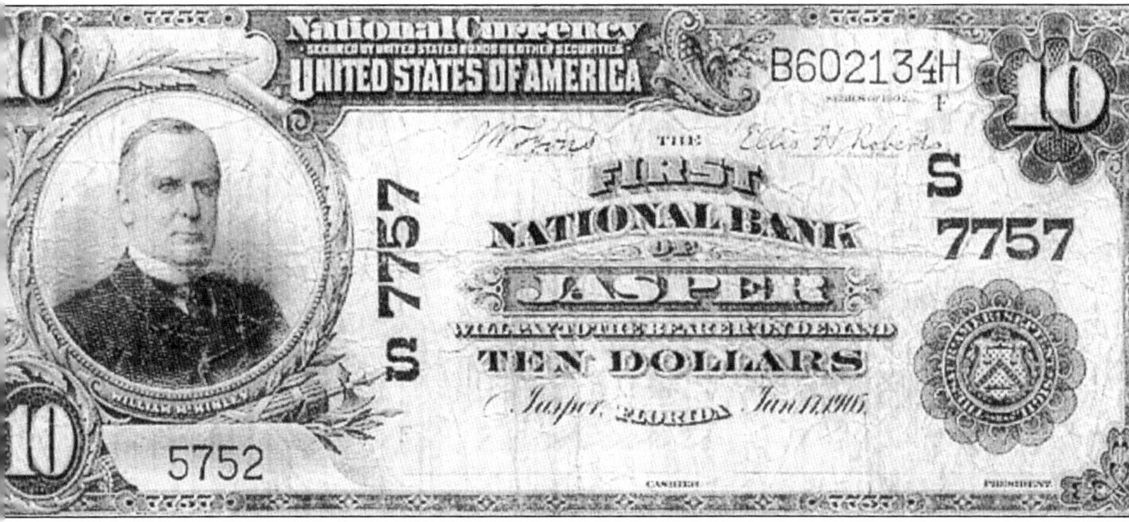

Currencies such as this one were issued by local banks, which then purchased government bonds and deposited them with the comptroller of the currency. This gave the bank the ability to give cash in exchange for the notes. The theory behind local currency was that a patron would buy the notes for a lesser amount than the face value, but the note would be worth the face amount in goods or services. The notes could be used around town with local merchants with the idea that it would boost the economy in the area. Although the notes were basically the same throughout the nation, each one bore the name of the local bank and the city in which it stood. (Alan Fouraker.)

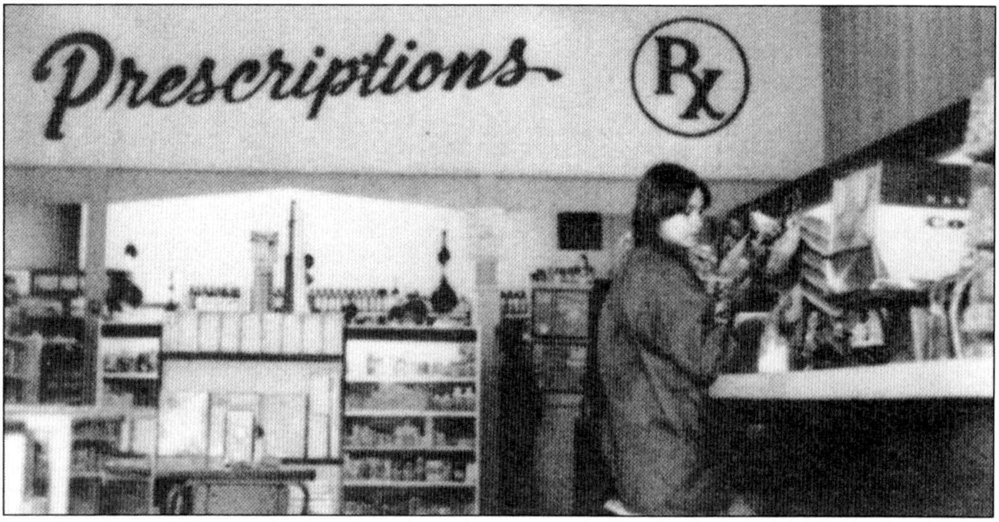

For 33 years, Clyde "Kayo" McGhin owned Kayo's Drug Store and soda shop in downtown Jasper. He sold it in 1993 to Rite Aid Drugs so he could spend more time with his family. The new company used his building until they completed construction of a new one at the corner of Hatley Street and Highway 41. His employees, Geneva Roper and Cissy Burnham, moved to Rite Aid Drugs in the new location, while McGhin retired. An unidentified customer stands at the counter. (Hamilton County High School.)

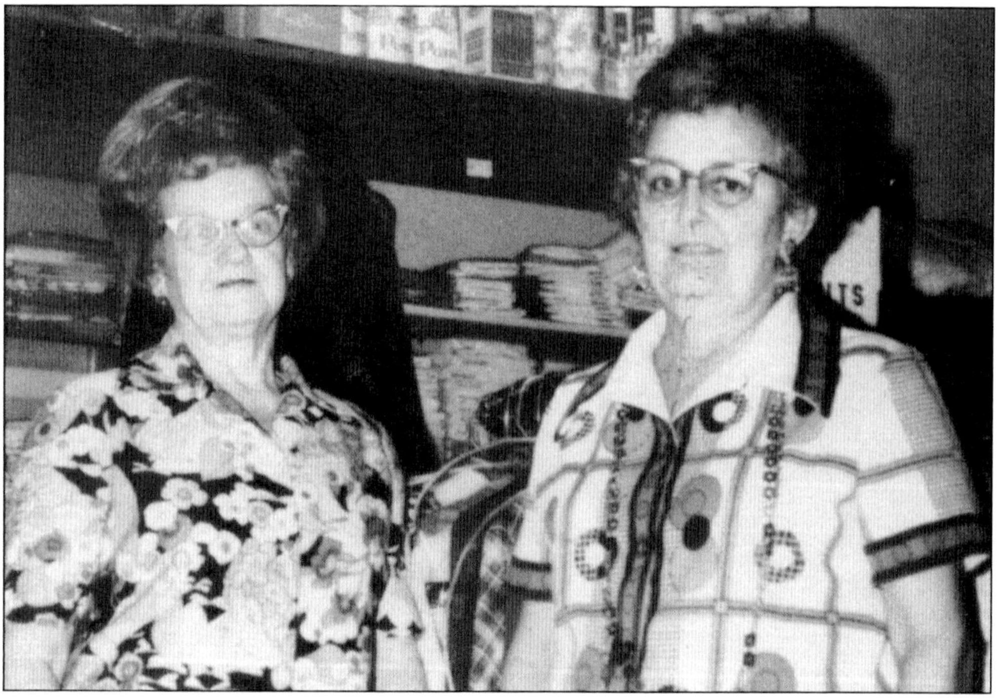

Eugene and Mary Lang operated Lang's Clothing Store, located on Hatley Street in Jasper, for nearly 50 years before selling the business to Albert and Mittie Deas in the late 1970s. The Deases owned the store for several more years before closing. Technically a small department store, it sold clothing, shoes, and household items, such as sheets and towels. Shown above is an employee and Mary Lang. (Hamilton County High School.)

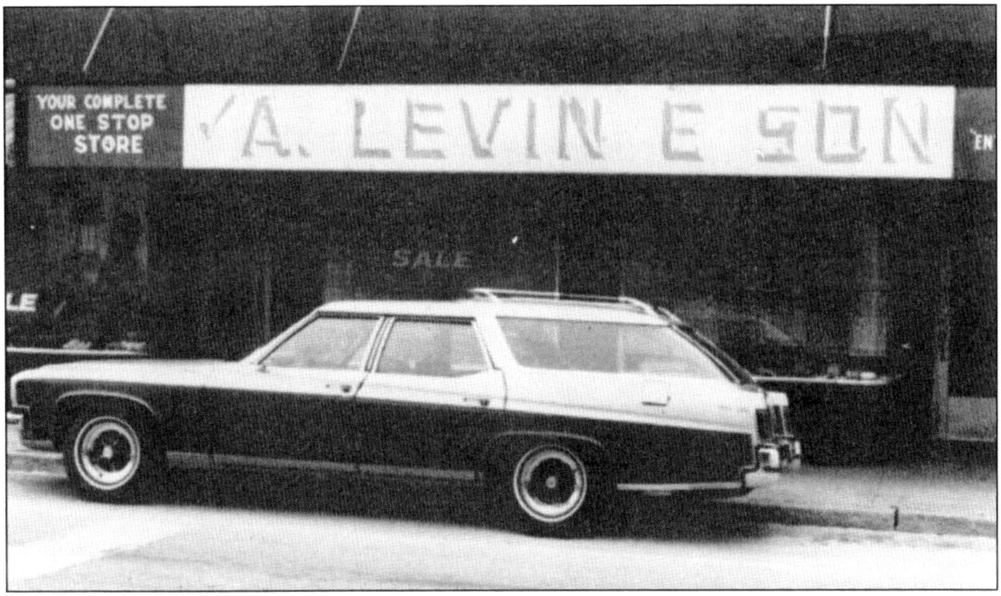

Charlie and Sylvia Levin owned A. Levin and Son Clothing Store, located in downtown Jasper for many years. The store opened on August 4, 1939, and the Levins owned it until the late 1970s or early 1980s, when they sold it to Norman Golivsky. The Golivskys operated the store until December 1990. Three of the first employees who ever worked in the store were Kirby Robinson, a Mr. Herndon, and Blanche Herndon. Once an employee was hired, if Levin liked them, he allowed them to stay for long periods of time. (Hamilton County High School.)

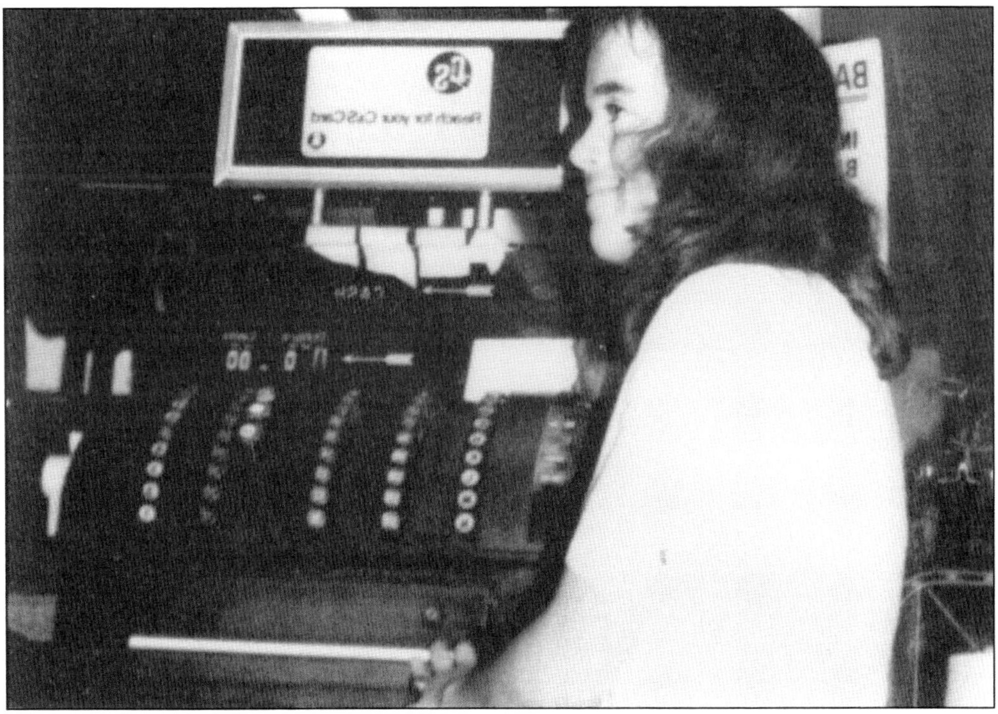

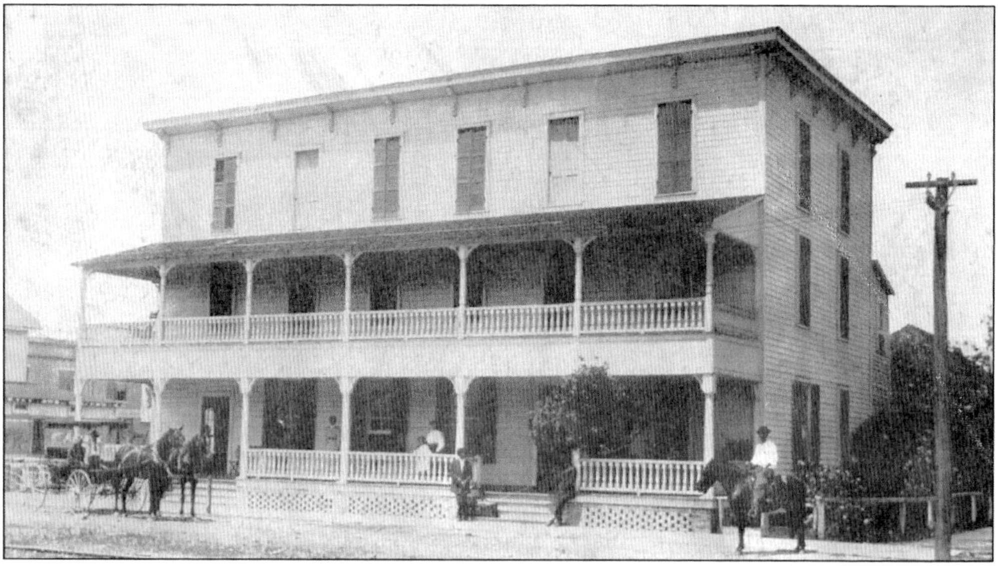

This 1920s photograph shows the Osceola Hotel on Central Avenue. Helen High changed the name to High Hotel when she purchased it in 1928. She also owned the High Café, and her daughter, Sara High, managed it for some time. L. M. Rhodes bought the café in May 1941. Helen High passed away June 1941 and was buried in Evergreen Cemetery. On March 31, 1942, the High Hotel burned to the ground, although some belongings of Nellie Frink, Katie Brown, Mr. and Mrs. E. N. Adicks, Mr. and Mrs. Overstreet, and other residents were saved. A small house owned by A. F. Hancock also burned. (Paul Marion and Alan Fouraker.)

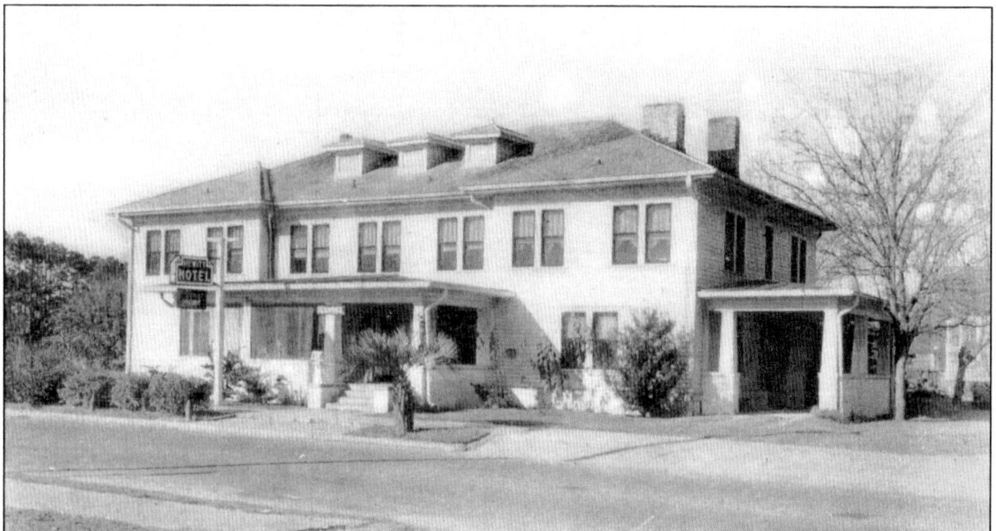

The Hewitt Hotel, built in 1926, was owned by Mr. and Mrs. Sydney Hewitt. In 1934, Ann Greer purchased it. "Miss Ann," as she was known, owned the hotel for 55 years. When she became ill, she moved to Surrey Place (an assisted living facility) in Live Oak, Florida. George Greer, Miss Ann's nephew, and later Johnnie Philman managed the hotel. It provided a place for those who had no family nearby, such as John Pearsall and John Gibson. Each July, Miss Ann would host tobacco field workers, feeding them and taking in their laundry until the season was over. The hotel is a private residence today. (Alan Fouraker.)

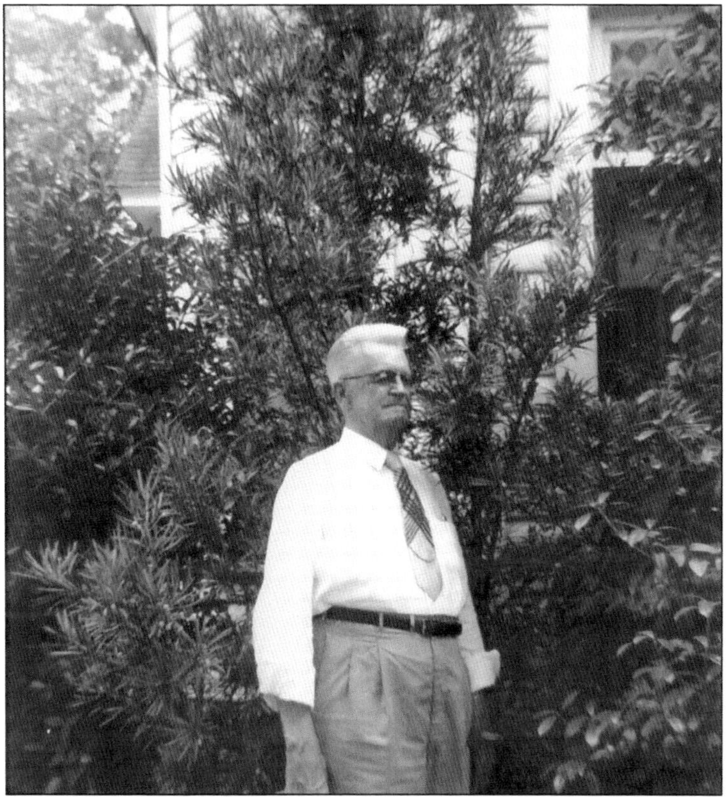

C. O. Shepherd (shown at right) lived a hearty life until April 27, 1974. He was 92 years old at the time and claimed to be surprised by the onset of old age. Moving here from north Georgia, Shepherd had one daughter, Mildred, who never married. During his time here, Shepherd was an avid businessman, for a while owning the Shady Brook Motor Court, located at the south end of Jasper. (Both Mildred Shepherd.)

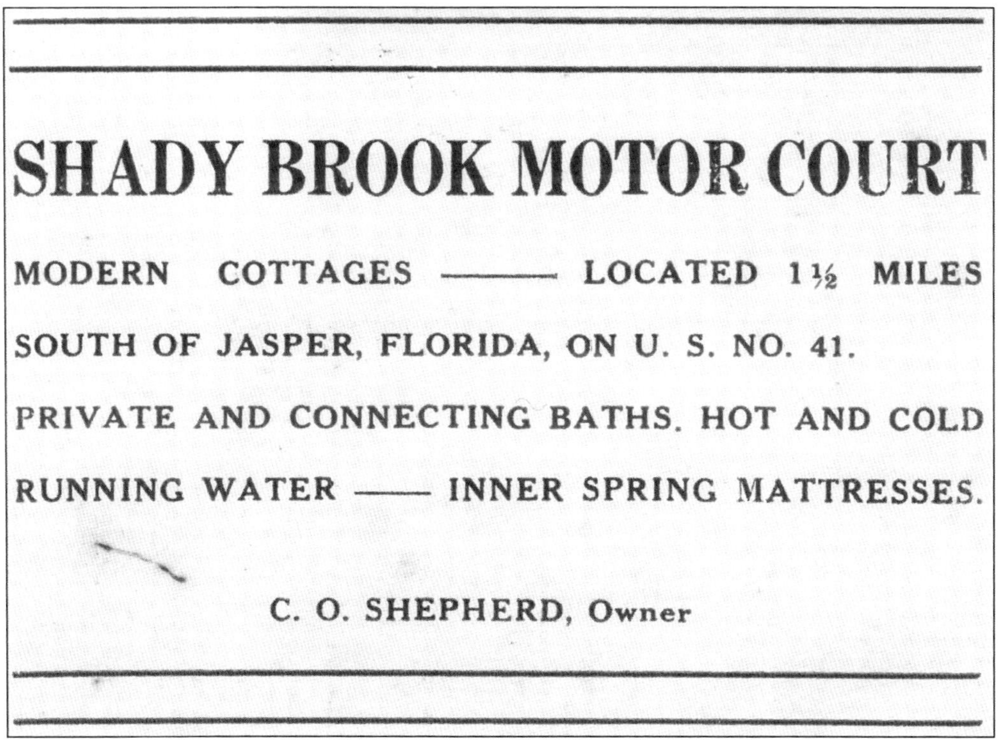

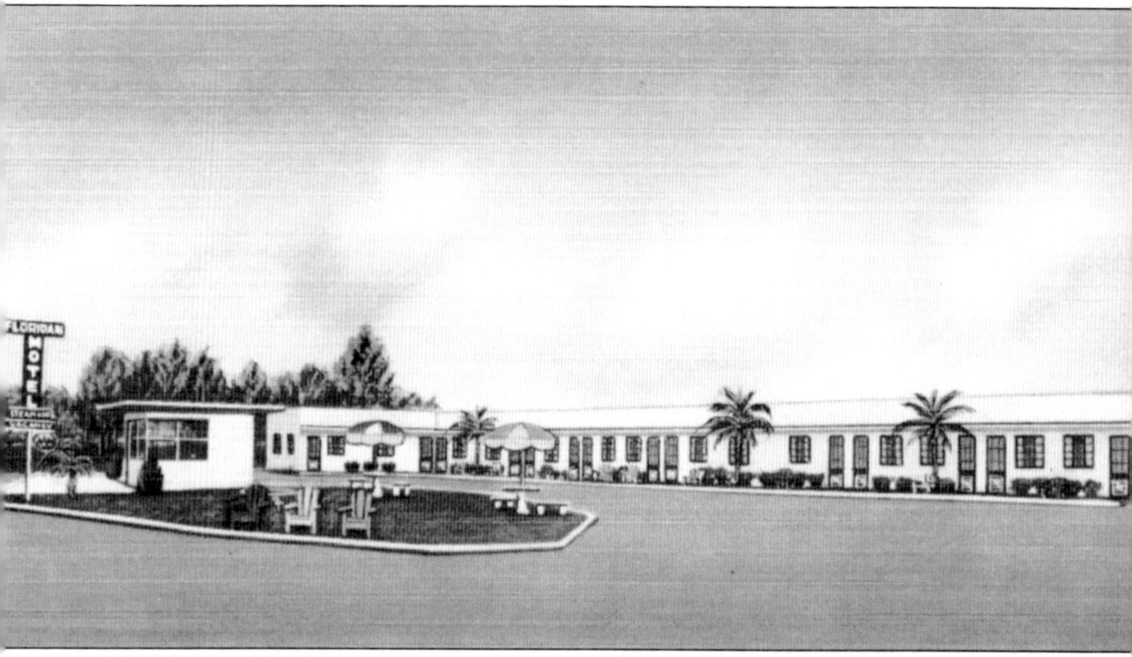

The Floridan Motel was constructed on the north end of Jasper by Eddie McGhin in 1951. He wished for all of the citizens of the town and county to see it, so he offered an open house in December of that year. Located at what is now the northernmost city limit of Jasper, the Floridan Motel was operated by Mildred L. and Fred Bischof for several years. Boasting air-conditioning and steam heat in the 18 rooms on-site, the motel was clearly one of the nicer locations of its time. (Author's collection.)

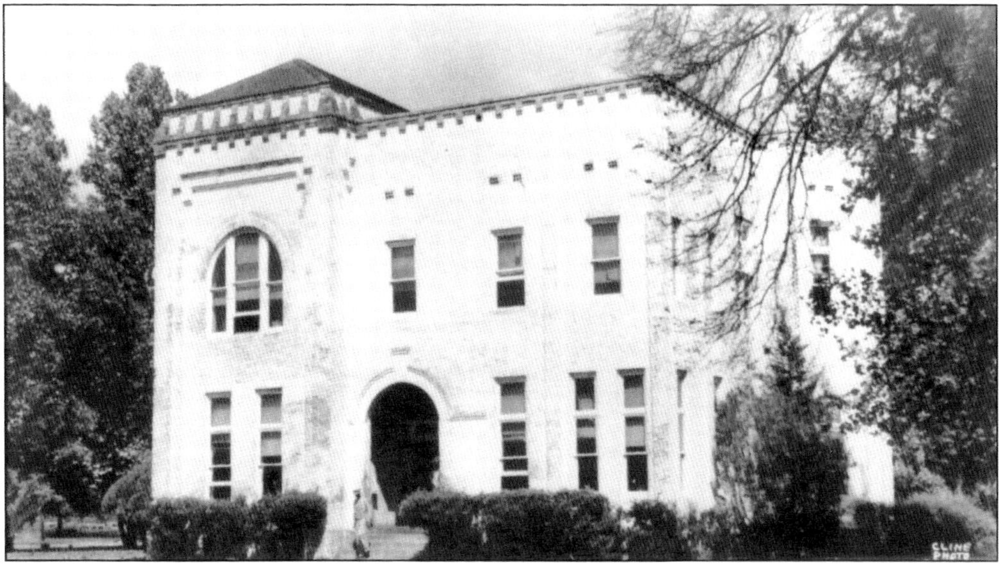

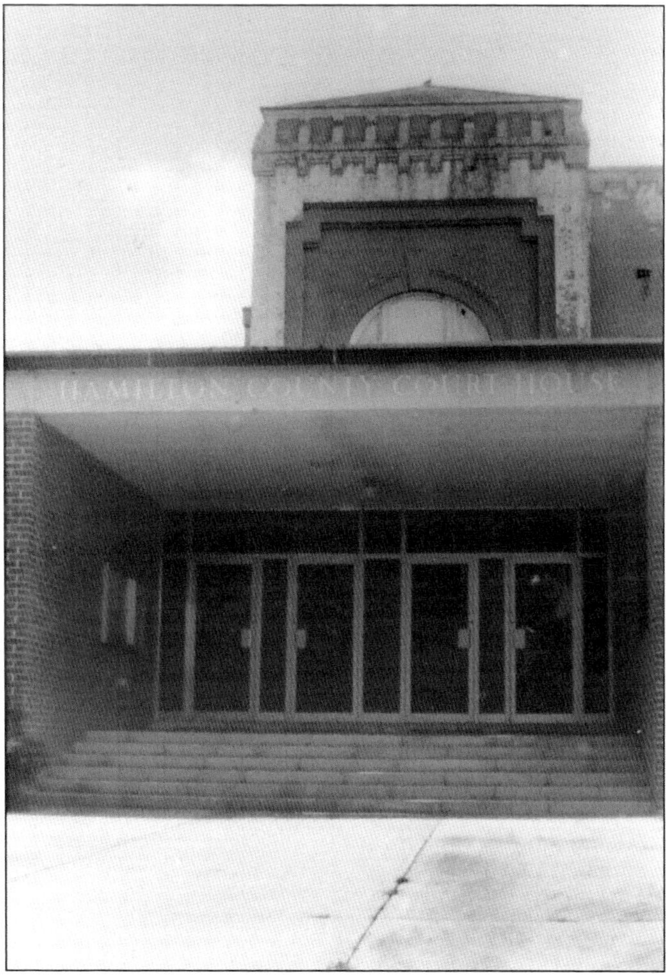

Jasper has been the county seat since June 1891; the current courthouse is the seventh to be built. Pictured is the sixth courthouse, completed in 1932, after the previous building was destroyed by fire in 1929. During the three years it took to rebuild, county officials maintained offices in the high school and privately owned buildings. The records remained intact, thanks to the fireproof vault installed in the courthouse in 1915. This "new" courthouse was built of brick and concrete by Bland and Foster for $14,485. It was remodeled in 1955 and 1968; eventually the offices were moved to the ground floor, and the upper floor of the building was removed. The above photograph was taken before the remodeling; the one at right shows the building afterward. (Above, Hamilton County Clerk of Court's Office; right, Marion Turner.)

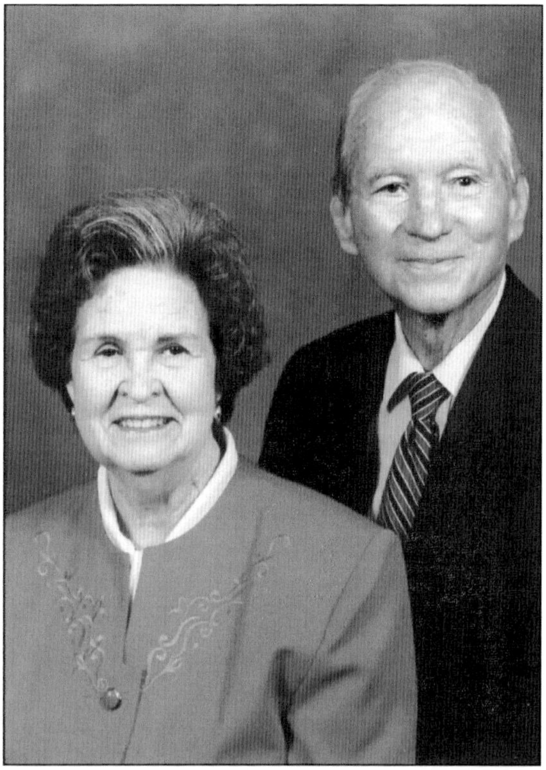

Harry Trammell Reid Sr. served as superintendent of public education from 1936 until 1944 and again from 1956 to 1968. On December 18, 1938, Reid married Mary Kathryn Harrell from Jennings. She was actively involved in the school system, clubs, and church. After graduating from the Cincinnati College of Embalming, Harry joined H. M. Tuten at Tuten's Funeral Parlor. In 1946, Reid started his own undertaking business, which he operated until his death in 2002. Mary Reid passed away October 1996. Both are buried in Evergreen Cemetery. (William S. Mitchell IV.)

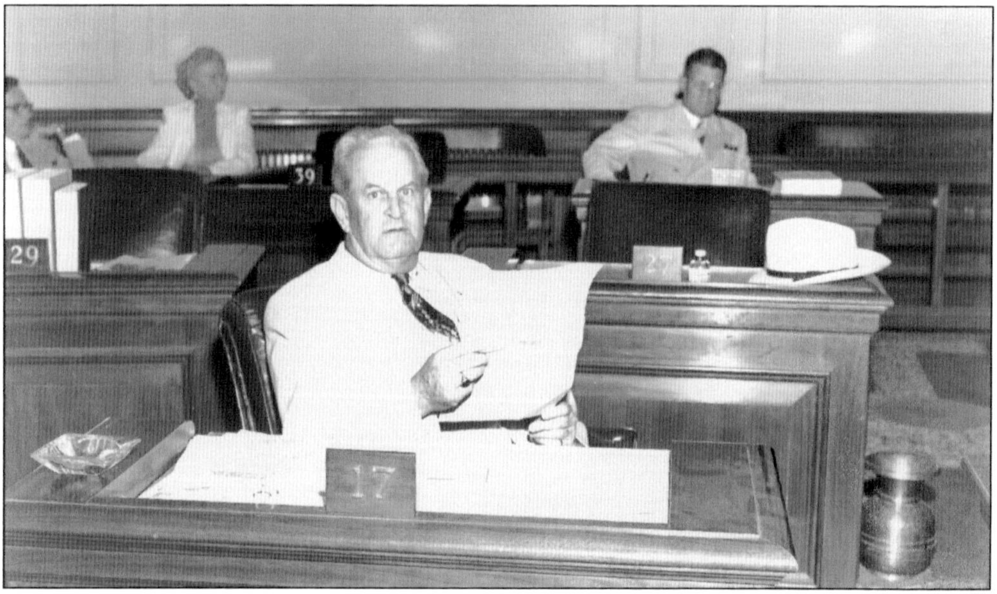

James Graham Black was born June 22, 1889. He fought in France during World War I, was elected to the Florida State Senate, and served on the Defense Committee during World War II. Black married Minnie Mabelle Vickers, daughter of Drew Luther and Minnie Smith Vickers, and they had one child, James Graham Black Jr. (1920–1978). Minnie Black was a member of several social clubs and organizations. She died January 3, 1984. All three are interred in Evergreen Cemetery in Jasper. (Florida Photographic Collection, State Archives of Florida.)

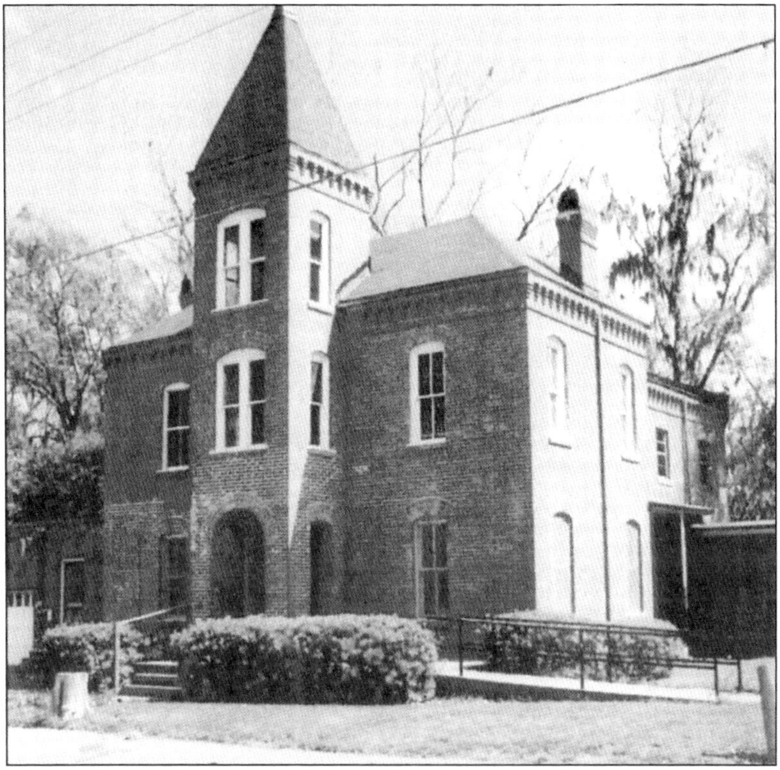

The Old Hamilton County Jail in Jasper was built in 1893 and housed prisoners for more than 91 years. The original hanging tower remains, where the last legal hanging in Florida was held. The sheriff and his family lived inside the jail to supervise the prisoners, cooking their meals and monitoring their visitors. The jail is currently listed on the National Register of Historic Places. (Marion Turner.)

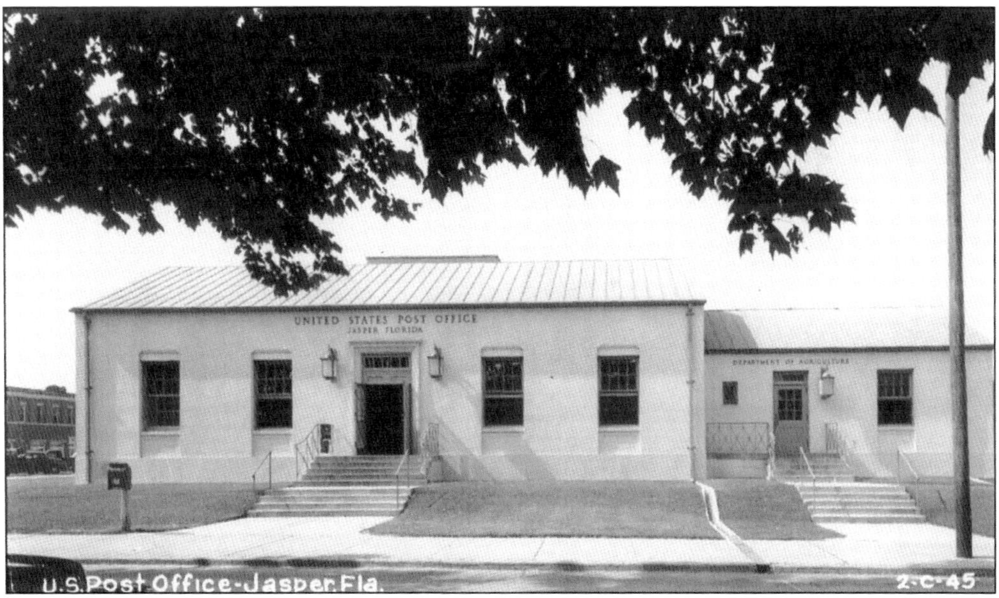

After earnestly lobbying for a post office building for Jasper, Congressman R. A. Lex Green telegraphed postmaster Kirby Lafayette Sandlin on behalf of Postmaster General James A. Farley and the state treasurer department officials in 1939—the county would receive $70,000 for a new federal building. One of the requirements for approval was the building had to house other federal activities, so the County Farm Agency office was located inside the post office to meet that requirement. (Paul Marion.)

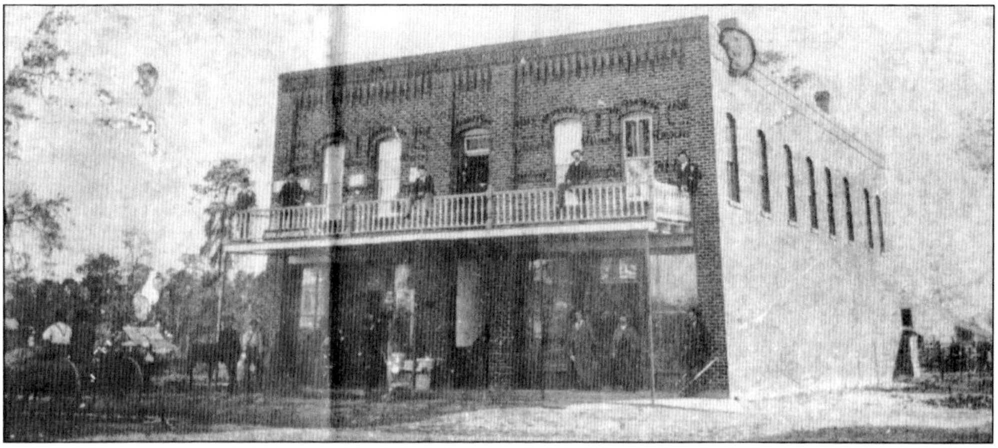

Joe Cox, a handicapped man who sold fish from his cart two days a week, is pictured above in the wagon to the left of the Horne and Greene Building in downtown Jasper. Shown from left to right are (upstairs) Braxton Small, George J. Graham, Chandler Reynolds, W. B. Roux, N. W. Marion, and Mallory Horne; (downstairs) E. C. Horne, W. H. Greene, C. W. Bradshaw, Barney Cheshire, and John M. Caldwell. (Marion Turner.)

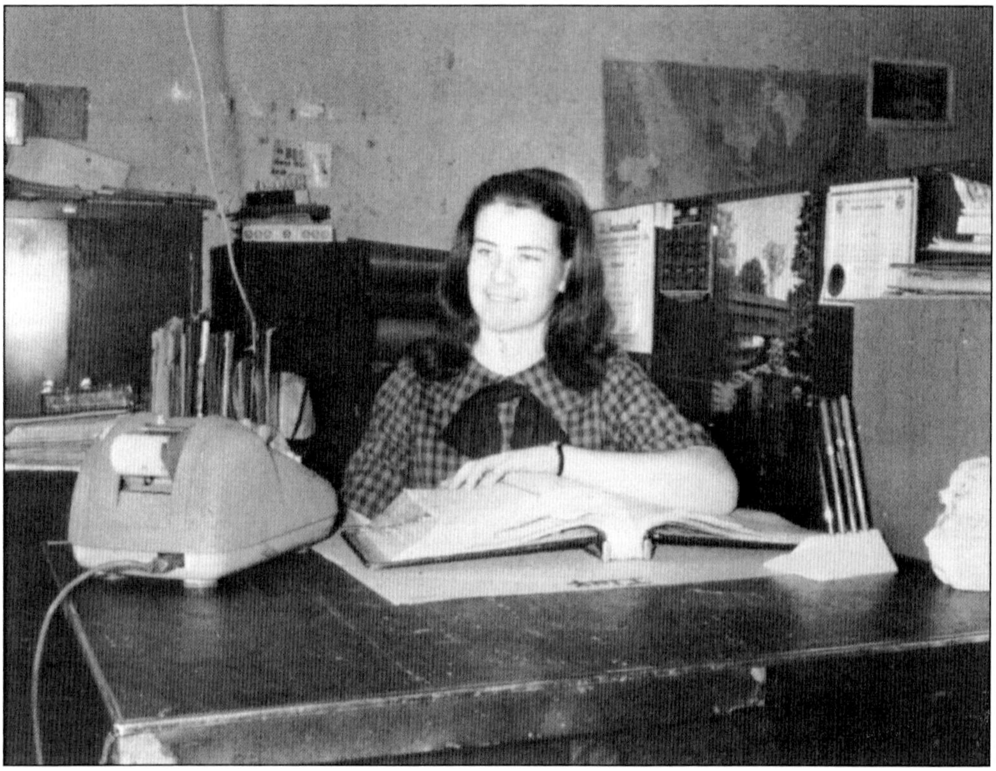

The *Jasper News* has been known by various names since its birth in the 1870s: the *Spirit of the Times*, the *Hamilton County Times*, and the *Weekly Courier*. In 1890, John M. Caldwell purchased the paper and renamed it the *Jasper News*, its current name. Since 1955, the paper has changed ownership several times: Robert Ehlert, Jack Taylor, Thomson South Georgia and North Florida, and Community Newspaper Holdings, Inc., (CNHI). Diana McDaniel (shown here) held an internship with the paper in 1967 under Robert Ehlert. (Hamilton County High School.)

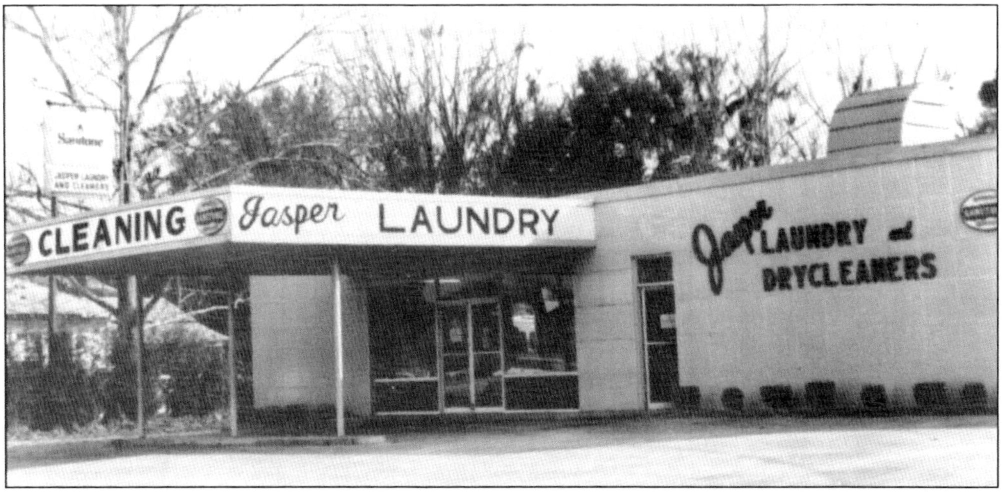

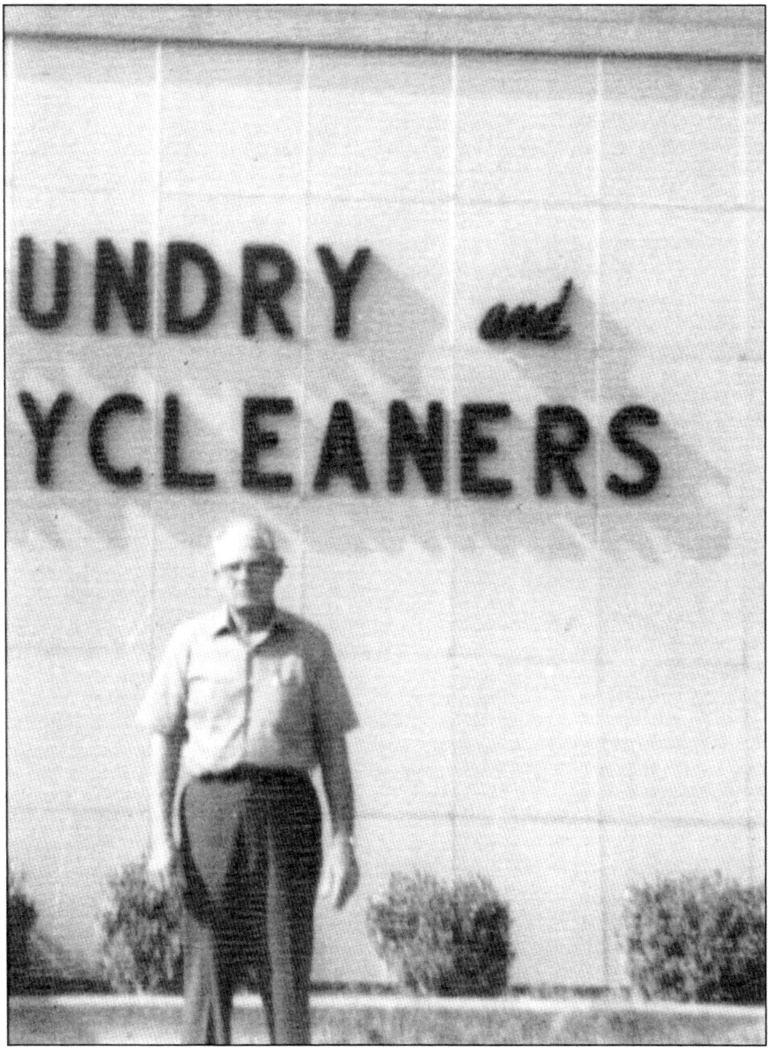

C. B. Barker (shown at right) and his half-brother, Archie Hicks, purchased the Jasper Laundry in 1946. It was already a laundry, and after the purchase, they increased the size of the operation. In 1961, there was a fire and the laundry was nearly destroyed. At that time, Barker bought Hicks's portion of the business, and Barker's son, David, joined him in the operation a year later. They rebuilt the business from that point on. Currently, the younger Barker is the owner and he has several employees. (Hamilton County High School.)

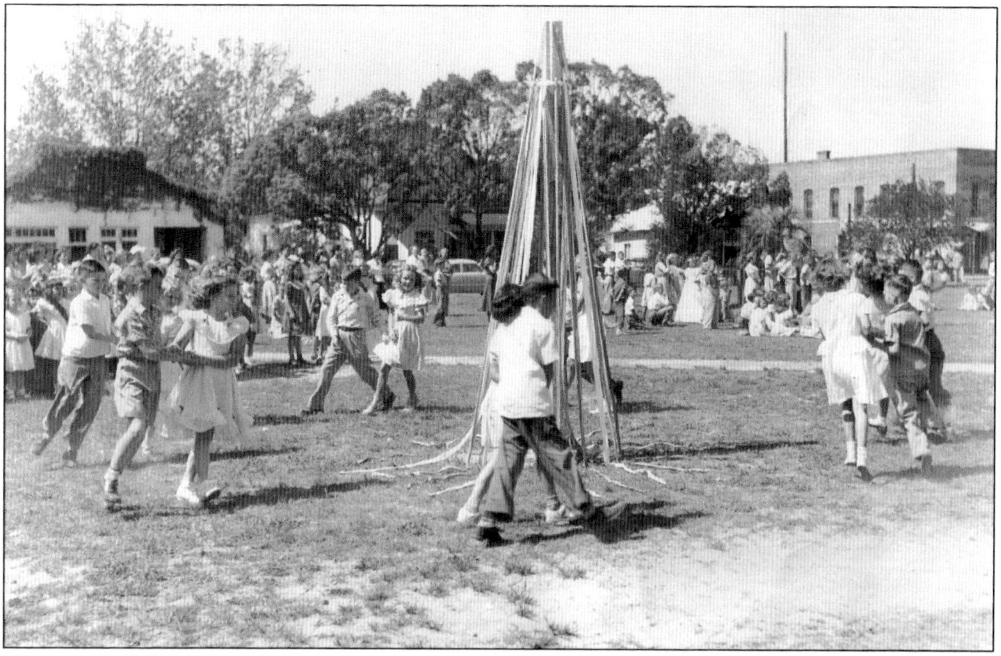

This view of the Jasper City Park in May 1951 shows the May Day Celebration hosted by the Jasper Woman's Club. Four sets of 16 children danced around four maypoles. The Jasper High School faculty chose the queen, Dorothy Hodges, for her scholastic excellence, and her throne was located at the center of the park. (Hamilton County Clerk of Court's Office.)

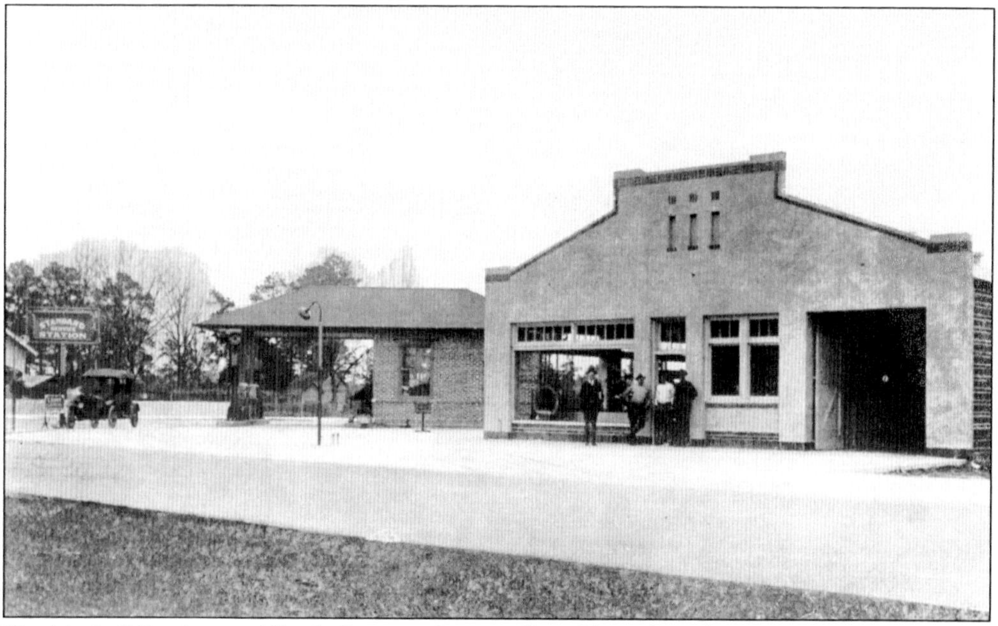

The Mitchell Brothers and Futch Company began selling Chevrolet vehicles in 1928. One longtime employee, George Dexter, opted to purchase the company in 1937 with Wiley Grantham. The partners operated the station under the original name for many years but changed it to the WG&D Chevrolet Company in 1949. The proprietors felt that Chevrolets were the finest vehicles on the road, and the shop was well known for its sales and prompt repair of vehicles. (Alan Fouraker.)

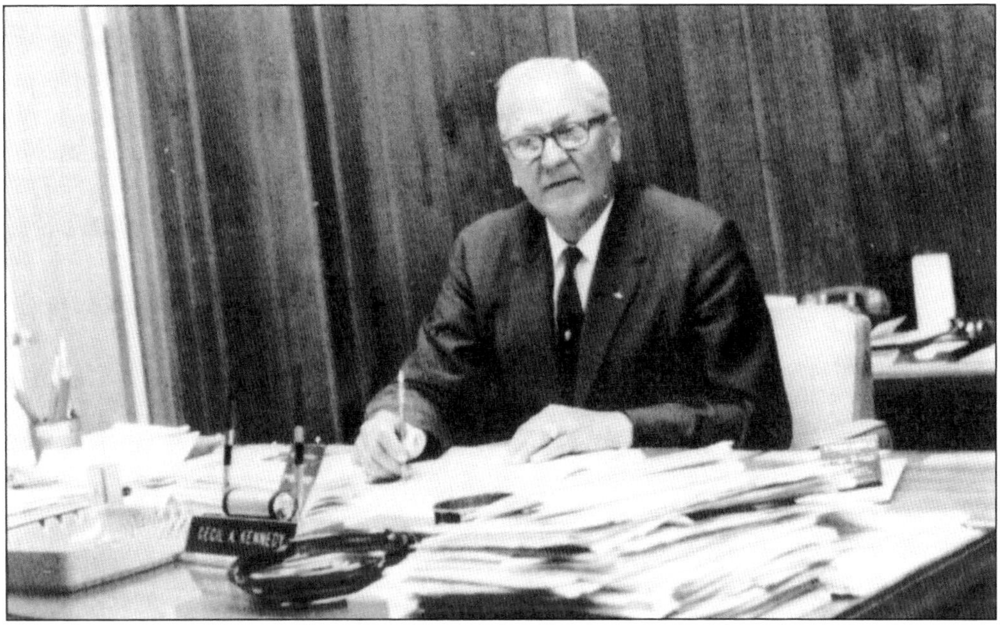

Cecil A. Kennedy purchased the Chevrolet dealership in the late 1960s from the WG&D Chevrolet Company and changed the name to C. A. Kennedy Chevrolet. For nearly 15 years, he peddled prized vehicles such as the El Camino, Chevelle S.S. 396, Corvette, Chevrolet II, Monte Carlo, Camaro, and pickup trucks over a half ton. In 1975, Bruce Gluek bought the dealership. (Both Hamilton County High School.)

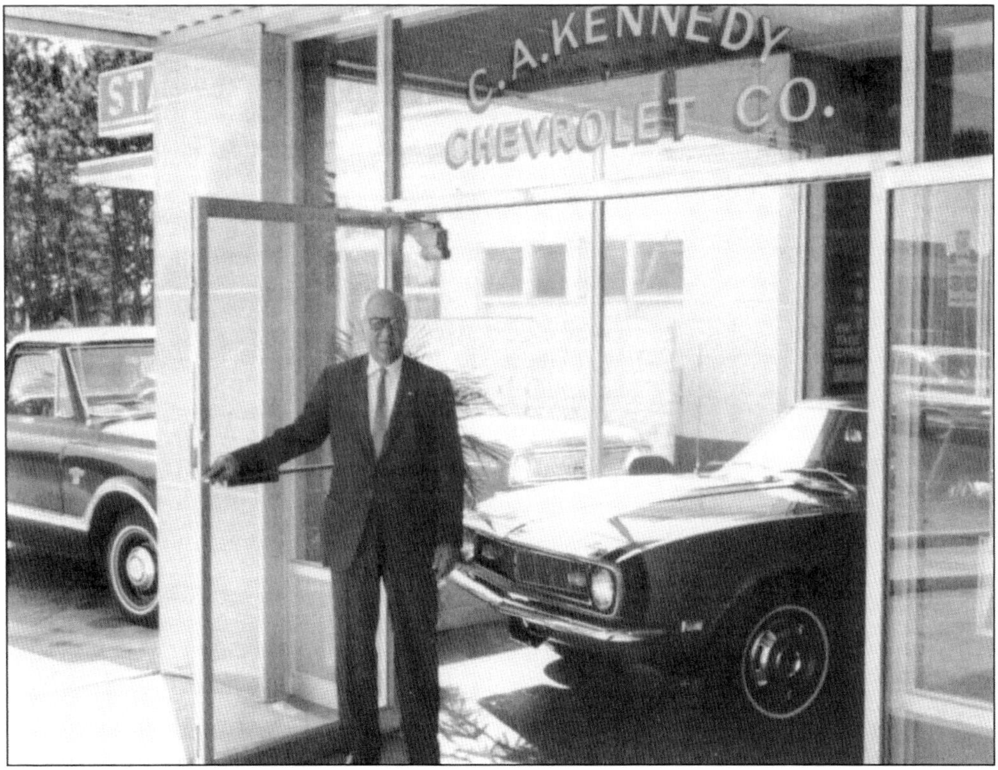

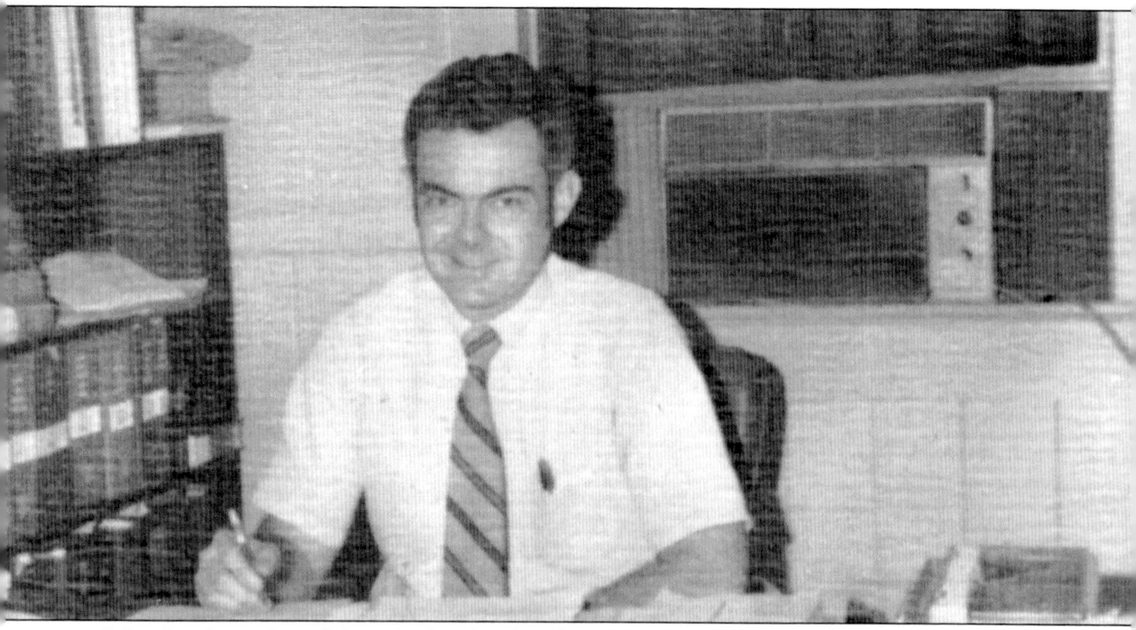

John Peach graduated from high school and went to the University of Florida to study history, knowing he would one day have his law degree. Leaving there in 1958 with his associate of arts degree, he joined the U.S. Army for a short stint before returning to college: first at Jacksonville University for his bachelor's in 1962, then to Mercer University for his bachelor of laws degree in 1965—a real lawyer. During his time at Mercer University, he met his soon-to-be wife, Lorena Williams. Practicing law with C. A. Avriett, he later opened his own practice. After six years, Peach set his sights on being a judge; he succeeded as county judge in January 1973 and moved up to circuit judge in May 1978. Peach retired in January 2009. (Hamilton County High School.)

John Hoyle McCormick was born in White Springs to Mr. and Mrs. C. H. McCormick. He has served as Hamilton County judge and mayor of White Springs. He has been county attorney since 1973. McCormick married Margaret Patricia McCall, a schoolteacher, in 1974. In this 1960s photograph, he is speaking at the Stephen Foster Memorial (currently the Stephen Foster Folk Culture Center State Park). (Florida Photographic Collection, State Archives of Florida.)

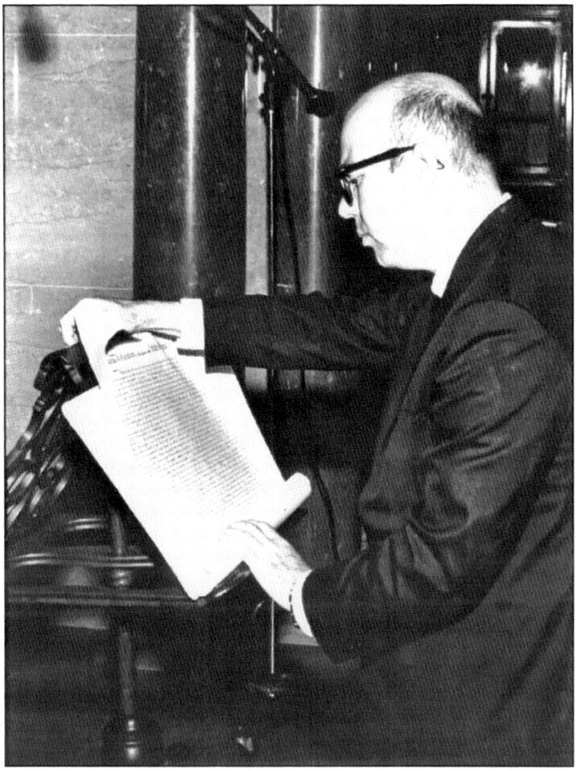

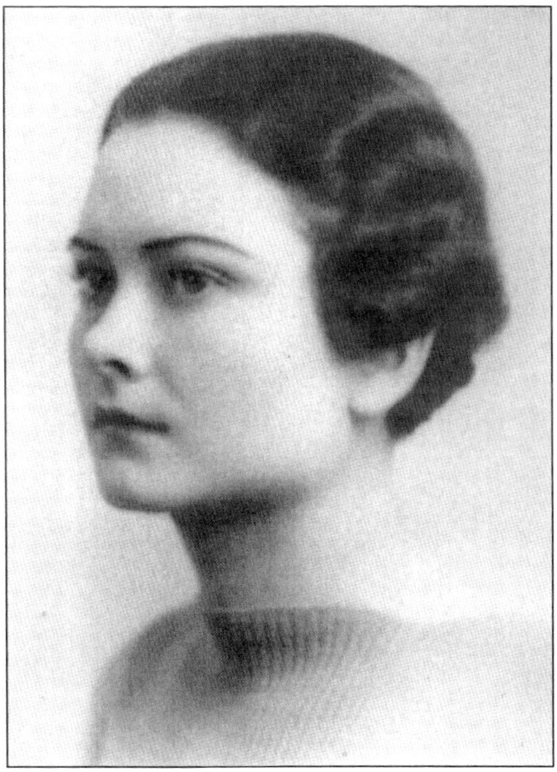

Jim Cassin Corbett Camp, daughter of James Alfred and Georgia Cassin Corbett Camp, was born October 2, 1915, and named after both parents. She attended the Jasper Normal Institute, graduated from the Jasper High School in 1933, and attended Florida State College for Women and Brenau College. "Ms. Jim," as she was known, married Raymond Judson Camp Jr. and was active in local organizations and social clubs. (William S. Mitchell IV.)

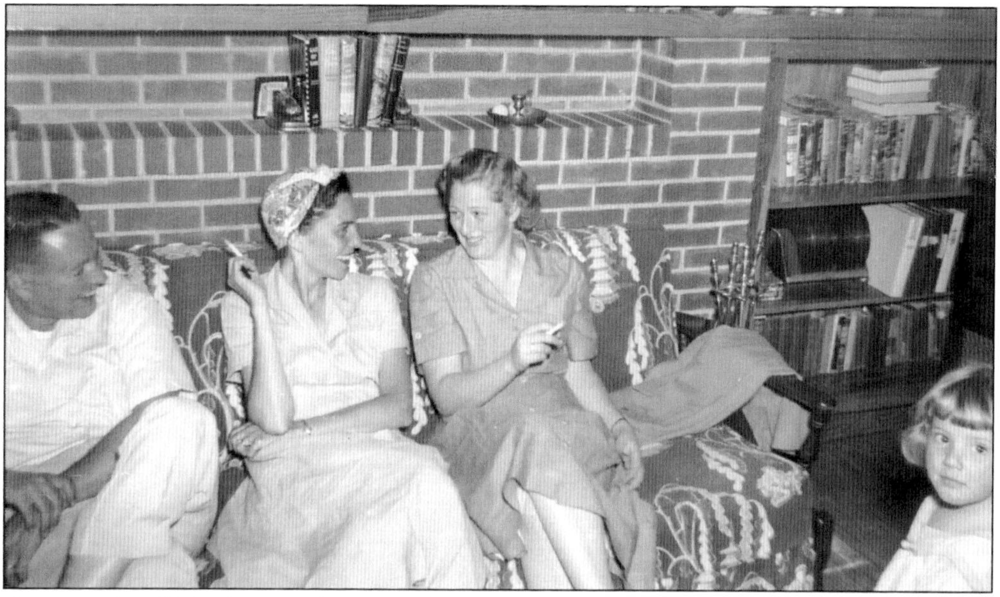

Shown in this 1950s photograph are members of the prominent Adams and Camp families. From left to right are Stanley Adams Jr., Bette Wisenbaker Adams, Ercel Anderson Camp, and Anne Camp Roberts. Stanley Adams Jr. married Bette Wisenbaker in the 1940s, and they had three children: Stanley Adams III, Cliff, and John. Ercel Anderson Camp married John "Buddy" C. Camp in 1939, and they had four girls: Sally Camp Mortiz, Ellen Camp Batcheldor, Anne Camp Roberts, and Bette Camp Conine. (Cliff Adams.)

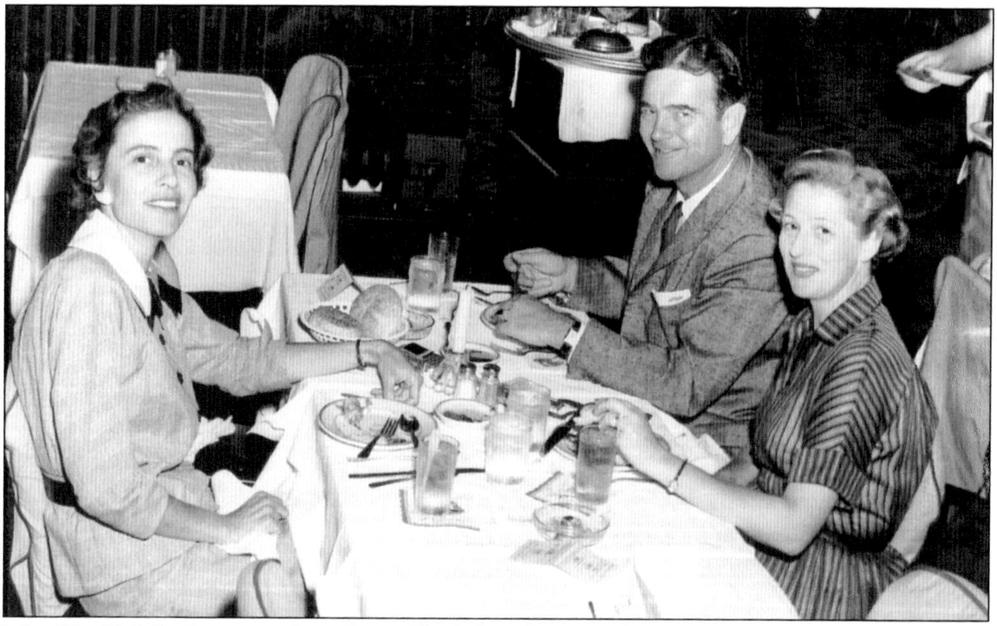

John "Buddy" C. Camp was born June 16, 1915, to Raymond and Sallie Powell Camp. His main occupations were naval stores, lumber, pulpwood, and forest farming. He served as chairman on several state boards. He passed away in 2008. Shown here in the mid-1950s, Camp, his wife, Ercel Anderson Camp (right), and Bette Wisenbaker Adams enjoy dinner together. The Camps are godparents to Cliff Adams, child of Bette and Stanley Adams Jr. (Cliff Adams.)

Many children wish to run away from home and do things for themselves. In this 1950s photograph, five-year-old Stanley Adams III (left) and three-year-old Cliff Adams (right) show their fearless side. At a time when hobos were still prevalent in society, the young boys found themselves among the ranks—bags packed and on their way to nowhere. (Cliff Adams.)

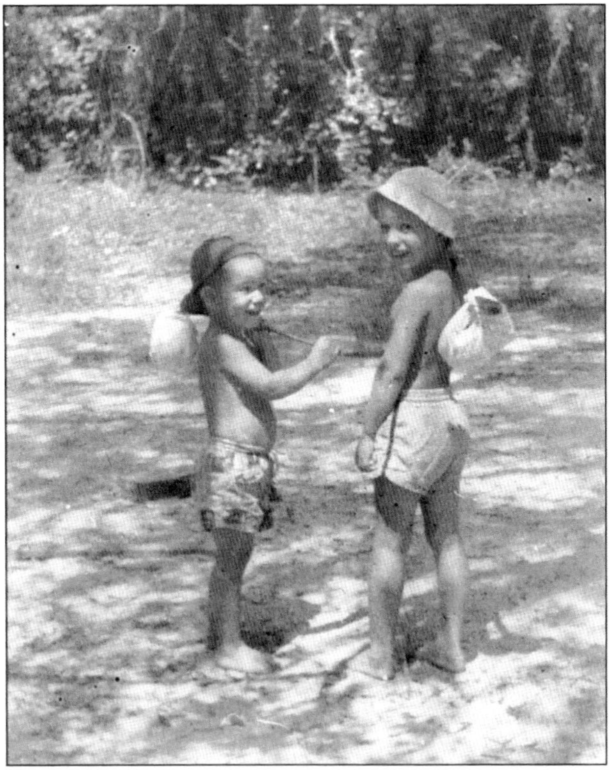

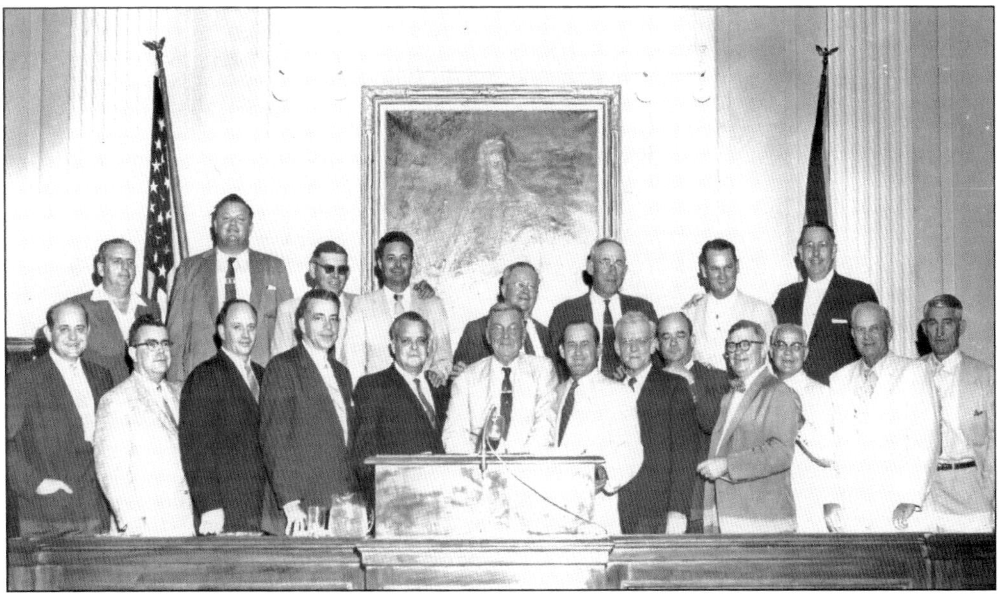

Originally each county in Florida had the same number of Senate and House representatives, so approximately 15 percent of the population elected a majority of the representatives that ultimately decided the laws. A former *Tampa Tribune* editor, James Clendenin, coined the name "Pork Chop Gang" because this group of legislators from north Florida took good care of their own districts. James Graham Black of Jasper (first row, second from left) was a member of the Pork Chop Gang in 1956. (Florida Photographic Collection, State Archives of Florida.)

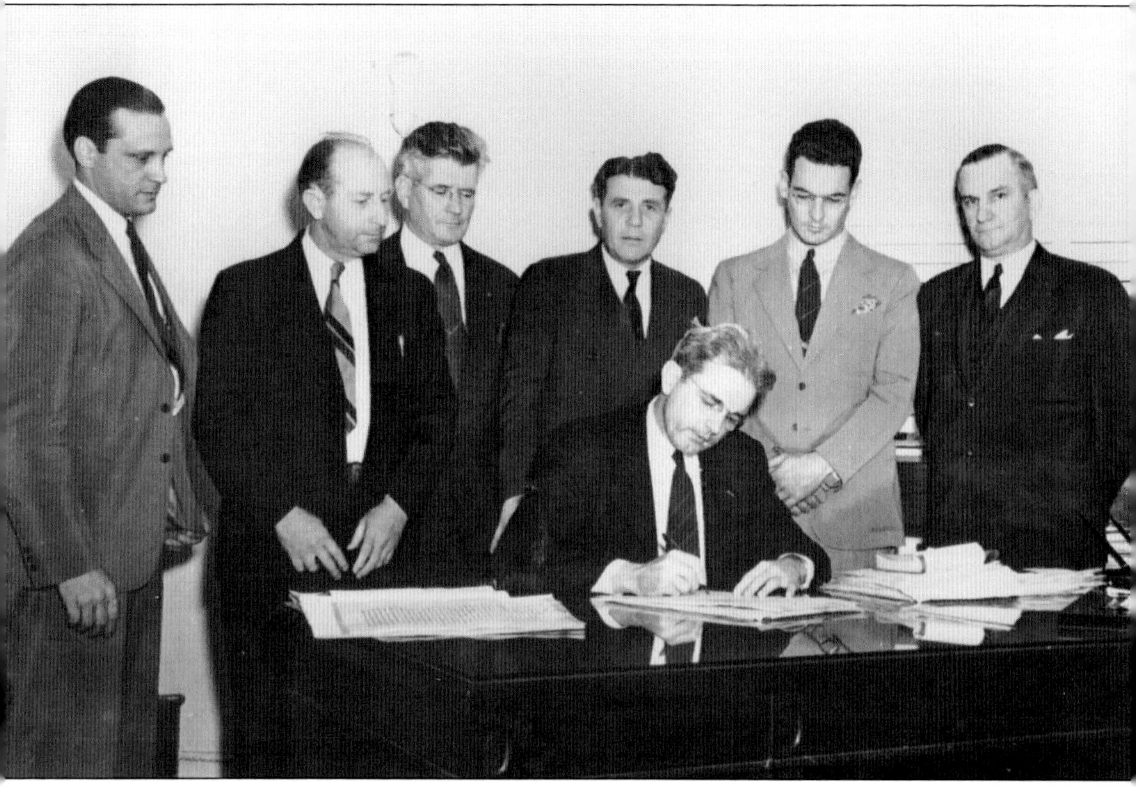

After an aggressive campaign across the state of Florida, Spessard Lindsey Holland (1892–1971) won the office of governor for the 1941–1945 term. Shown here on May 13, 1941, mere months after taking office, he is signing a bill. Looking on are, from left to right, Sen. Addison Drummond from Bonifay, Rep. Frank Bamberg Harrell from Jasper, Sen. Raeburn C. Horne from Madison, Rep. Loomis Chapman Leedy from Orlando, and Rep. Daniel McCarty from Fort Pierce. Frank Bamberg Harrell was born on May 17, 1893. He served as a representative from Hamilton County for several years. In 1939, during his term, he was chosen as the chairman of the Finance and Taxation Committee for the House of Representatives. Harrell died on October 10, 1966. Both he and his wife, Avvie Watson Harrell, are buried in Evergreen Cemetery in Jasper. (Florida Photographic Collection, State Archives of Florida.)

Six

Jennings

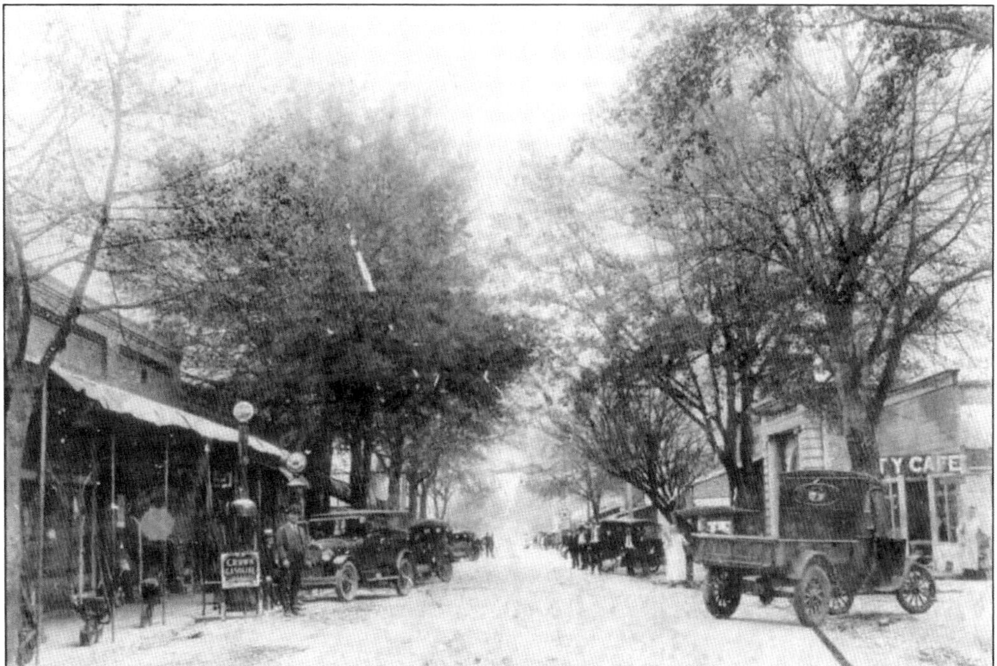

This photograph shows Jennings around 1924. As the largest community in the county at the time, Jennings boasted a large commerce base for the era. Three cotton gins were located in the town, shipping their wares to Savannah, Georgia, and Jacksonville, Florida, via the Georgia Southern and Florida Railway. Two drugstores had four physicians to send patients on their way. Thirty-six stores provided enough business to maintain two banks. All of these provided valuable employment for the citizens of the community. Many of the buildings have been long destroyed, but a few remain today. (Marian Deas.)

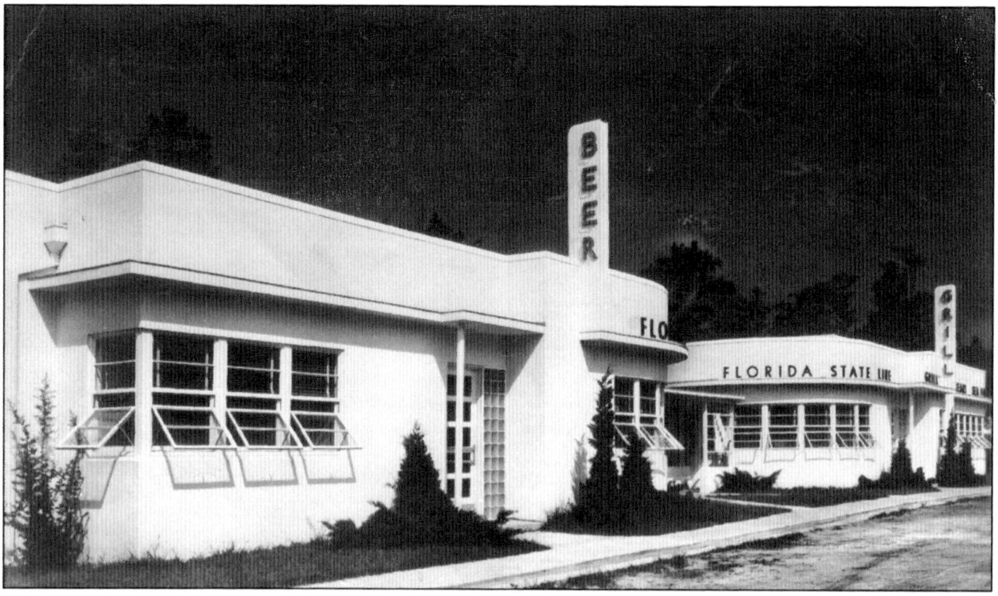

Boasting steak, seafood, and other meals on the Georgia side, and alcoholic beverages on the Florida side, the Florida State Line Grill was located with half of the building in each state. The restaurant was in operation from the late 1930s until the mid-1950s, when Hamilton County was voted to become a dry county, and the Florida side could no longer sell alcohol. It was very popular with tourists, who enjoyed the fact that they could visit both states in one stop. The above photograph shows the outside of the restaurant; below is the dining room. (Author's collection.)

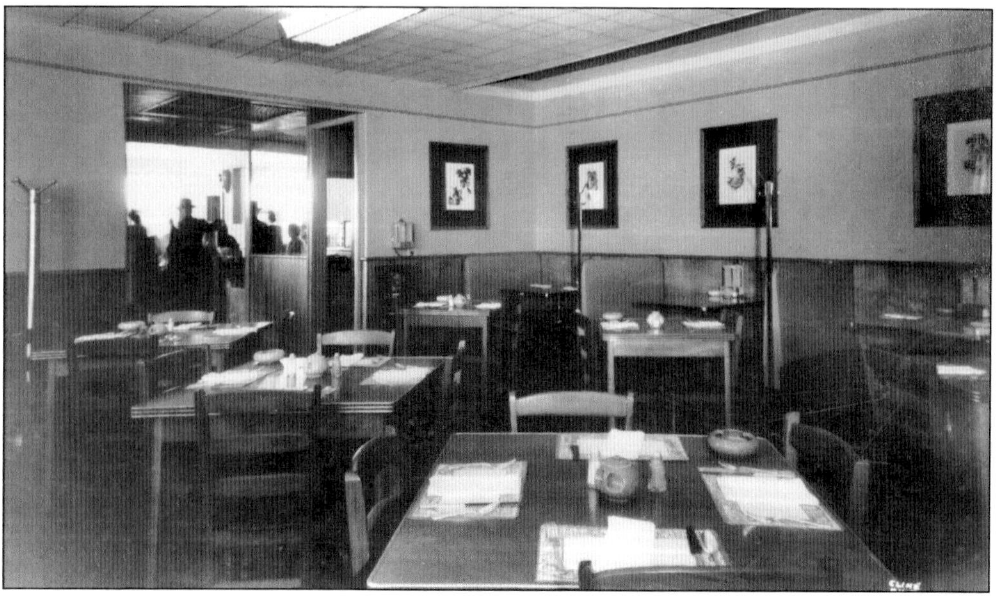

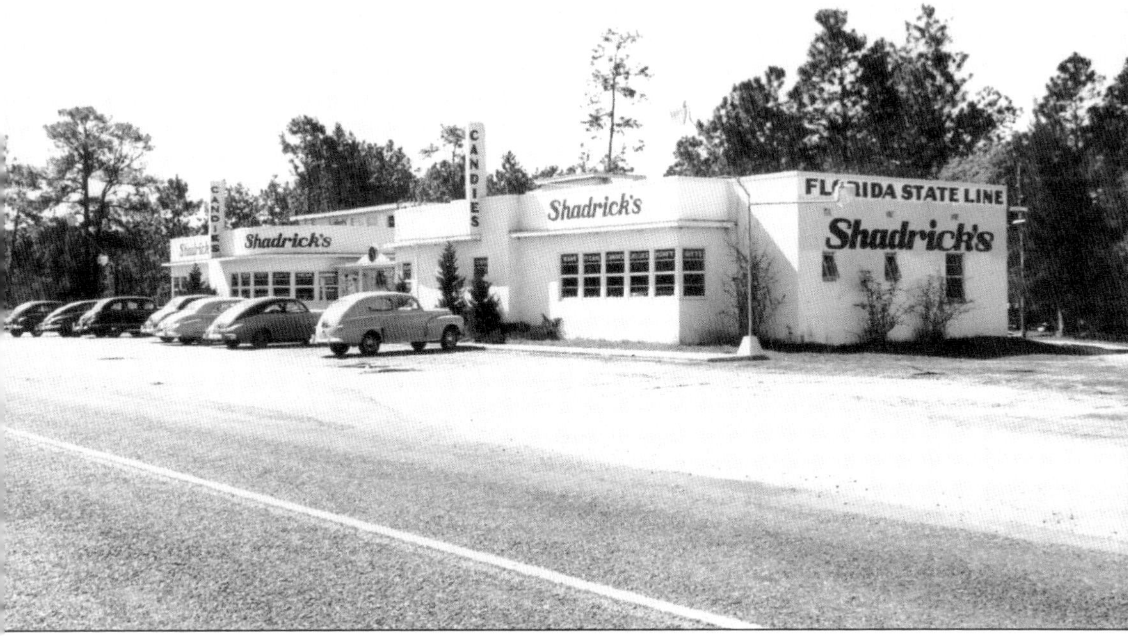

This building is located on the Florida-Georgia state line on Highway 41 and remains standing today as a private residence. Known as Shadrick's Candy and Gift Shoppe, it was in operation from the mid-1950s to the mid-1960s. Shortly after the interstate was constructed, the business closed from lack of patrons. (Author's collection.)

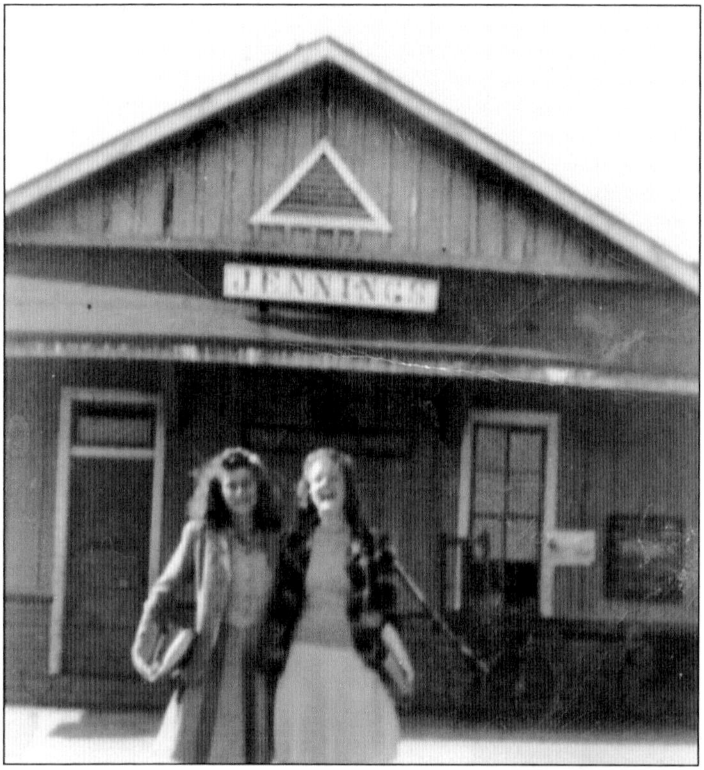

The Georgia Southern and Florida Railway (GS&F) Jennings Train Depot was a popular stop for the railroad, where citizens would board the train and head north to Valdosta, Georgia, for a day of shopping. Another popular day trip for citizens was to White Springs for a day of swimming and picnicking at the springs. The tracks for the GS&F were laid in 1889–1890 from Macon, Georgia, to Palatka, Florida. After some financial difficulties in 1891, the line fell under the supervision of the Southern Railway and then Norfolk Southern Railway 100 years later. (Contributor.)

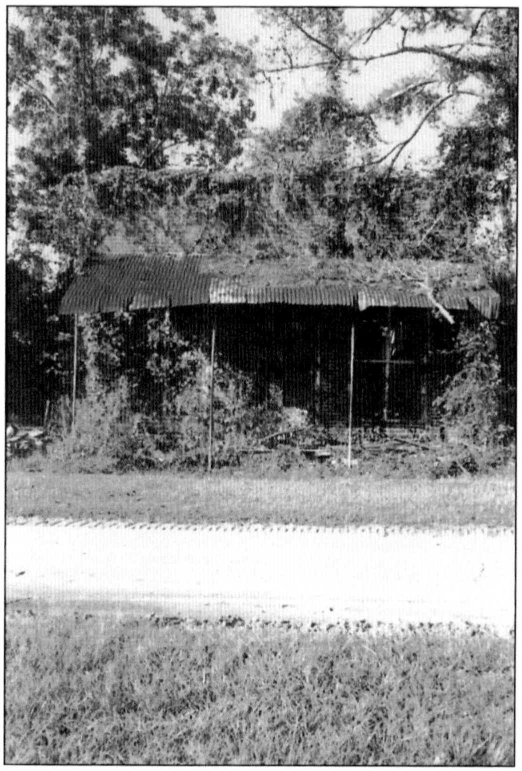

Located in the heart of Jennings, this building was a grocery store for several years, owned by Mellie and John Deas Sr. The family decided to move out of town and sold the grocery store. After a few more years of life as a grocery store, the building changed hands several times and eventually fell into decline. Although it is still standing today, the front entrance area has been destroyed; it is completely covered in vines and has been rendered unusable. (Marian Deas.)

T. P. "Tom" and Alice McCulley moved to Hamilton County in the early 1900s, settling on a farm on County Road 143. With six children—Leonard, Dalton, Lawton, Luther, Ernest, and T. C.—it was necessary to work full-time on the farm to survive. With luck, McCulley would be able to sell excess crops and livestock at local markets. After Alice's death, he married Mattie Gill (pictured here) and had another child, Bobby Ray, who died in infancy. T. C. McCulley and his son, Richard McCulley, have turned the McCulley Farm into a successful horse riding and camping location. (Richard McCulley.)

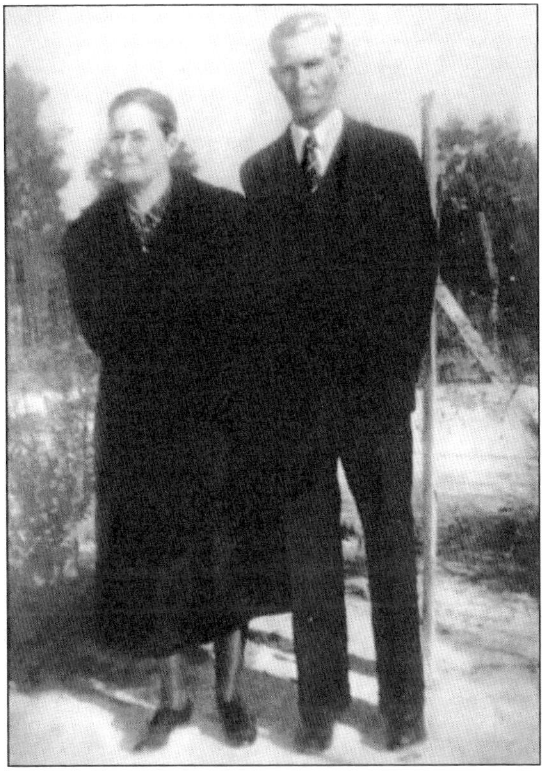

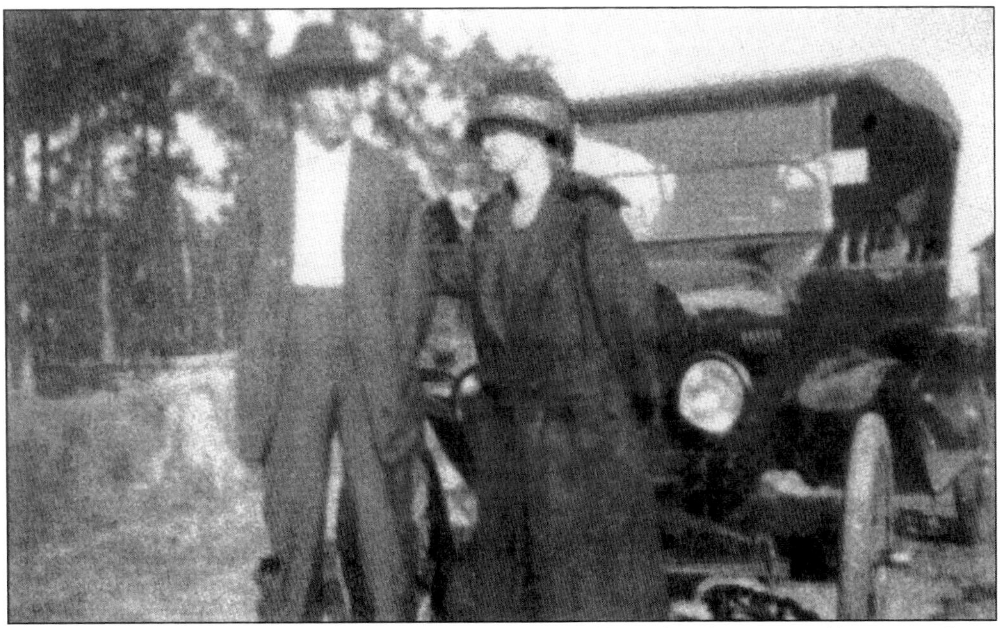

This 1920s photograph shows Bradford Washington Wells and Leila Dees Wells. He was born in 1878, in the cabin that his father, Alexander G. Wells, built. Wishing to remain close to his parents, he built a cabin nearby. He and Leila had three children: Verner, Nita, and Kirby. He died in 1956, and she lived nearly 20 years without him, dying in 1974. Both are buried in New Hope Cemetery. (Richard McCulley.)

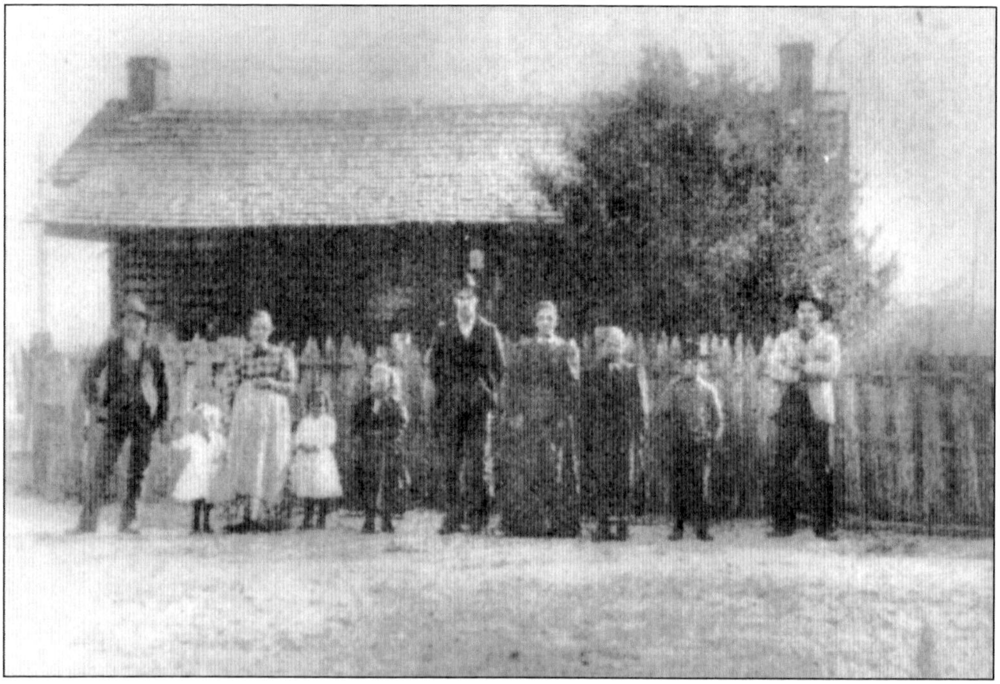

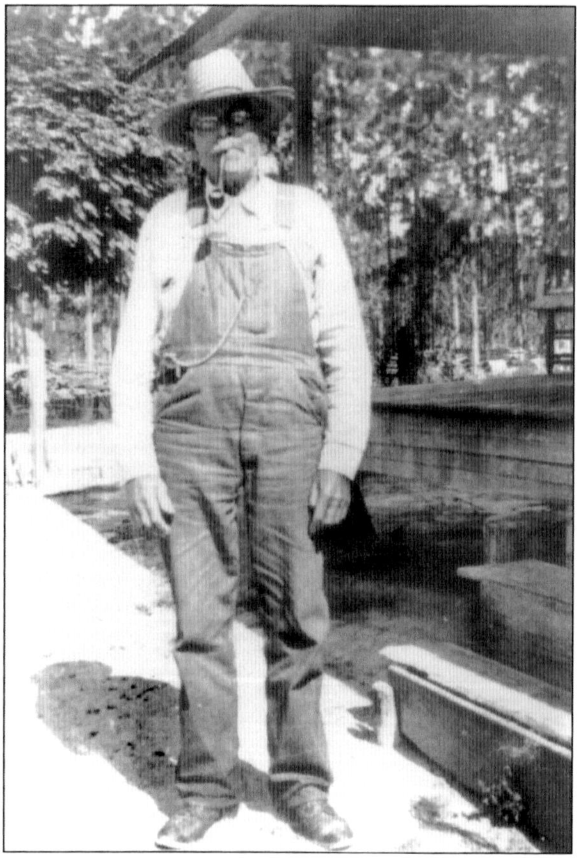

Alexander G. Wells arrived in Hamilton County with his parents, Jacob and Rebecca Wells, and their family, around 1860. About 10 years later, he married Sarah Ann Waters and built a pine log cabin for his family. They had the following children: Sarah Chloe Ann, Jacob A. Monroe, Ida Ruby, Henry Franklin, Georgia Pearl, Rosa Louvinia, Mattie, Minnie, Bradford Washington, and William. In the above photograph, Alexander Wells is the first man pictured on the left, and Sarah Wells is the first woman on the left. Several of their children are shown, but it is unknown which ones. At left, Alexander Wells is shown in his later years. Both are buried in the Wells Cemetery, along with two of their children and several grandchildren. (Both Richard McCulley.)

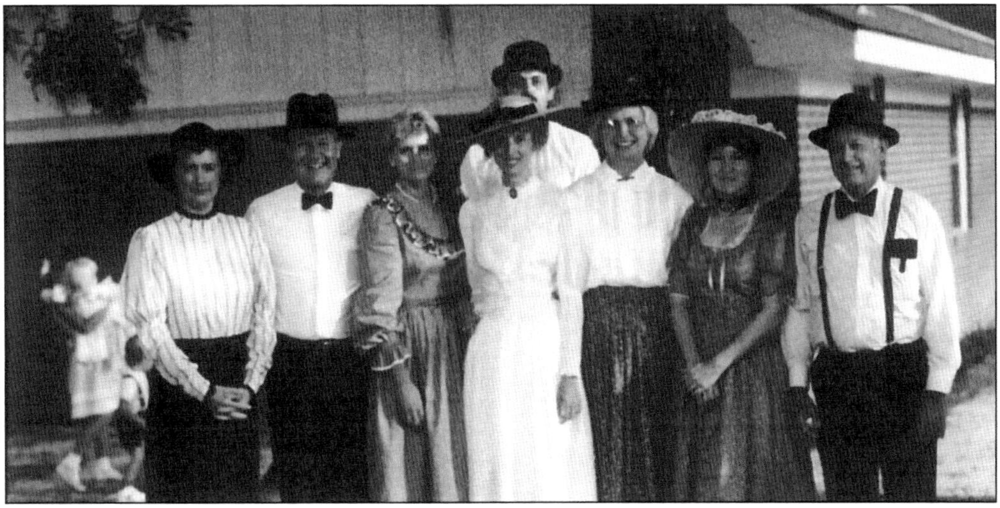

On August 28, 1988, Burnham Christian Church had their Homecoming and Centennial Celebration. Church services were conducted much in the same way as those of 100 years before. The men sat on the left side of the church, the women sat on the right, and the children sat with the parents of the respective sexes. To aid in authenticity, church members dressed in the same style of clothing that would have been appropriate in 1888. The above photograph shows, from left to right, Marian Roberts, Wayne and Pat Niederhuth, Louie and Susan Goodin, Marian Deas, Kathy Burnam, and James Deas Jr. The below photograph shows, from left to right, Pat Niederhuth, Marian Roberts, Marian Deas, Susan Goodin, and Kathy Burnam. (Both Marian Deas.)

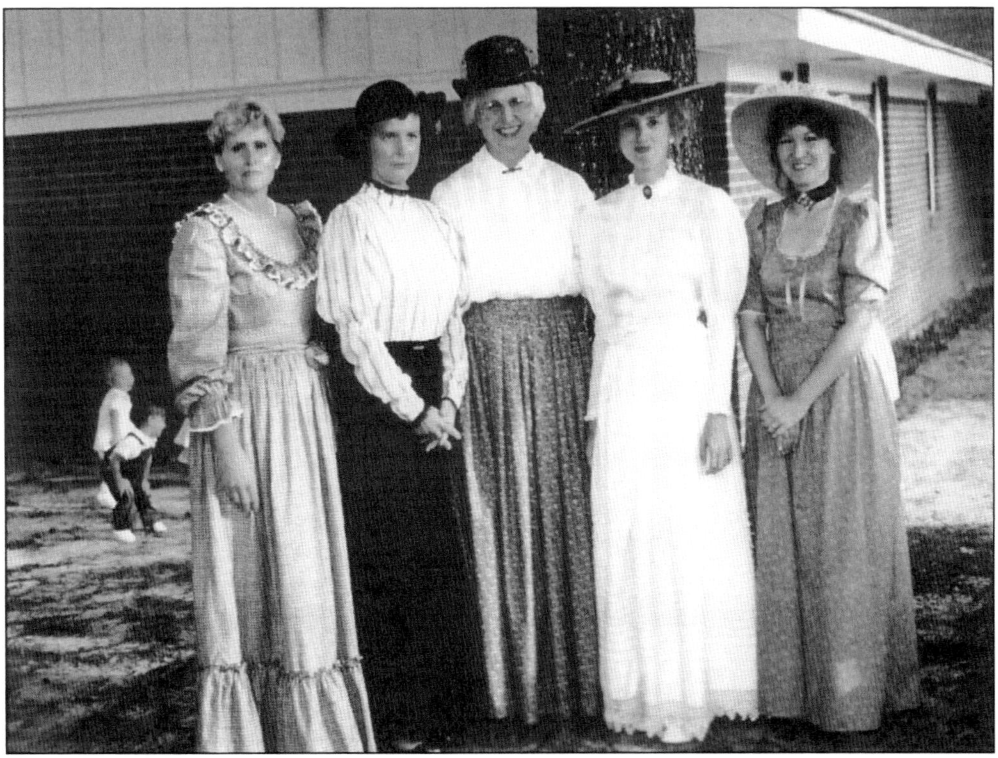

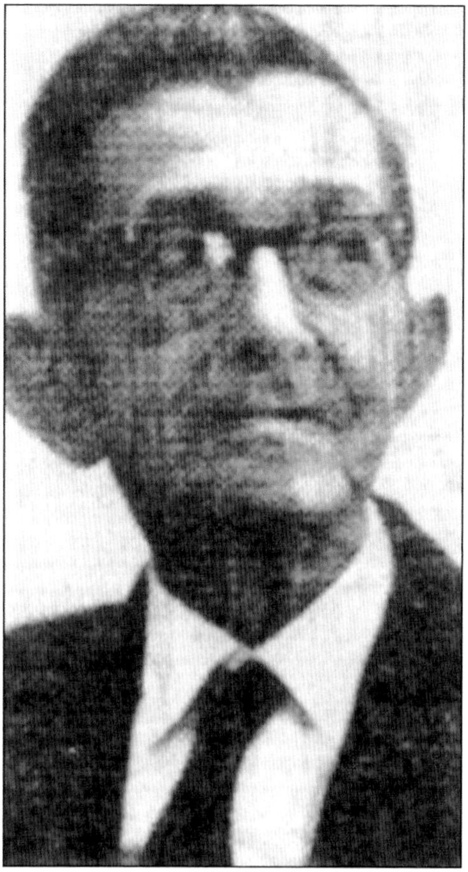

Isaac "Ike" Shiver, son of Abraham Edwin and Serena Jane Shiver, was born on January 18, 1884. Shiver came from a farming background, which he continued into adulthood. He was a deacon and elder for Burnham Christian Church, drove a school bus for 14 years, and served as a member on the school board for two terms. In addition, he owned a grocery in Jennings for several years. Shiver passed away February 3, 1979, and was interred in Burnham Christian Church Cemetery, next to his wife, Hattie. (Marian Deas.)

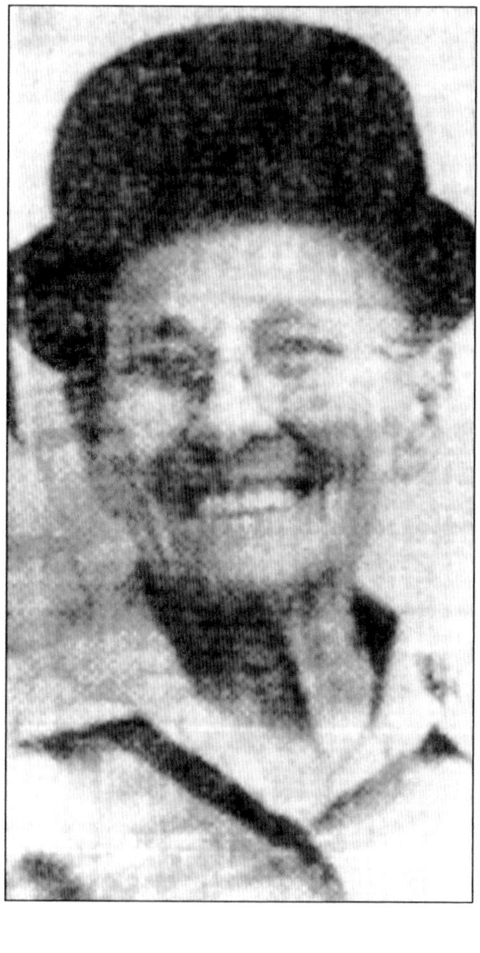

On November 4, 1884, Hattie Irene Padgette was born to John Daniel and George Ann Padgette. Becoming a member of Burnham Christian Church at age 14, Shiver was active in church activities. She made the Communion, a weekly ritual, for nearly 50 years, baking bread without leavening and canning grape juice from her own grapes. She taught at a local country school for five years and later in the public school system, retiring at age 87. She passed away March 4, 1977, and was interred in Burnham Christian Church Cemetery. (Marian Deas.)

The first formal wedding in Burnham Christian Church was on September 4, 1905: Isaac Shiver and Hattie Irene Padgette. He fixed a little house for her about 5 miles from the church. She made her own wedding dress and the dinner for the wedding party and reception. Their honeymoon was a moonlit buggy ride, but at 21 and 20, respectively, they did not want for anything more in those simpler times. (Marian Deas.)

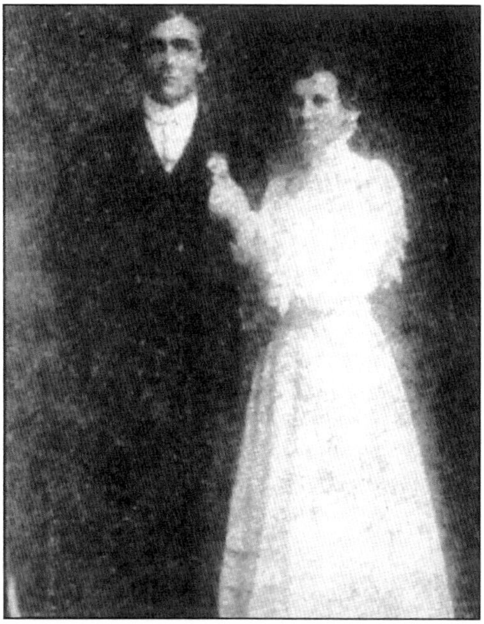

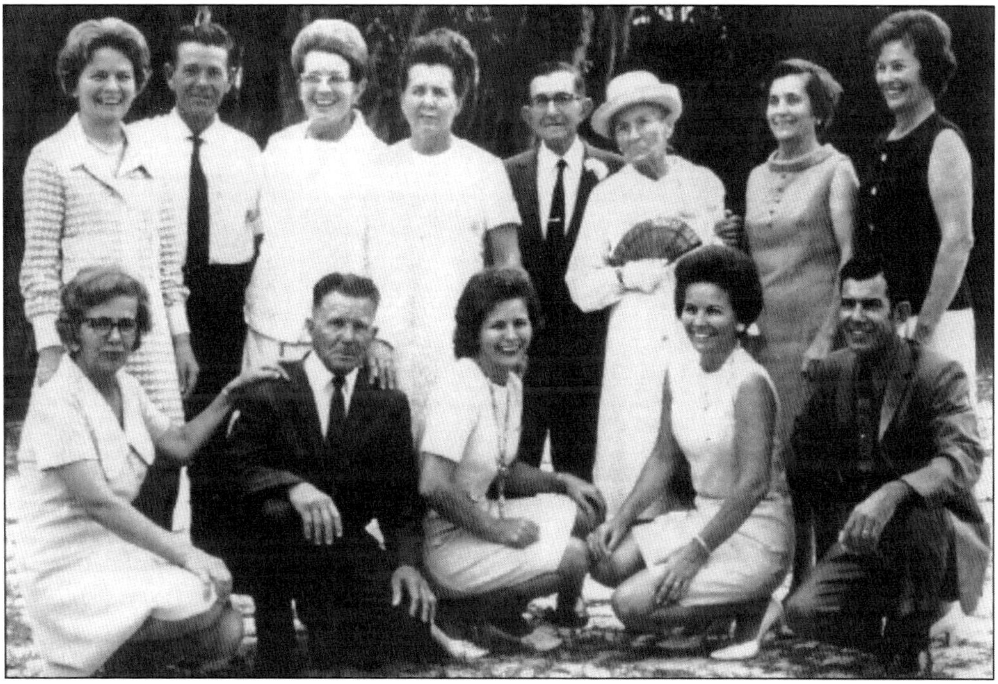

Here are the 11 children of Isaac and Hattie Shiver on their 65th wedding anniversary, when they hosted a grand party for their parents at Burnham Christian Church. In attendance were all of the children and spouses, 37 grandchildren, 23 great-grandchildren, and numerous friends. Shown from left to right are (first row) Christine Bogan of Pensacola, Florida; Kenneth of Palatka, Florida; Marian Hudson of Lake City, Florida; Amaryllis Burchette of Orlando, Florida; and Ike Jr. of Fernandina Beach, Florida; (second row) Ruth Lindauer of Valdosta, Georgia; John of Jennings; Nellie Tyre of Crestview, Florida; Mildred Shiver of White Springs; Isaac; Hattie; Edith Johnson of Jennings; and Helen Brand of Jacksonville, Florida. (Marian Deas.)

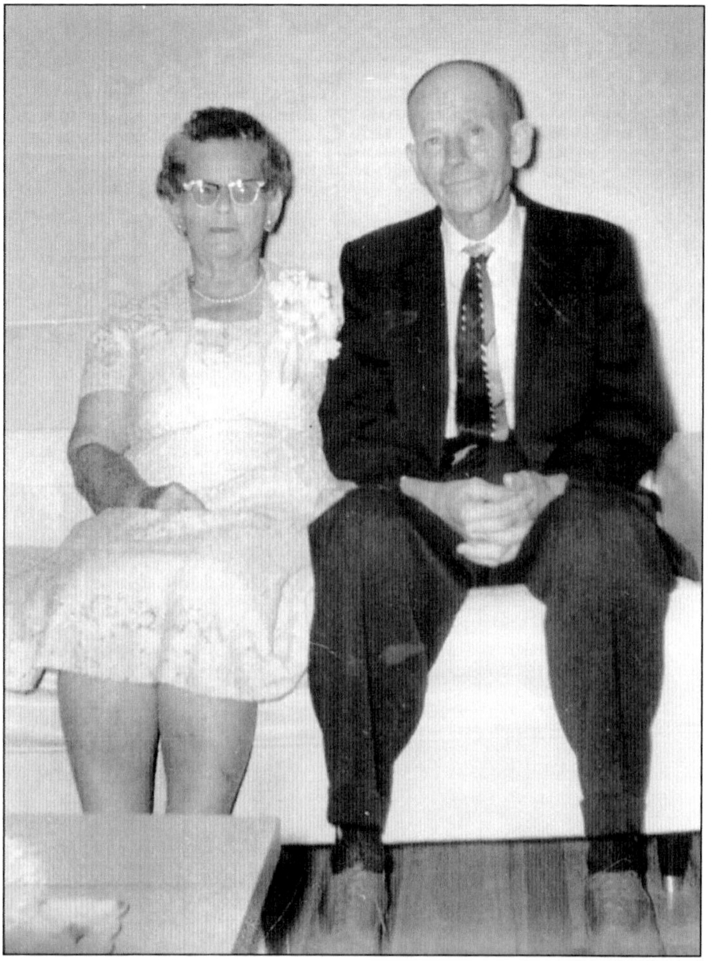

Together James Bryant and Carrie Mae Cunningham Deas (left) had 10 children over a span of 19 years: Mary Lucium, Lois, James Curtis, Rachel Madeline, Quinteen, Hazel Iona, Ruby Mae, Betty Bonita, Albert Waldron, and Patricia Ann. James Bryant Deas was born on November 11, 1893, and died December 20, 1973, at the age of 80. His wife, daughter of John Thomas and Rachel Alderman Cunningham, was born February 7, 1896, and passed away December 27, 1990, at age 94. They are buried side by side in the Burnham Christian Church Cemetery, along with several other family members. Shown below are all of the Deas children and their mother in the late 1970s. (Both Marian Deas.)

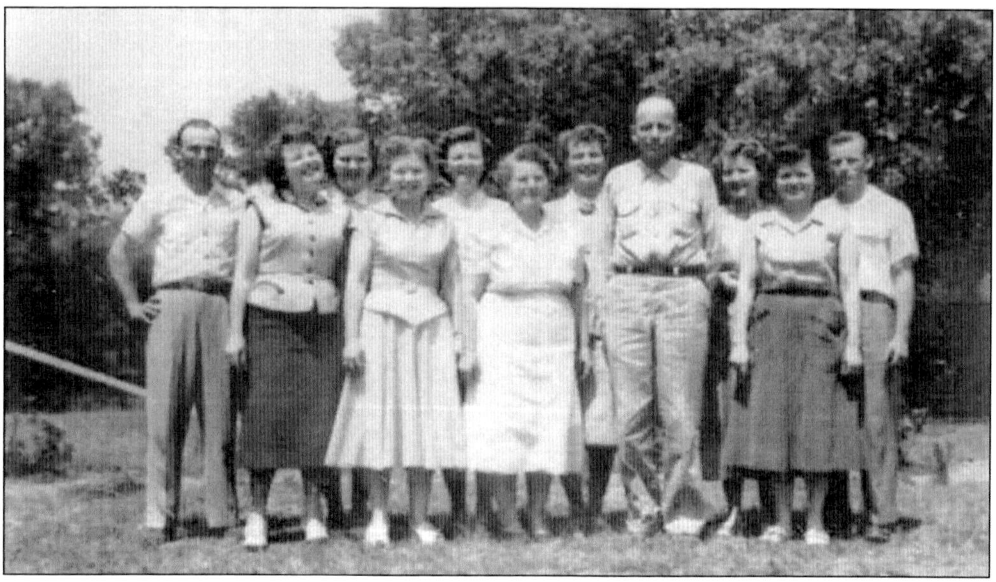

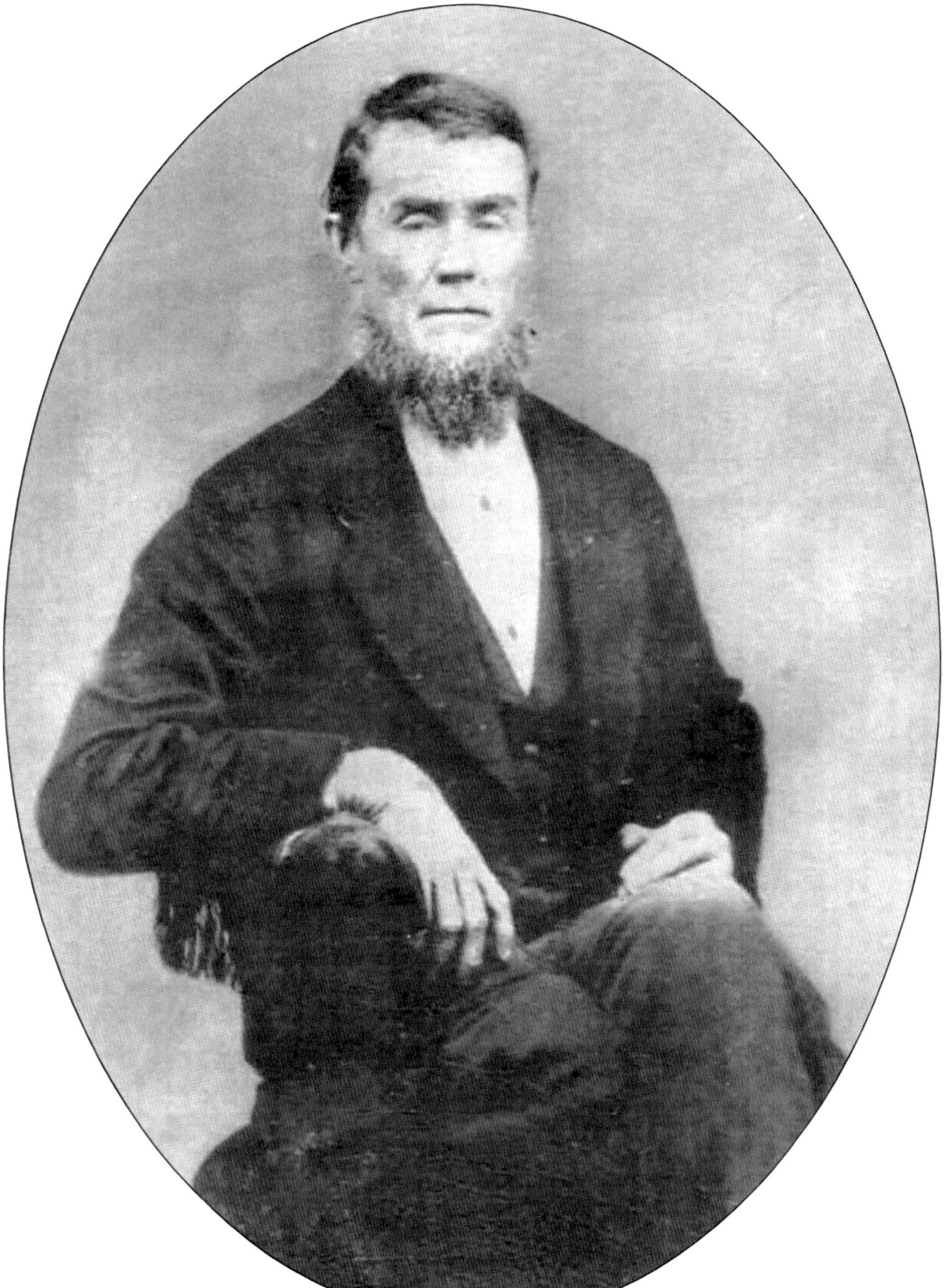

Perhaps James Bryant Burnham's most important contribution to the community was the donation of a 3-acre plot of land, to be used for the church building and cemetery of Burnham Christian Church, which was named in his honor. He later married Eliza Zipperer and they had five children throughout their marriage: James Bryant Jr., Betty, Eliza, Mary Ann, and Emily. (Marian Deas.)

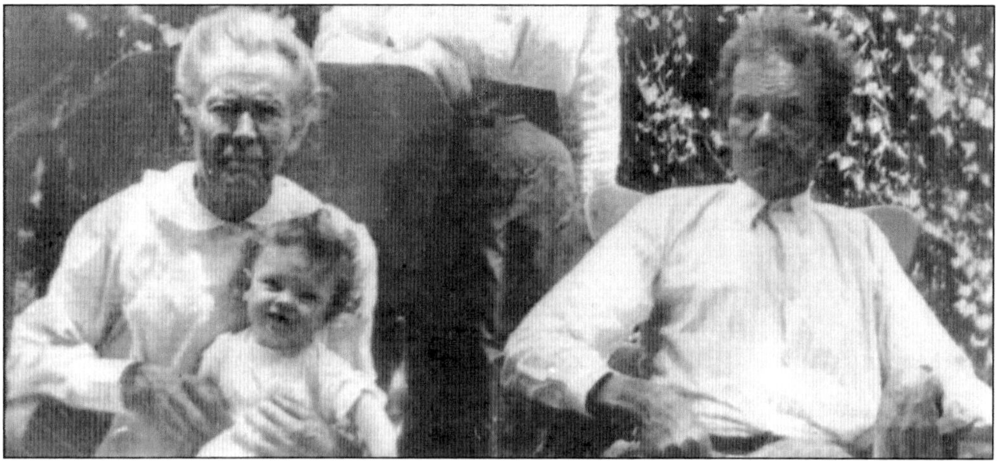

Alexander and Eliza Zipperer were two of the 20 charter members of Burnham Christian Church who were baptized in Frank Zipperer's pond to commemorate the church. In the photograph above, the couple is shown with their granddaughter, Baby Marie. They had a total of six children—Hattie, Albert (shown below), Mamie, Ida, Will, and Mary Francis. Albert, their son, is shown below with his wife, Mollie. Albert and Mollie were active in the church, continuing the association of the Zipperers and Burnham Christian Church. In the mid-1930s, Mollie Zipperer helped organize the first Christian Women's Fellowship at the church. (Both Marian Deas.)

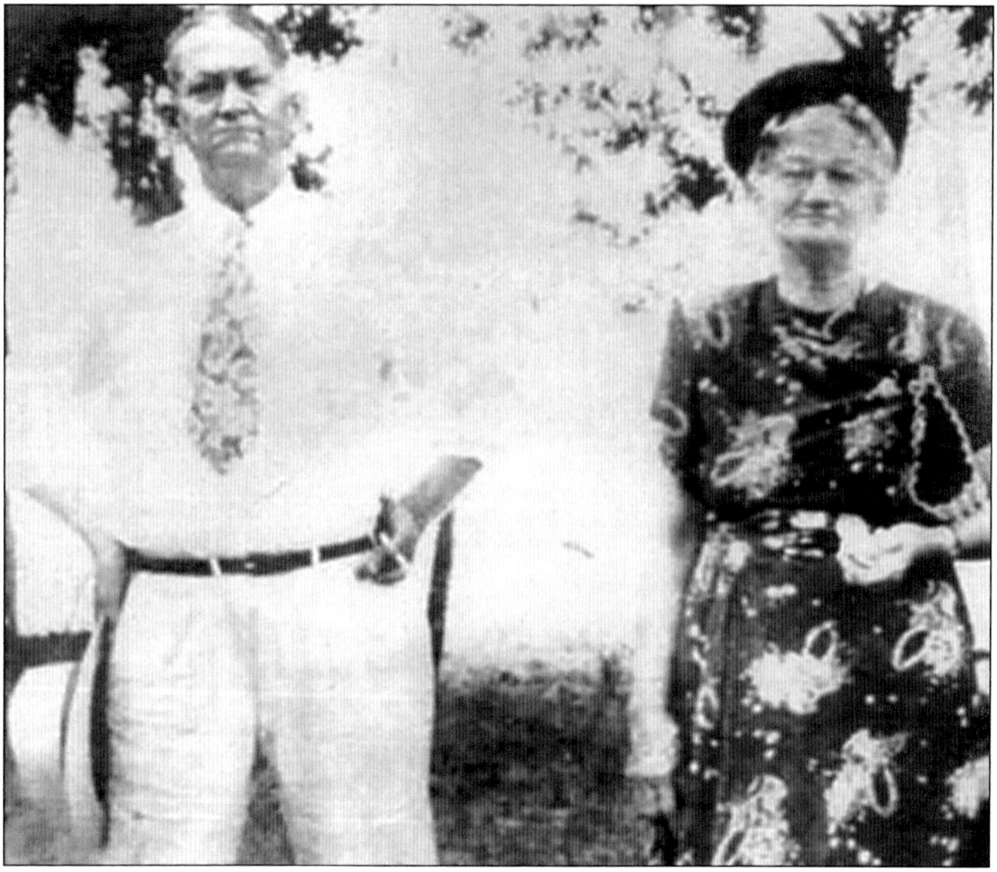

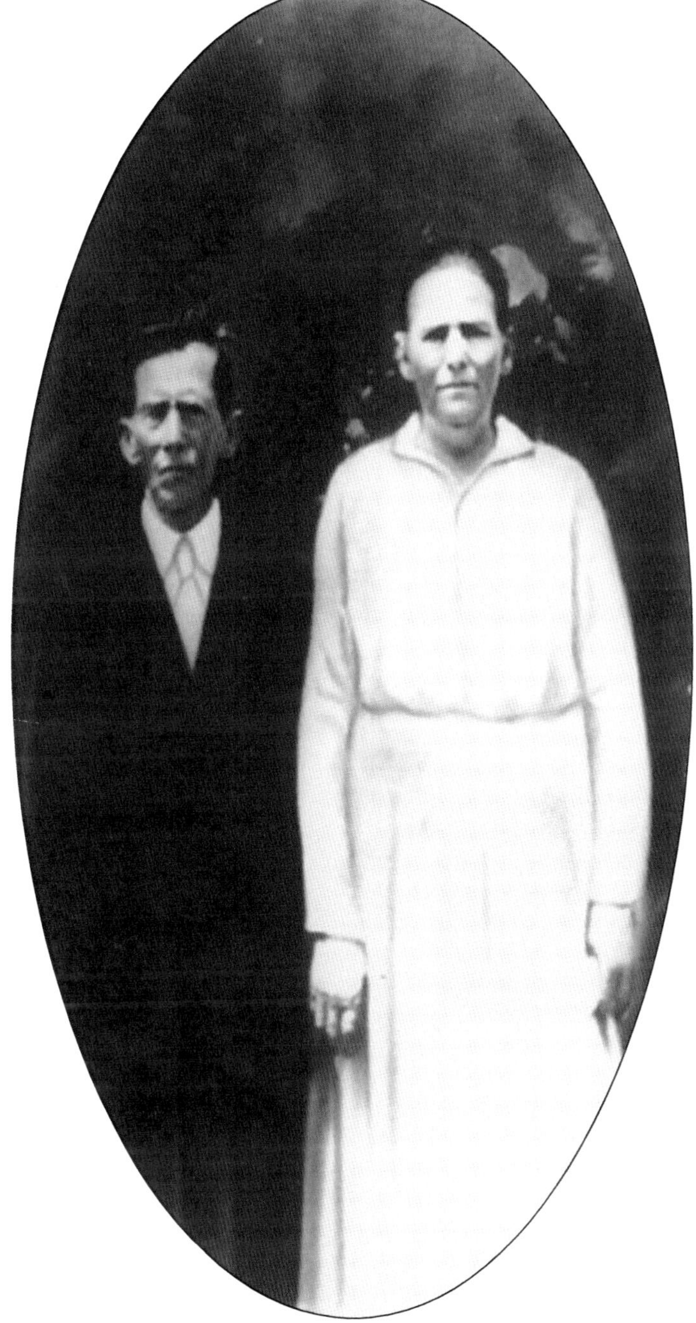

Mary Francis Zipperer, daughter of Eliza Burnham and Alex Zipperer, married Santanna M. Deas. Together they had 12 children, five of whom died in childhood. They include Alexander, Mary Eliza (died at age seven), Mathue (died in infancy), James Bryant, John Hall Sr., Clyde, Clayton (died at age one), Myrtle "Mertie" (died at age six), Maude (died at age 12), R. M., Santanna Mathew "SM" Jr., and Julia Allene. Mary Francis passed away February 12, 1939. A little more than a year later, Santanna passed away as well, perhaps from grief. Both are interred at Burnham Christian Church Cemetery, along with several of their children. (Marian Deas.)

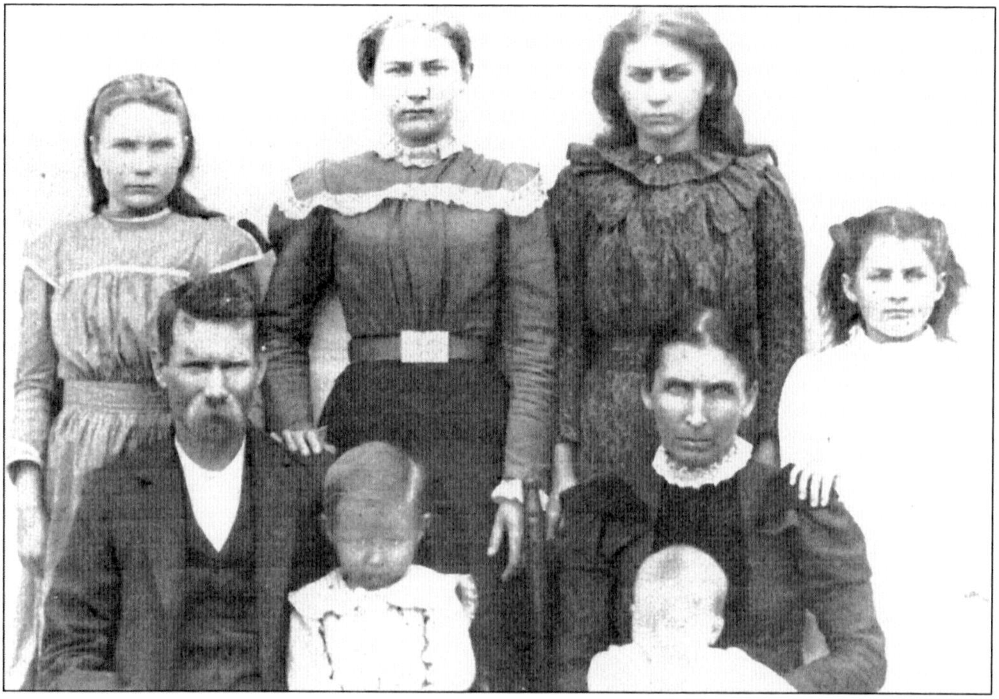

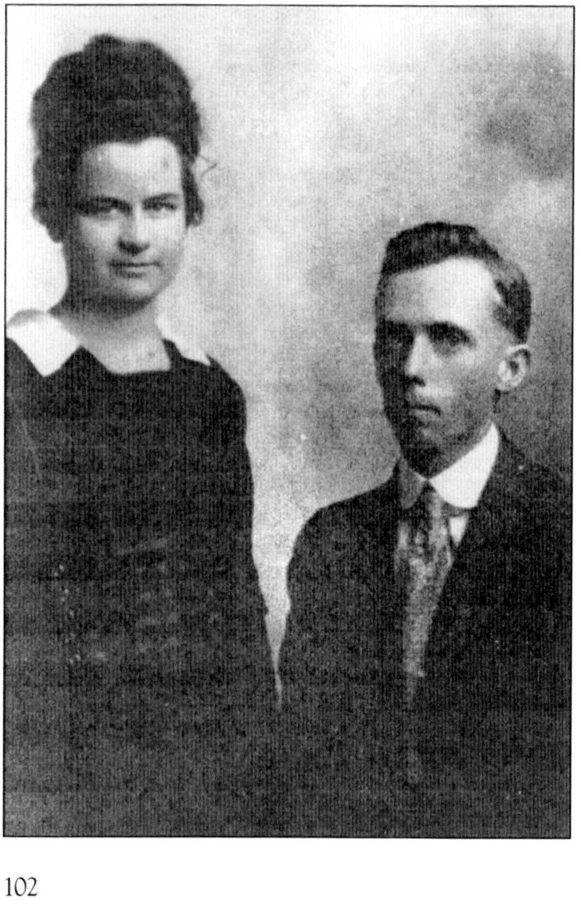

The Aldermans were early settlers of the Jennings area. After a time, four Alderman siblings married four Cunningham siblings. The result was a larger number of Aldermans and Cunninghams dispersed throughout the northwest portion of the county. Shown here are, from left to right, Rose, Bertha, Effie, Julia, Robert "Bob" (father), Johnnie, Sarah Cunningham (mother), and Leater Alderman. (Marian Deas.)

Lottie Alderman, daughter of Amanda Cunningham and Barzilla Alderman, married Henry Blair. Together they had five children: Leon Lanier (1920), twins Hazel Imogene and Herman Eugene (1923), Henry Wesley (1938), and Betty Anne Blair (1940). (Marian Deas.)

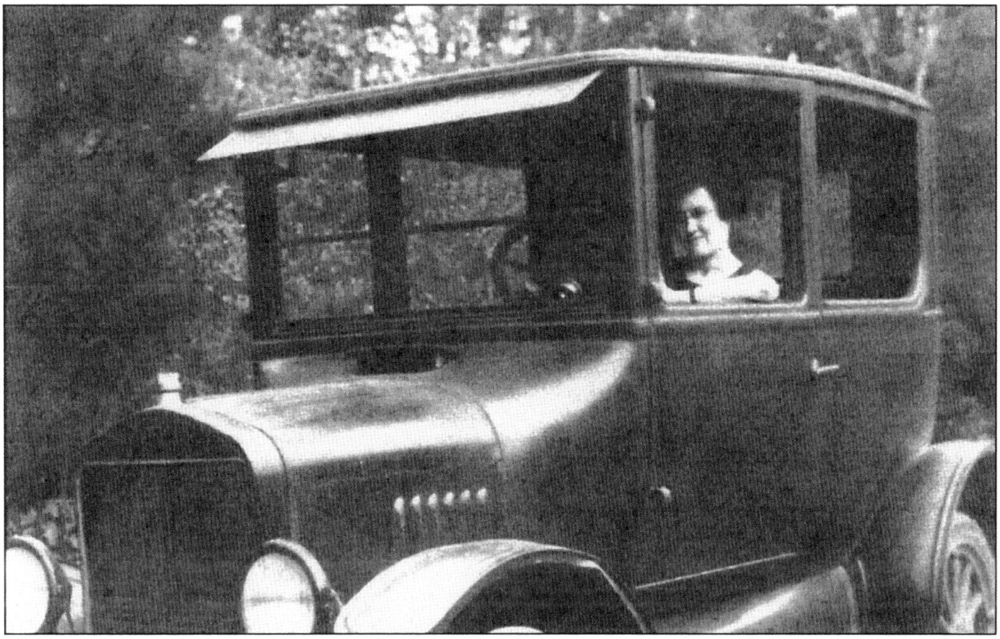

Mamie Alderman, daughter of Barzilla and Amanda Alderman, shows off her lovely Ford Model A in the late 1920s. Later in life, Alderman moved to Tampa, Florida, where she lived alone, never marrying. Before her death on December 20, 1932, she made all of her funeral arrangements, including choosing her casket and attending to minor details. Her remains were transported from Tampa to Jennings, where she was buried. (Marian Deas.)

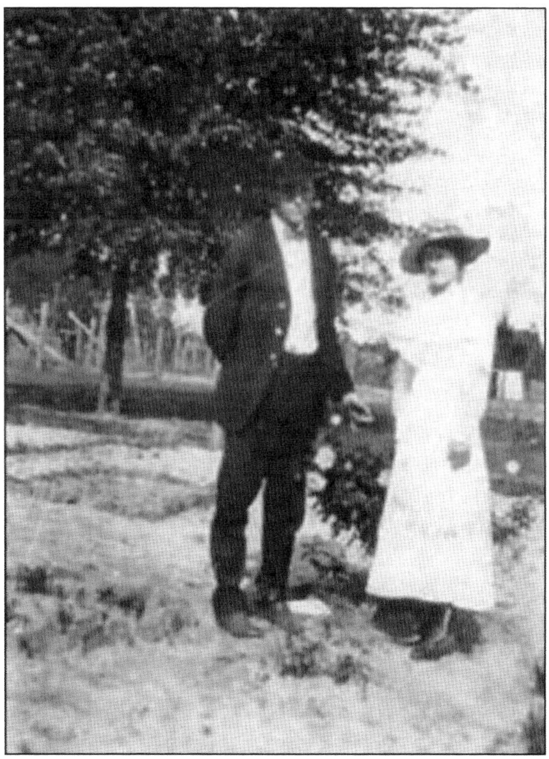

John Hall Deas Sr. was born January 24, 1896. At age 20, he married Mellie Alderman, daughter of Barzilla and Amanda Cunningham Alderman. They had a number of children, many of whose descendants remain in Hamilton County or the surrounding areas. The children were Eloise, Dorothy, Juanita, John Hall Jr., James Franklin "Brother," Amanda "Mandy," Bobby D., and Wanda. John Hall Sr. died December 8, 1960, at 64 years of age, while his wife followed him in death 33 years later on December 4, 1993. (Marian Deas.)

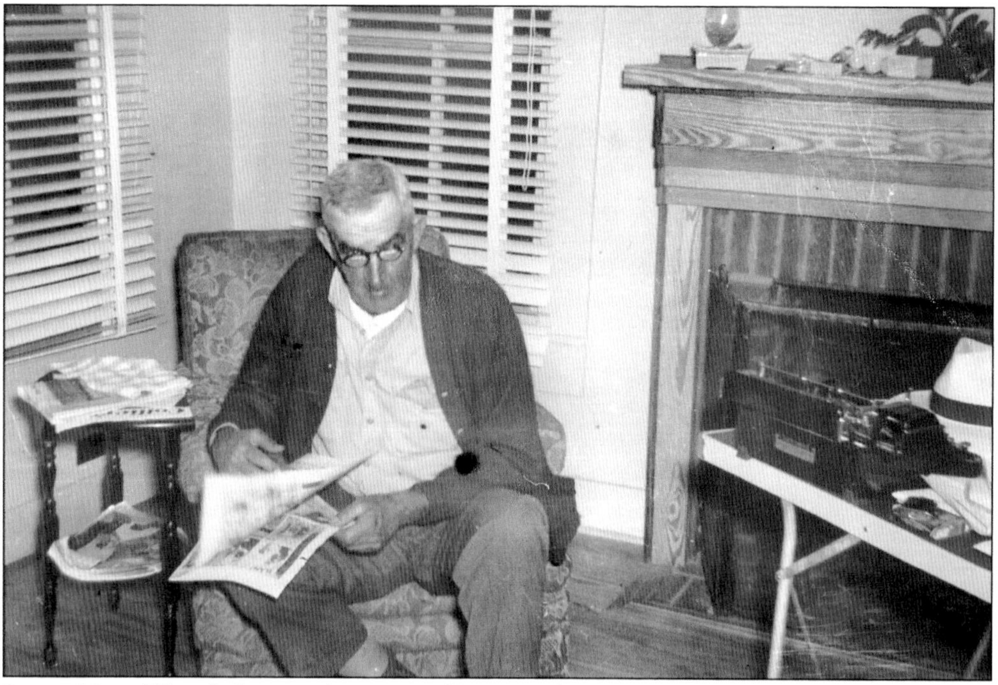

Peyton Harry Wisenbaker was the mayor of Jennings during the late 1950s and early 1960s. One of his shining moments during his time in office was the introduction of telephones to the city of Jennings. This 1951 photograph shows Wisenbaker at his home, relaxing. (Cliff Adams.)

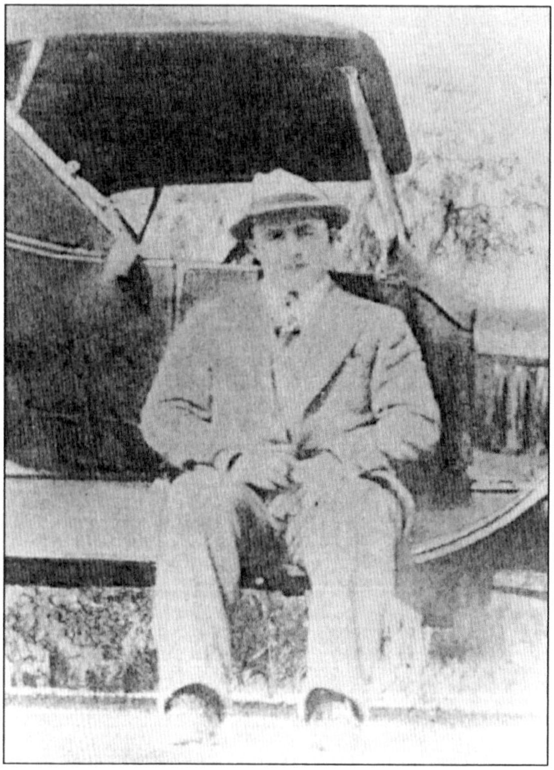

Like many young men of the time, Pennywell Kelley worked for a cotton gin in Jennings. After a horrible accident at work one day, he walked nearly 8 miles carrying his severed arm, seeking medical attention. After he was pronounced dead by the local doctor, the undertaker was summoned, and he found Kelley sitting upright in bed. His arm could not be saved, but Kelley survived the incident without further harm. This 1925 photograph was taken before the accident, when Kelley was about 21 years old. He married Ora Lee, and they had 11 children: Sudie Selph, Lavern Harris, Pennywell Franklin Kelley Jr., Wes Kelley, Christine Ulrich, Jerry Kelley, Christlee O'Dwyer, Roy Kelley, Shiryl Norris, Rhonda Hancock, and Terry Kelley. The family of Sudie and Cleveland Selph still resides in Hamilton County; many of the others live in nearby counties. Kelley passed away in 1978. (Sudie Kelley Selph.)

Seven

White Springs

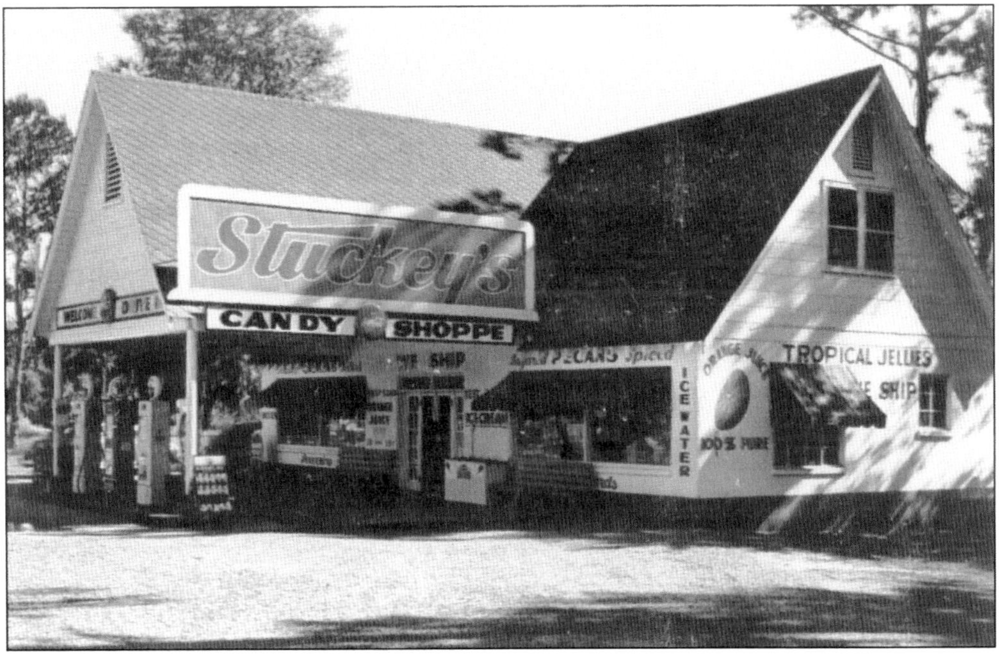

This Stuckey's Candy Shoppe located on U.S. Highway 41, just outside the city of White Springs, opened in the early 1940s and closed around 1960. The Stuckey's owner moved away from Hamilton County, and an individual purchased the building. For quite a while, it was operated as a drinking establishment, until the owner decided to make the building his personal home. Dramatic renovations have been made to the building, leaving the roof as the only recognizable sign that it was ever a Stuckey's Candy Shoppe. (Alan Fouraker.)

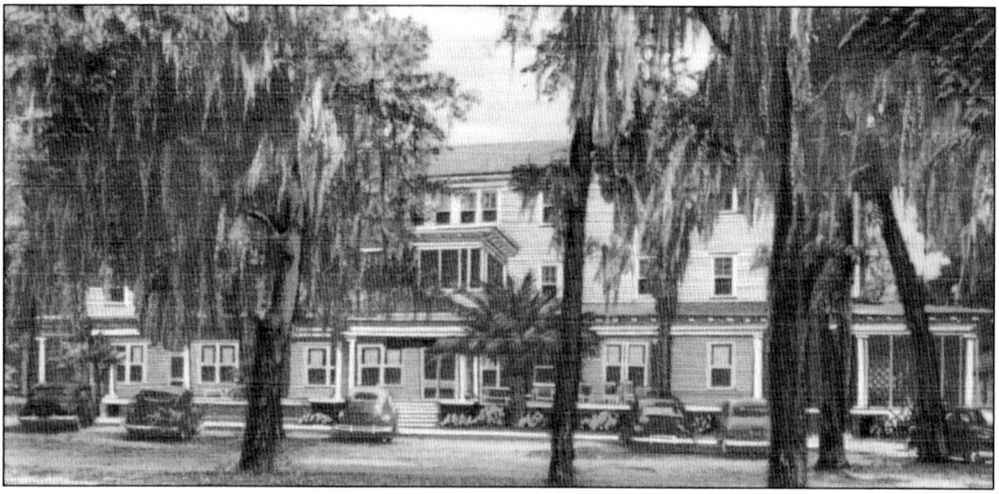

The year 1960 marked a turning point for an important area of White Springs. Watkins A. Saunders and A. F. Saunders made the decision to sell their property to Claude A. Thompkins, a part-time resident of Jasper and Jacksonville. The Colonial Hotel, the Suwannee River Motor Court, and the Spring House were included. The Saunders family, heavily involved in the community, had no way of knowing their prized properties would soon be demolished. A short 10 years after the sale, ownership of the property was transferred to the State of Florida, and the Spring House was torn down. After a small fire in 1973, in which the damage could have been repaired, the state demolished the Colonial Hotel and, shortly after, the Suwannee River Motor Court. (Above, Alan Fouraker; below, author's collection.)

The Colonial Hotel

WHITE SPRINGS, FLORIDA

On the Beautiful Suwannee River

AAA Approved — Automatic Sprinkler System

Excellent Cuisine — American and European Plan

A small hotel of exceptional comfort located on U. S. Highway No. 41 twelve miles north of Lake City, Florida.

Many of the Colonial's guests are business men and their families who spend their vacations here to enjoy the quiet homey atmosphere and pleasant surroundings. Swimming in the Spring Pool, Horse Back Riding, Canoeing, Fishing and Boating Trips on the Suwannee River as well as Hunting in season add to the pleasure of the guests.

Suwannee River Court

WHITE SPRINGS, FLORIDA

Member Quality Courts and United AAA Approved Court

All rooms are large, well ventilated with private tile bath, steam heat, electric fan, comfortable furnishings and private porches overlooking the Suwannee River.

Guests of Suwannee River Court have the privilege of the Mineral Springs drinking water and Recreation Room without cost.

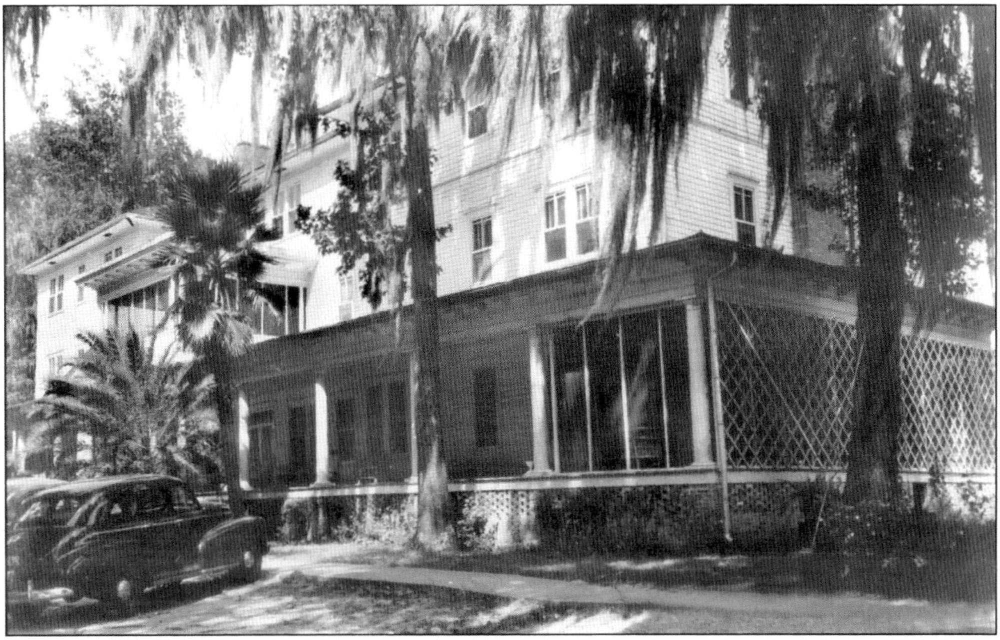

The Colonial Hotel, located one block away from the springs, was built in 1912. It was operated as a hotel by W. A. Saunders until 1960, when the property was sold. Facing the Suwannee River, guests could eat in the dining room, feasting upon hot meals of country ham, roasted turkey, and mouth-watering biscuits. Boasting exceptional comfort, the Colonial Hotel drew patrons from miles around. Local citizens visited the Colonial Hotel to utilize the excellent services of the dining room, while businessmen from afar (Charleston, Atlanta, Chattanooga, and Tampa) arrived with their families in tow, ready for a vacation packed with relaxation and activities such as horseback riding, canoeing, fishing, boating trips on the Suwannee River, and, of course, swimming in the famous spring a block away. (Above, Alan Fouraker; below, author's collection.)

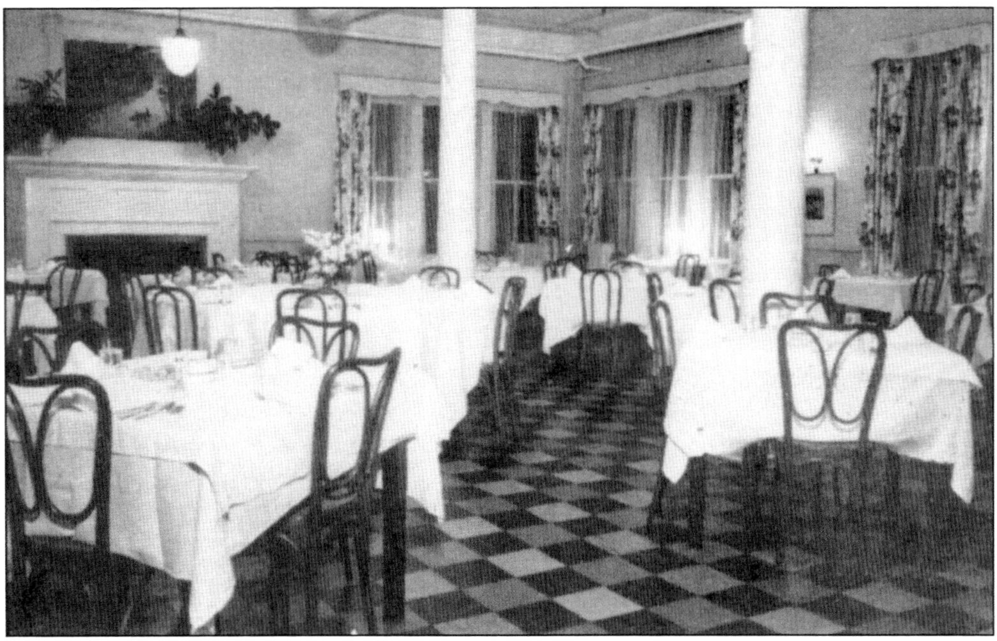

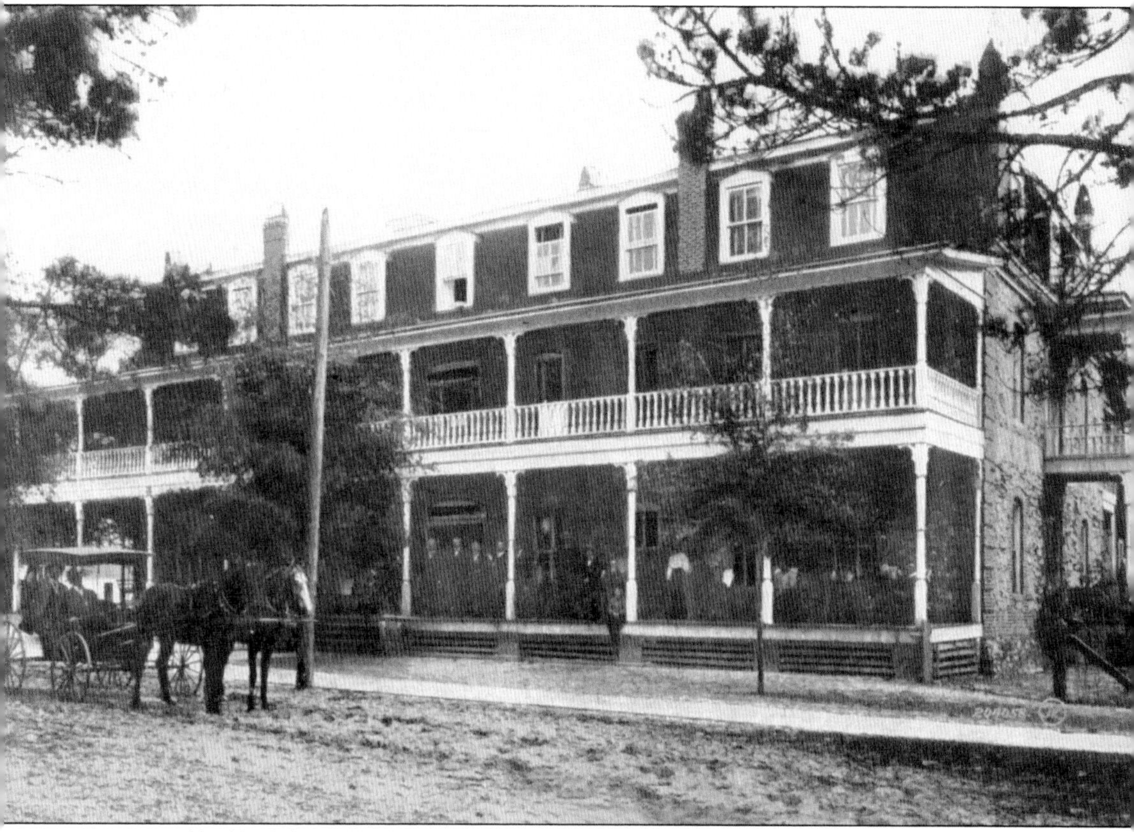

W. B. Telford had the Telford Hotel built in 1902, by J. W. Bynum, using a combination of Georgia brick and river rock excavated from the nearby Suwannee River. Upon its completion, the hotel boasted its own acetylene-powered lighting system and water plant. The three-story hotel had 40 rooms available for guests and covered more than 15,000 square feet, with porches on the first and second floor, although they have been removed. The rooms have been reconstructed to be larger, often by combining two or more rooms, while maintaining the original style. The above photograph depicts the Telford Hotel in the early 1900s, not long after it was constructed. (Alan Fouraker.)

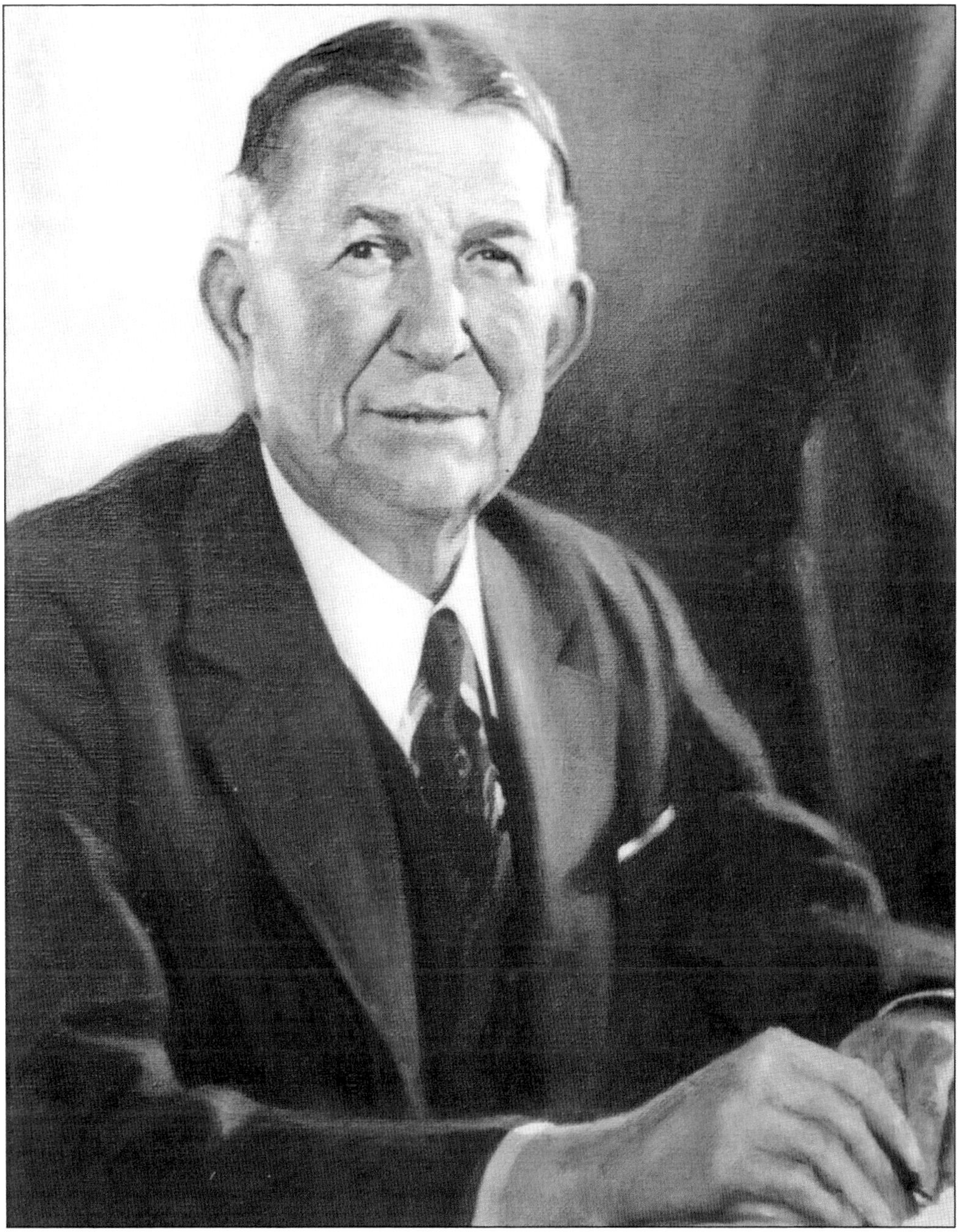

Frederick Preston Cone attended the Florida Normal College, located in White Springs, and later the Florida State Agricultural College in Lake City. After finishing his schooling, he became a teacher in a rural schoolhouse and decided he would like to be a lawyer. For three years, he was an assistant law clerk to Judge H. C. Palmer and then was admitted to the bar in 1892, to practice law on his own. The Florida State Senate saw him as a member for two terms, during which he helped establish a uniform system of textbooks for schools in Florida. In 1937, Cone was appointed governor of Florida. He served for one term and then moved to Lake City, where he died in 1948. Cone was buried in Primitive Prospect Baptist Church with his wife, Mildred Thompson Cone. (Florida Photographic Collection, State Archives of Florida.)

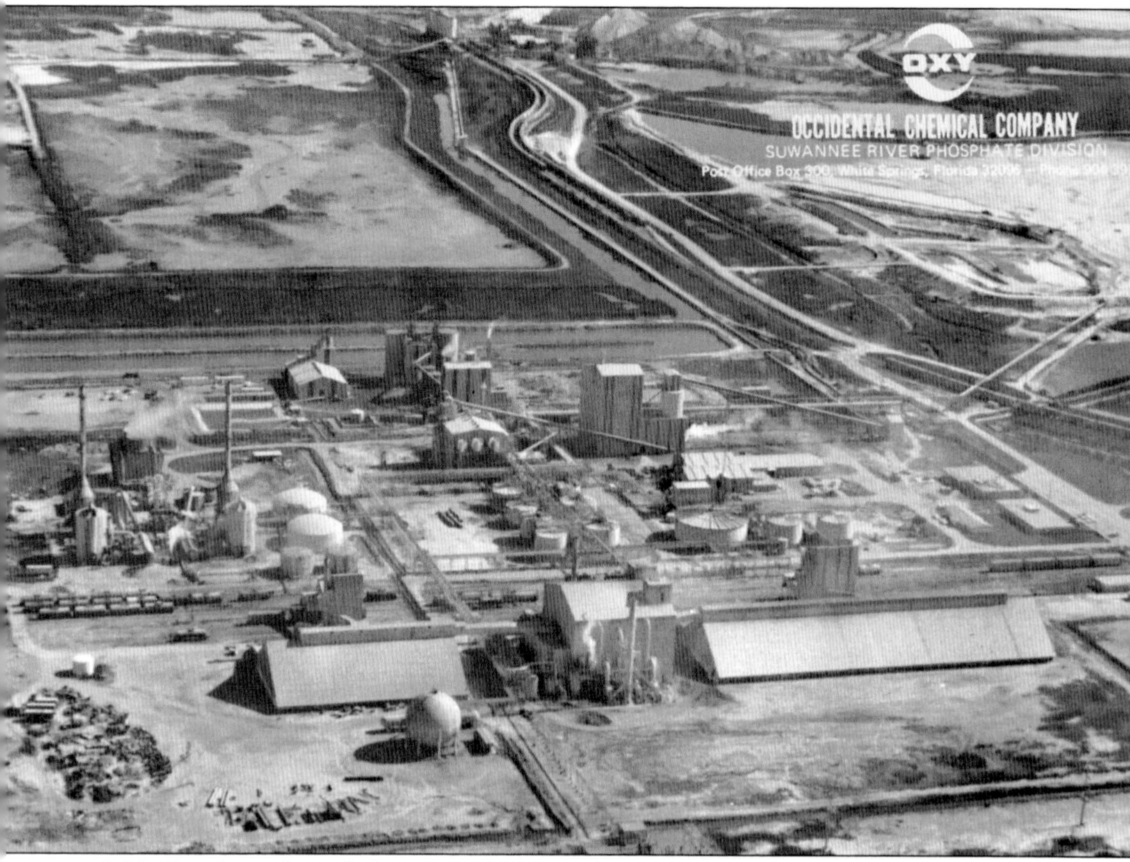

PCS Phosphate, formerly known as Occidental Chemical Corporation or "OXY," has been in operation in Hamilton County since 1964. A common practice in Central and South Florida, mining was not done in northeast Florida until OXY opened its plant. Each day, dozens of 100-ton hopper cars carry phosphate mined in the White Springs area to a Jacksonville, Florida, terminal, where it is then shipped to outlying locations. In the early 1990s, OXY sold the company to PCS (Potash Corporation of Saskatchewan) Phosphate. They are still one of the largest employers of the area, with an average of 900 employees in 2006. (Hamilton County High School.)

Eight

The Spring House

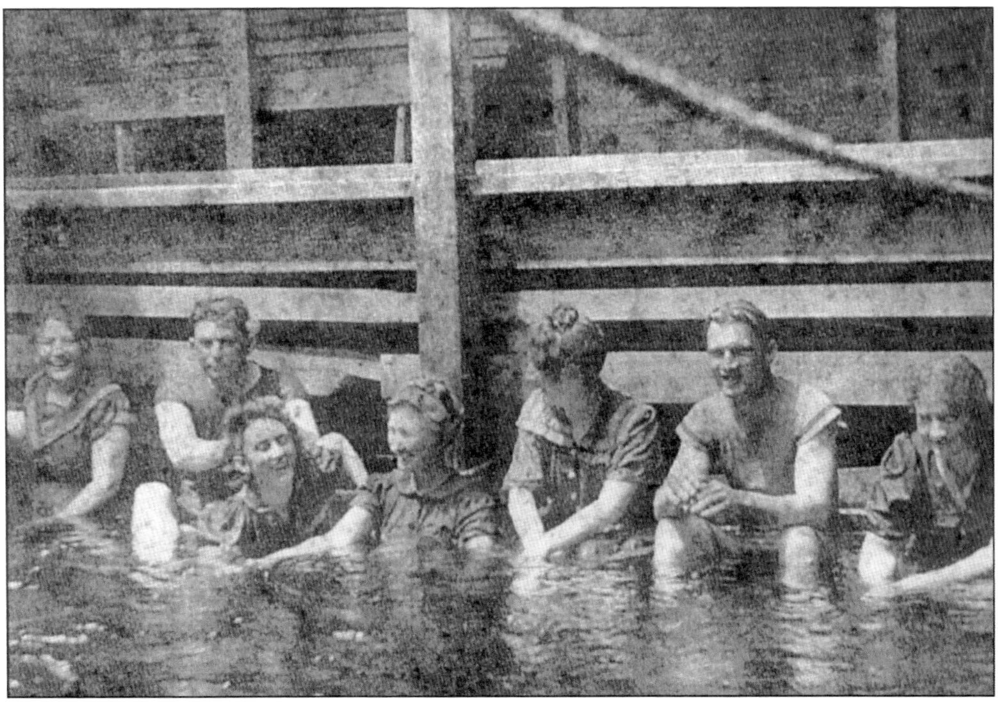

This 1895 photograph is one of the earliest of the Spring House in White Springs. Taken when Bryant Sheffield owned the spring, it shows the most popular activity of the area—swimming. Shown in the photograph are Mary "Minnie" Adams Strickland (first woman on the left), Robert Watkins Adams Jr. (on the left), and Nathaniel "Nat" Adams (on the right). The other women in the photograph are unidentified. Minnie Adams married Allen Strickland, of Valdosta, Georgia, and moved from the area. (Cliff Adams.)

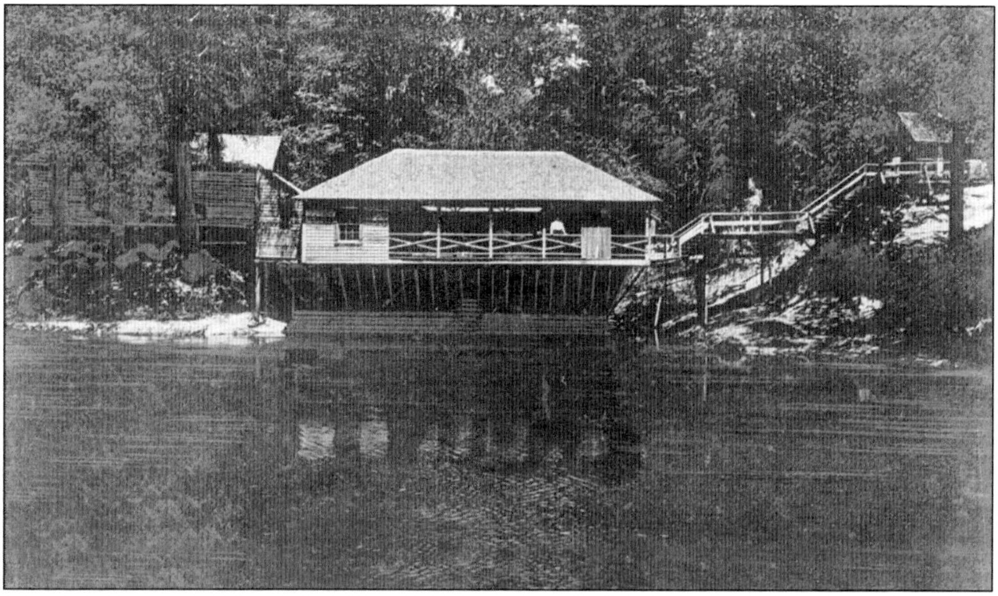

Bryant and Elizabeth Sheffield purchased nearly 1,000 acres in the White Springs area in 1835, including much of what is now the city of White Springs. Shortly after, Sheffield discovered the refreshing properties of the spring water and built a log cabin for guests. The waters were said to relieve rheumatism, kidney troubles, gout, nervousness, dandruff, insomnia, indigestion, and other ailments. The family continued to own the springs until 1887, when they sold it to Wight and Powell of Cairo, Georgia. (Alan Fouraker.)

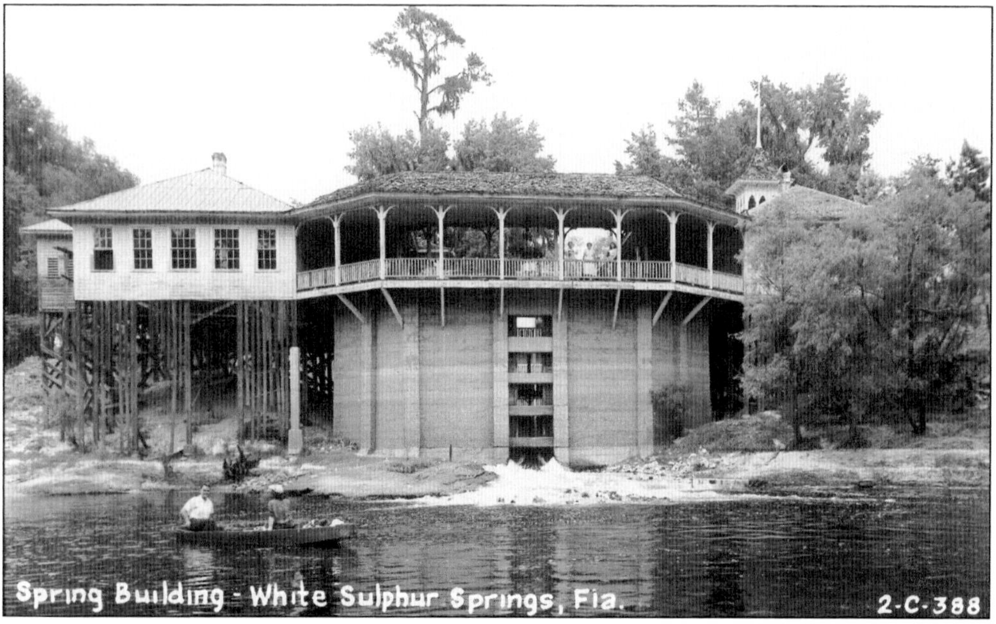

In 1903, Minnie Mosher Jackson and her brother, Dr. Mosher, built a concrete and coquina wall around the spring. The wall was meant to protect it from the rising waters of the Suwannee River during floods. On the wall was a three-tiered structure housing treatment rooms, dressing rooms, a concession area, and an elevator. The Spring House became the social center of White Springs, where people went to play cards and visit. (Alan Fouraker.)

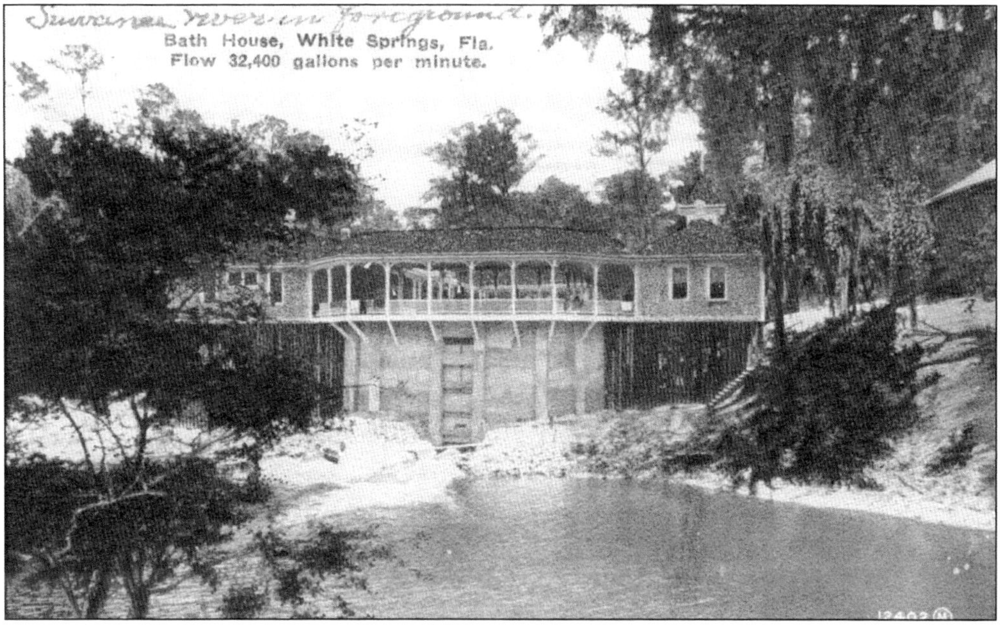

Dr. Mosher and Minnie Mosher Jackson sold the spring in 1916 to Amy C. Mathers and her brother, Doctor D. N. Cone. During their time of ownership, Mathers had the spring water chemically tested. An advertisement was disbursed throughout the state of Florida extolling the benefits of the springs, including the chemical analysis of the water and the water flow of the time, 32,420 gallons per minute. (Paul Marion.)

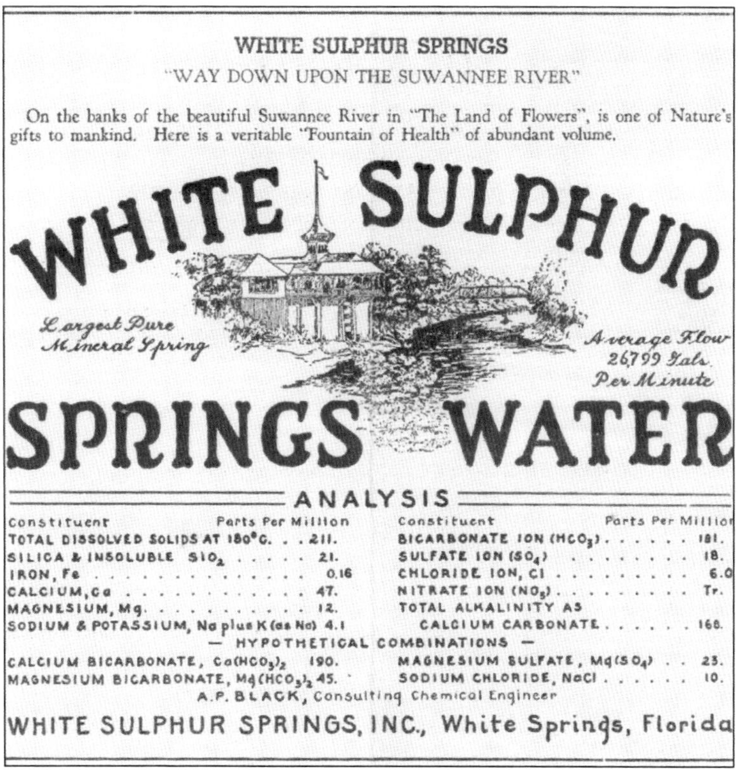

This advertisement boasting the water analysis of the White Springs sulphur water circulated for several years, until at least the late 1950s. The advertisement lists a number of "curing" chemicals and elements, including iron, calcium, sodium, potassium, and calcium bicarbonate, analyzed by A. P. Black, chemical engineer. Although the curing properties of the spring have never been proven, guests flocked to the location with high hopes of leaving illness free, relaxed, and rested.

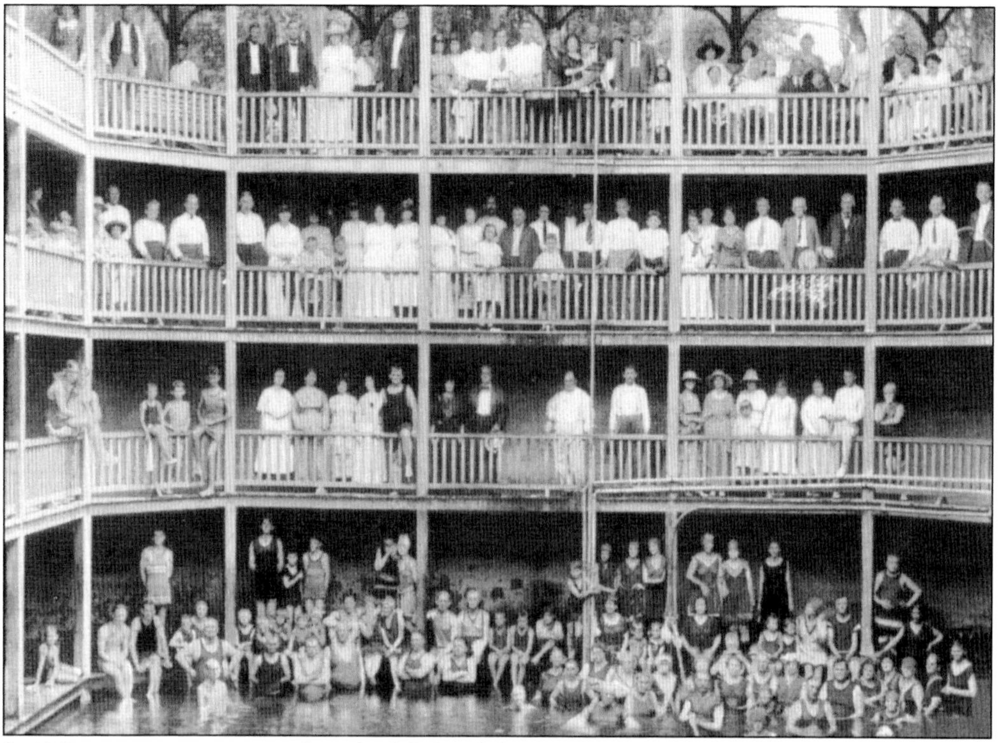

In 1962, a new swimming pool was built behind the Spring House for the enjoyment of locals and tourists alike. These photographs show the Spring House as it was until the early 1970s, when it ceased to be one of the most popular tourist destinations in Florida. The current owners of the spring, the State of Florida, purchased the property from Claude A. Tompkins and his daughter, Carol Tompkins Cassidy, around 1970. For a short time after, it was still used as a swimming area, but the Spring House had begun to fall into disrepair. The state ultimately removed the original Spring House. In its place, they duplicated the upper floor of the original Spring House, leaving the lower area open. (Both Alan Fouraker.)

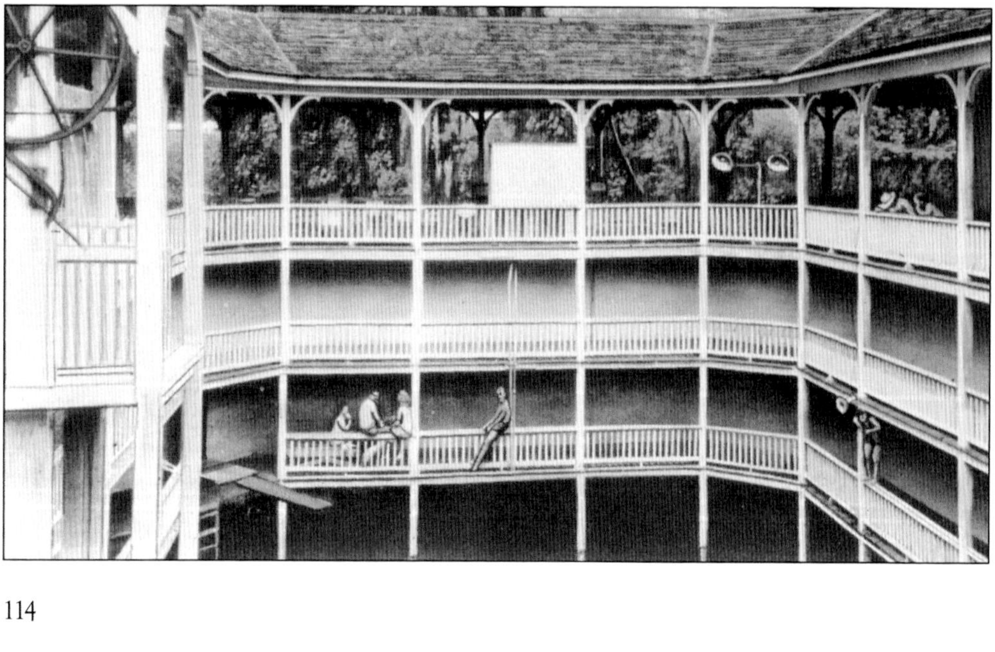

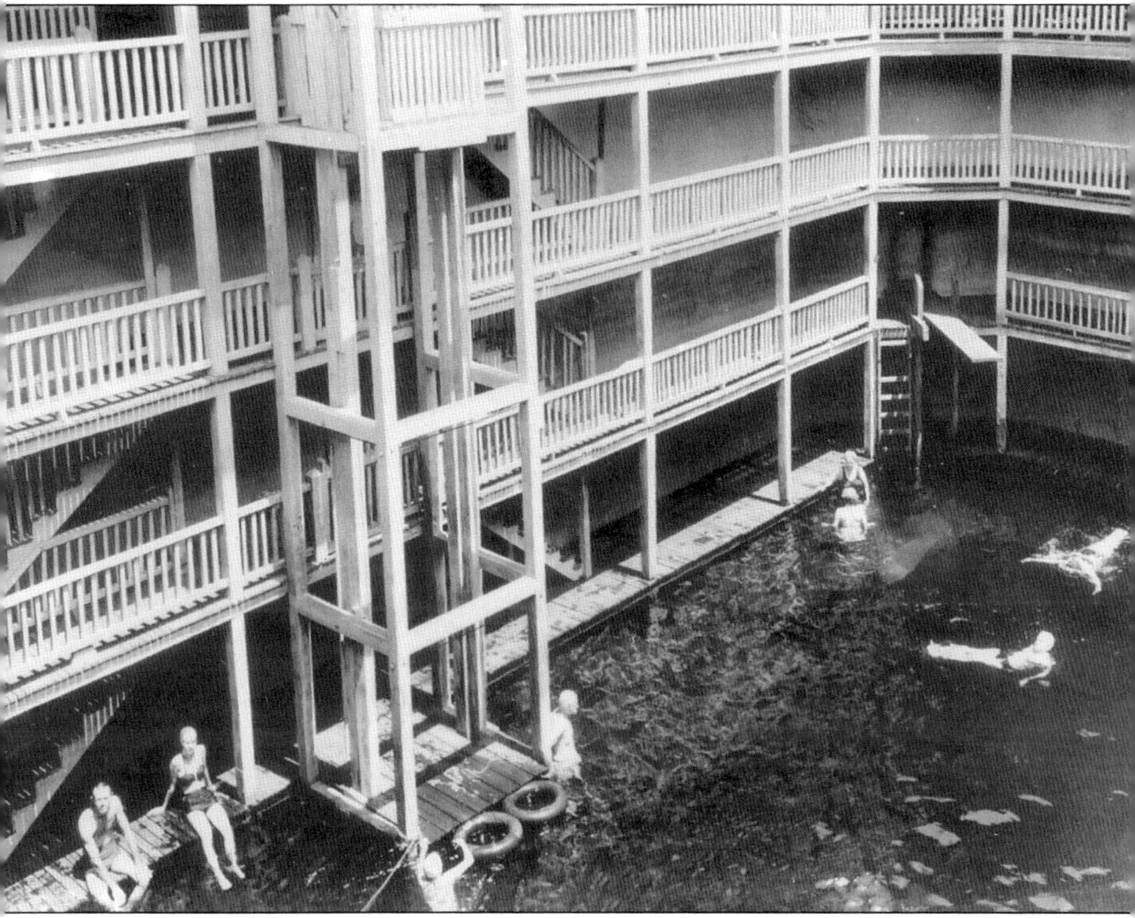

The Spring House is one of 85 historically significant buildings in the White Springs Historic District. The 120-acre area covers much of downtown and includes residential buildings, the Spring House, and Stephen Foster Folk Culture Center State Park. The area was listed on the National Register of Historic Places in 1997. (Alan Fouraker.)

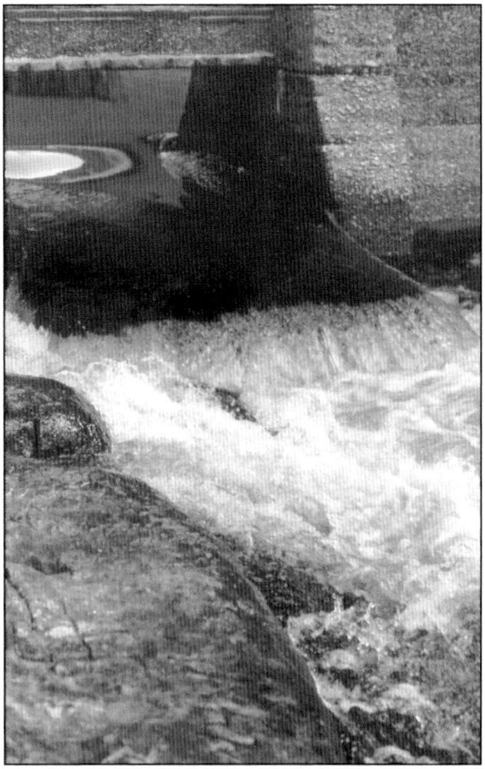

The White Springs area has long been considered to be a sacred healing ground. As early as the 1700s, warring Native American tribes, such as the Timucuans and the Apalachees, would come to the waters of the spring to rest and recuperate from their struggles. Putting aside their disagreements, the rival tribes would bathe in and drink the mineral waters in peace. Although the second magnitude spring no longer flows, the area retains an aura of peace. (Florida Photographic Collection, Florida State Archives.)

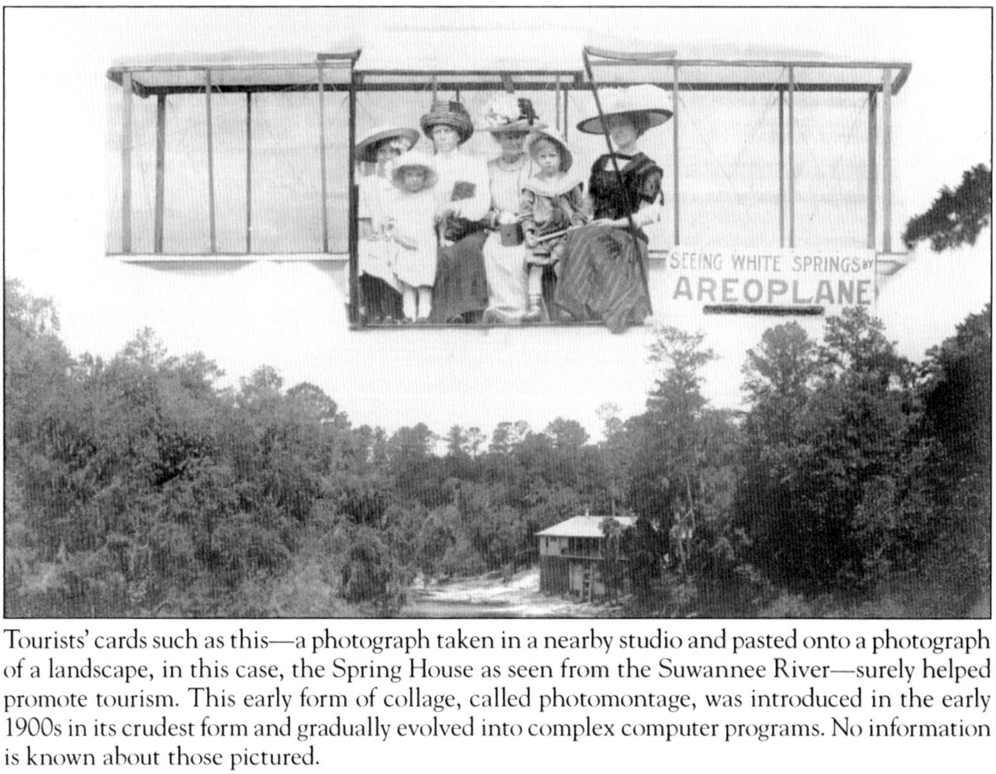

Tourists' cards such as this—a photograph taken in a nearby studio and pasted onto a photograph of a landscape, in this case, the Spring House as seen from the Suwannee River—surely helped promote tourism. This early form of collage, called photomontage, was introduced in the early 1900s in its crudest form and gradually evolved into complex computer programs. No information is known about those pictured.

Nine

Stephen Foster Folk Culture Center State Park

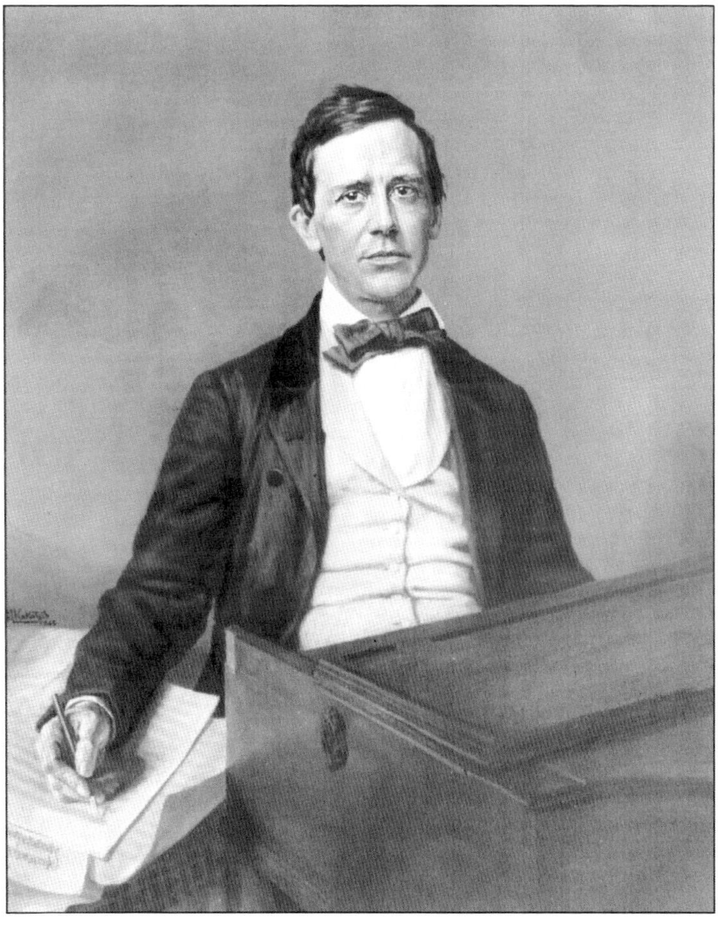

Stephen Collins Foster generously gave Florida their former state song, "Old Folks at Home (The Suwannee River)," in 1851. He later sold the song and its rights to Edward P. Christy, who then produced a series of postcards depicting various songs written by Foster. Throughout his lifetime, Foster wrote more than 200 songs, beginning with "Open Thy Lattice Love" at age 18. His last song, "Beautiful Dreamer," was composed just days before his death on January 13, 1864. (Florida Photographic Collection, State Archives of Florida.)

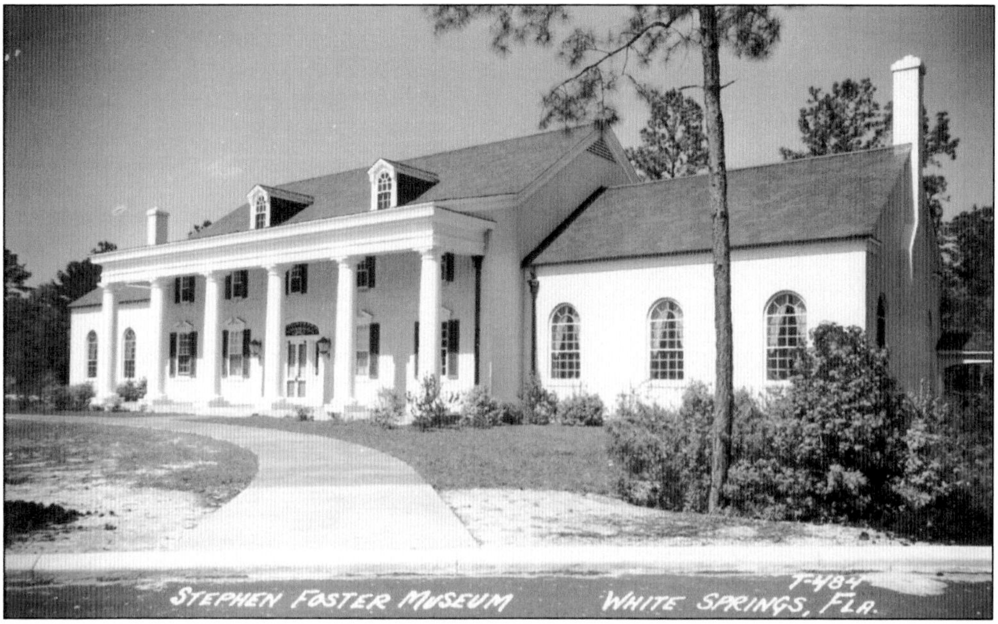

The Stephen Foster Museum was the first of several components of the Stephen Foster Folk Culture Center State Park. Templin's, Inc., of Lakeland, Florida, won the bid to construct the museum and curator's dwelling a short distance from the Suwannee River, for $195,091. The museum houses dioramas and paintings that depict various scenes from Foster's songs. Mackey W. White, formerly of Live Oak, Florida, furnished the architectural drawings for the buildings.

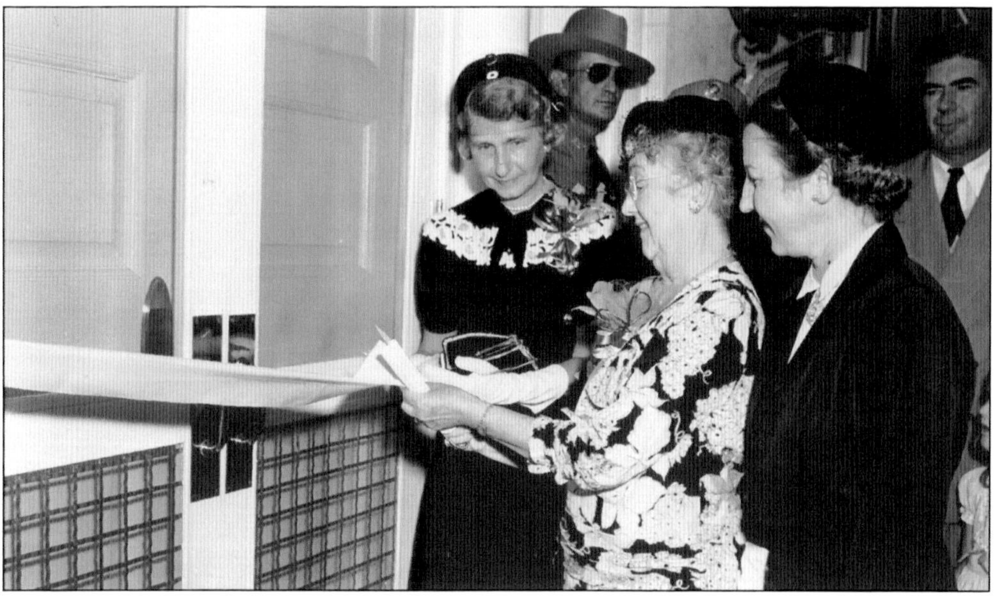

The Florida Agricultural and Mechanical College provided a 100-voice choir to sing Foster's ballads and melodies at the dedication on October 4, 1950. This was the climax of the celebration, with Jessie Welsh Rose, Foster's granddaughter, cutting the ribbon draped across the entrance of the museum building. As the ribbon fell, after a hand clap of praise, thousands of visitors were admitted to view the dioramas and memorabilia of Foster. (Florida Photographic Collection, State Archives of Florida.)

These paintings of Stephen Foster by Howard Chandler Christy are showcased at the Stephen Foster Museum. *Beautiful Dreamer* (right), painted in 1948, shows Foster daydreaming at his desk, with scenes from three of his songs: "Beautiful Dreamer" (1862), "Jeanie With the Light Brown Hair" (1854), and "Old Folks at Home" (1851). The postcard below shows *Many Happy Days I Squandered*, painted in 1950. Another interpretation of "Old Folks at Home," the painting shows Christy's idea of Foster as a young boy enjoying an outing with his young female friend, referencing days of carefree youth. The second verse of "Old Folks at Home" has the line, "many happy days I squandered, many the songs I sung," hence the title of the painting. Christy received $5,000 compensation for each of the 62-square-foot paintings. (Author's collection.)

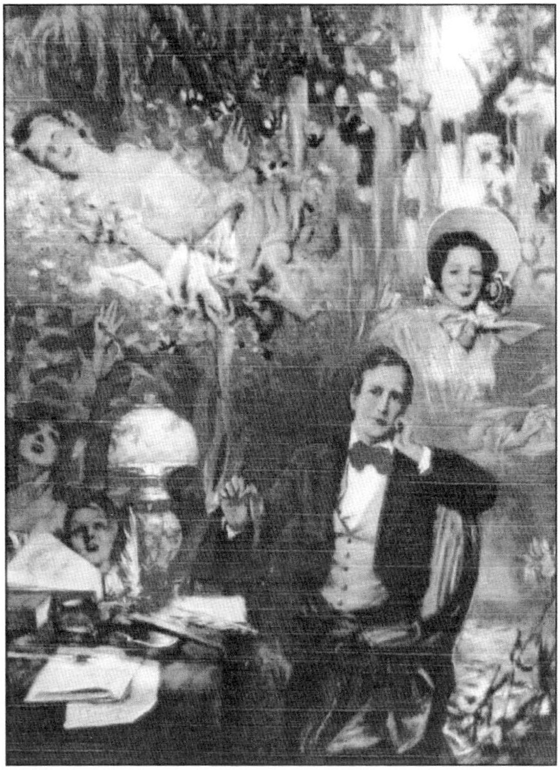

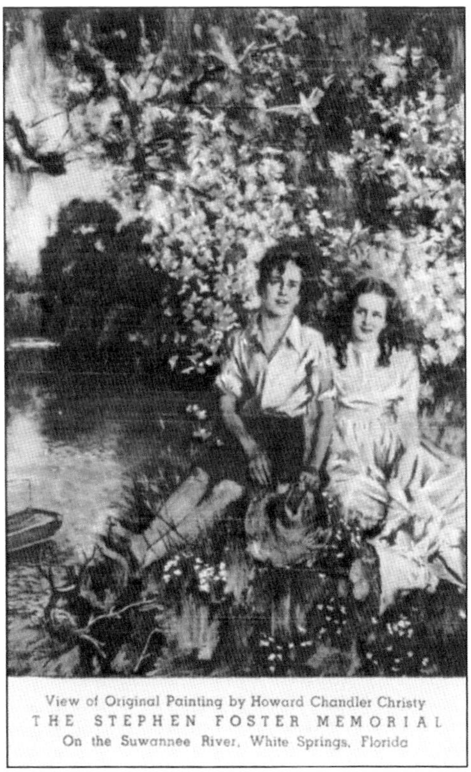

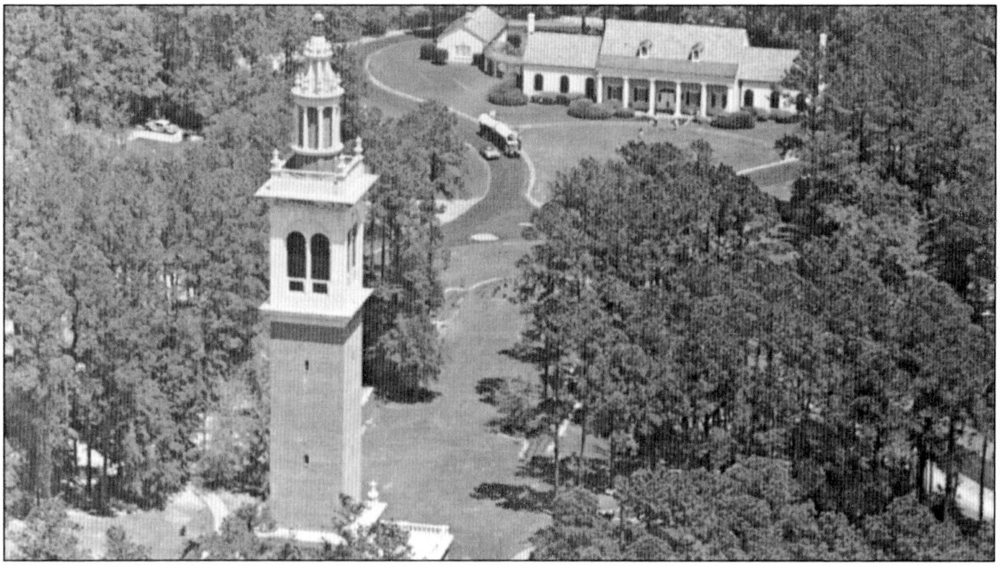

The idea of the Stephen Foster Folk Culture Center State Park was born in 1931 in the mind of Frank Groover of Jacksonville and Josiah K. Lilly of Indianapolis, Indiana. Groover determined the most appropriate area for the memorial was on the Suwannee River at White Springs. The Florida Federation of Music Clubs adopted the idea and purchased the land. Later the project was turned over to the state-sanctioned Florida Stephen Foster Memorial Commission, which then budgeted $500,000 for the memorial. This 1978 photograph shows a bird's-eye view of the Stephen Foster Folk Culture Center State Park. (Author's collection.)

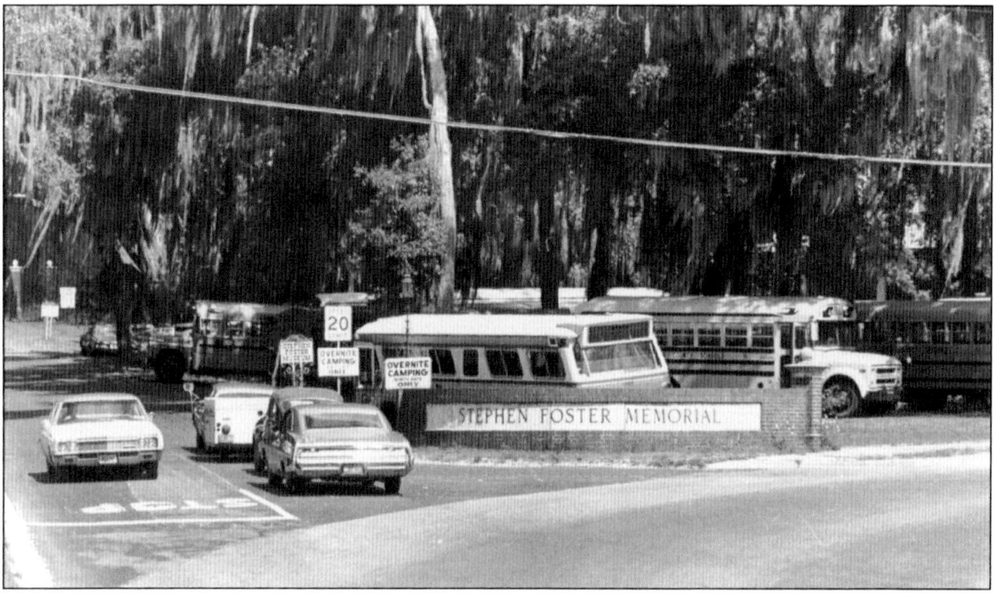

This 1972 photograph of the Stephen Foster Folk Culture Center State Park shows the entrance during the Florida Folk Festival. As can be seen, the festival drew large numbers of people from the beginning. Otherwise, it would never have grown into the renowned festival it is today. In 1972, attendance for the festival rose to more than 100,000—the most ever recorded. Throughout the years, attendance has hovered around 20,000–40,000 people. (Florida Photographic Collection, Florida State Archives.)

Before any work could be done for the carillon tower, as with all projects, plans had to be made. Architects generally attempt to give their backers a feel for what the completed project will look like; this is what has been done here. This sketch was used on several advertisements prior to its completion to show potential and current visitors what was to come. The 200-foot carillon tower was completed in 1956. (Author's collection.)

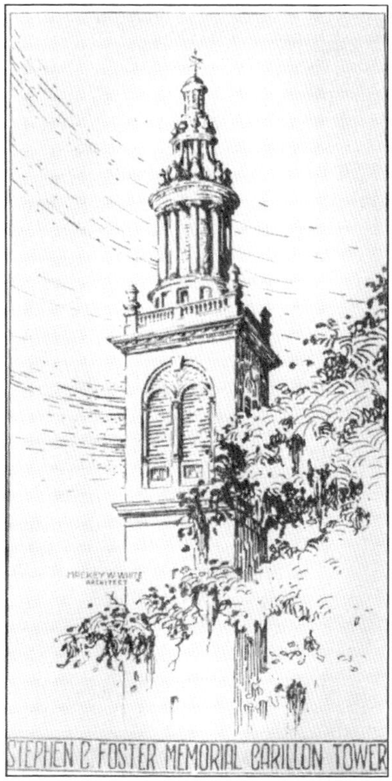

A year after the order was placed with the J. C. Deagan Corporation of Chicago, the world's then-largest bells arrived at the Stephen Foster Folk Culture Center State Park in 1958. The bells costs $119,000 and took approximately one month to install. Consisting of tubular bells ranging in length from 3 feet to 18 feet, the carillon has a broad range of over four octaves and can be played either manually or mechanically. Concerts have been played nearly every day since the carillon bells were officially "on," with melodies composed by Stephen Foster himself being featured. (Florida Photographic Collection, State Archives of Florida.)

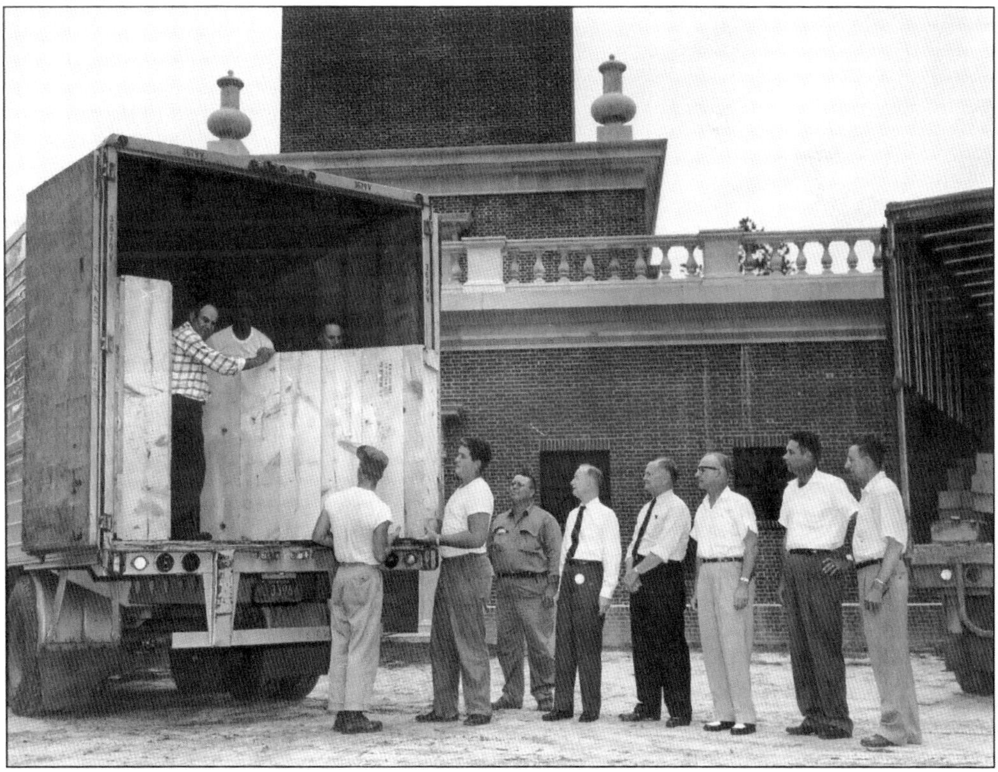

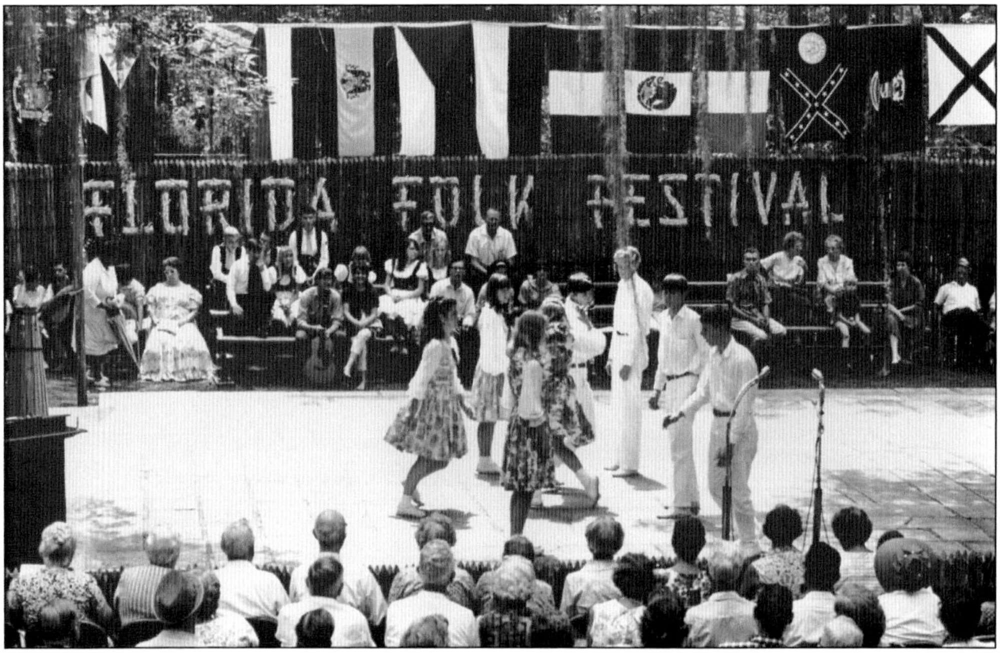

Hundreds of performers arrived at the Florida Folk Festival in White Springs each year. Among the performers were outstanding dance groups such as this one. This 1970s photograph shows a group getting ready for their performance, as other performers and fans look on from the stands. (Florida Development Commission.)

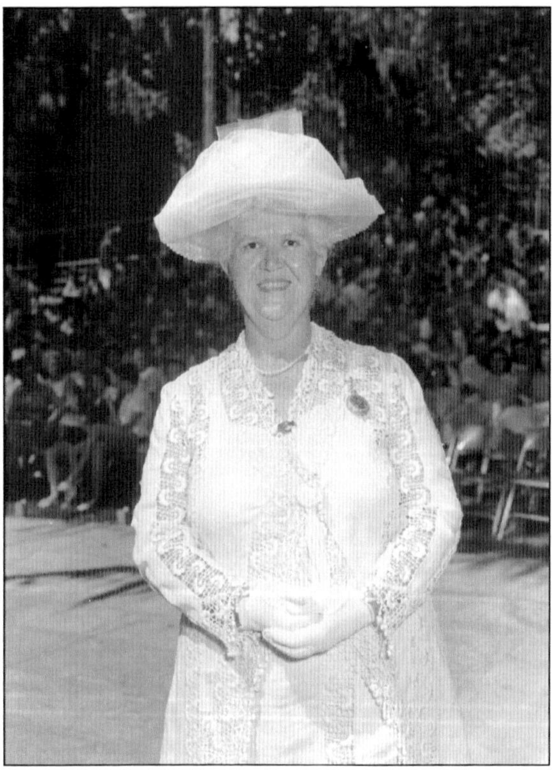

For the first two years of the Florida Folk Festival, Thelma Ann Boltin, "Queen of Florida Folk Life," participated as a storyteller. In 1954, she was asked to direct the festival. She worked year-round to ensure there were plenty of participants for the festival. Although she was unable to direct the festival toward the end of her life, she remained actively involved until her death in 1992. (Florida Photographic Collection, State Archives of Florida.)

Maude McCall Havener spent most of her life in the school system—either as a student or a teacher. Completing the first eight years of her schooling at Jennings High School, she moved on to higher education, eventually receiving her master's degree in education. She married Walter Robert Havener of Clearwater, Florida, and, upon his retirement, returned to Hamilton County. She is shown here (front, far left) with her class of students in 1960, attending the Florida Folk Festival. (Florida Photographic Collection, Florida State Archives.)

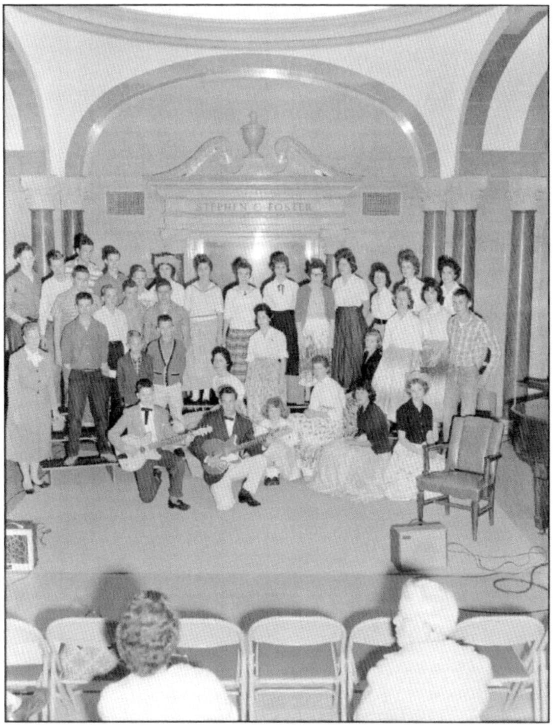

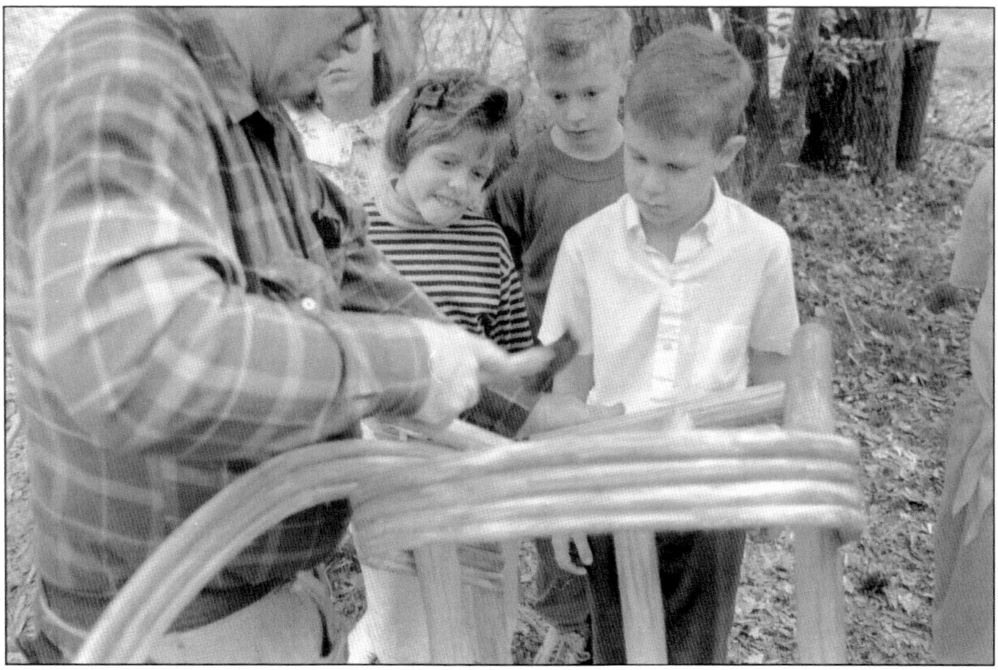

Dr. Elbert Charlton "Skeeter" Prather of Jasper worked with the Florida Public Health System for 35 years until he retired in 1987, holding the positions of secretary of the department, state epidemiologist, and district state health officer. Dr. Prather's main hobbies were woodworking and blacksmithing. He is shown in this 1993 photograph at the Florida Folk Festival, demonstrating his skills. (Florida Photographic Collection, Florida State Archives.)

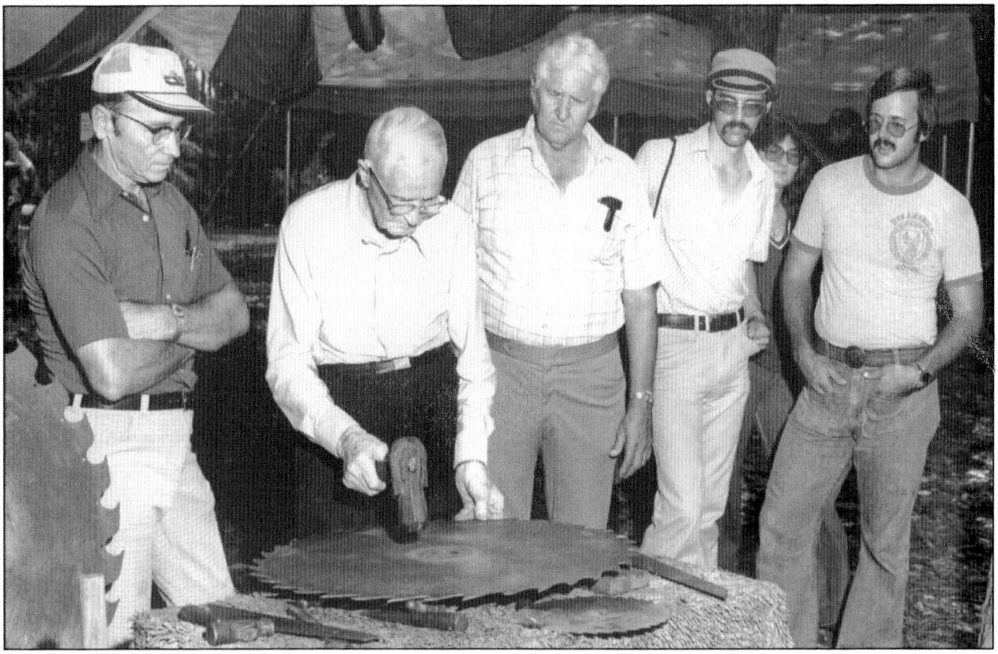

Willoughby Herbert Hammack was born on December 2, 1884, and died on October 23, 1984, at the age of 99. He was skilled in the art of metalworking—a job he performed nearly his whole life. The above photograph, taken when Hammack (second from left) was about 93 years of age, shows him setting saw teeth at the 1978 Florida Folk Festival, held annually in White Springs. The other men in the photograph are unidentified. The photograph below shows Hammack alone in front of his metal working shop in 1979. (Both Florida Photographic Collection, State Archives of Florida.)

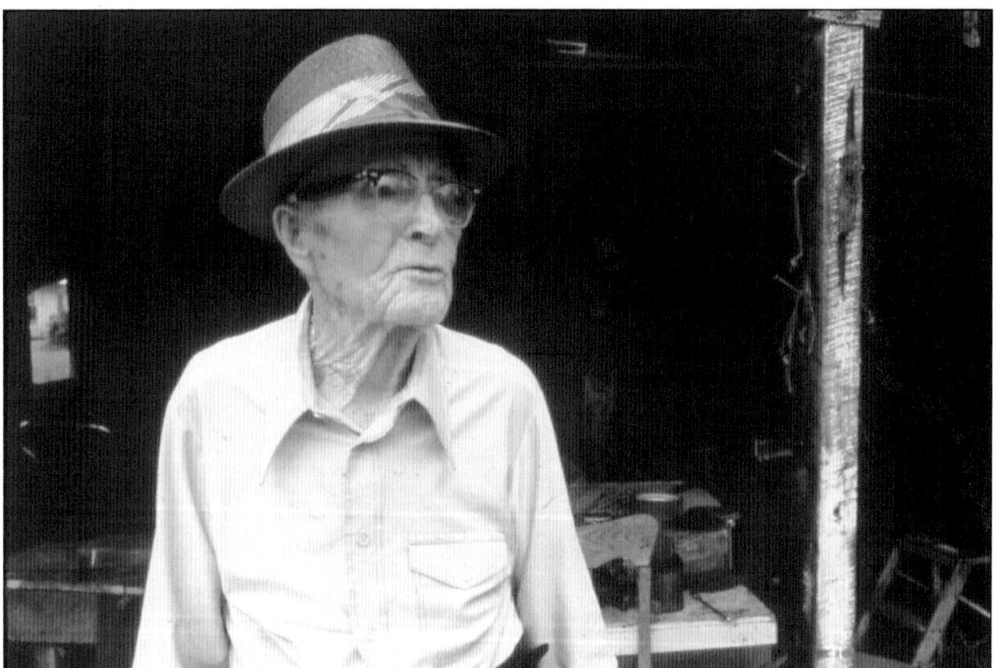

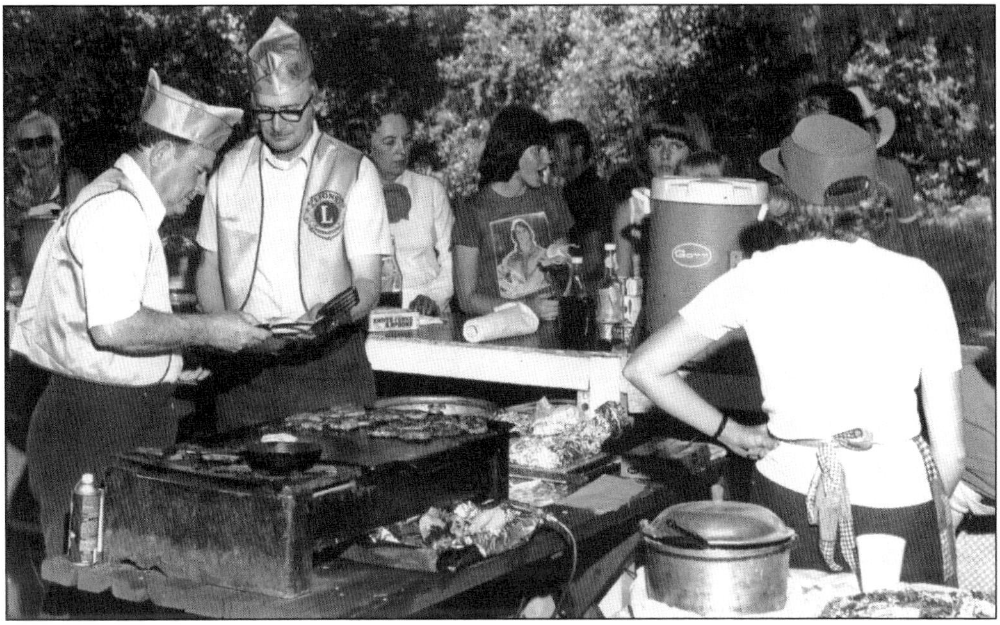

The annual Pancake and Sausage Breakfast, hosted by the Lions Club of Jasper, attracted dozens of diners each year. In this 1978 photograph, the Lions Club opted to hold the breakfast at the Florida Folk Festival. Through the years, the time has been changed, and the Lions Club now hosts a Pancake Dinner, usually held at the former J. R. E. Lee Middle School, and serves hundreds of people. (Florida Photographic Collection, State Archives of Florida.)

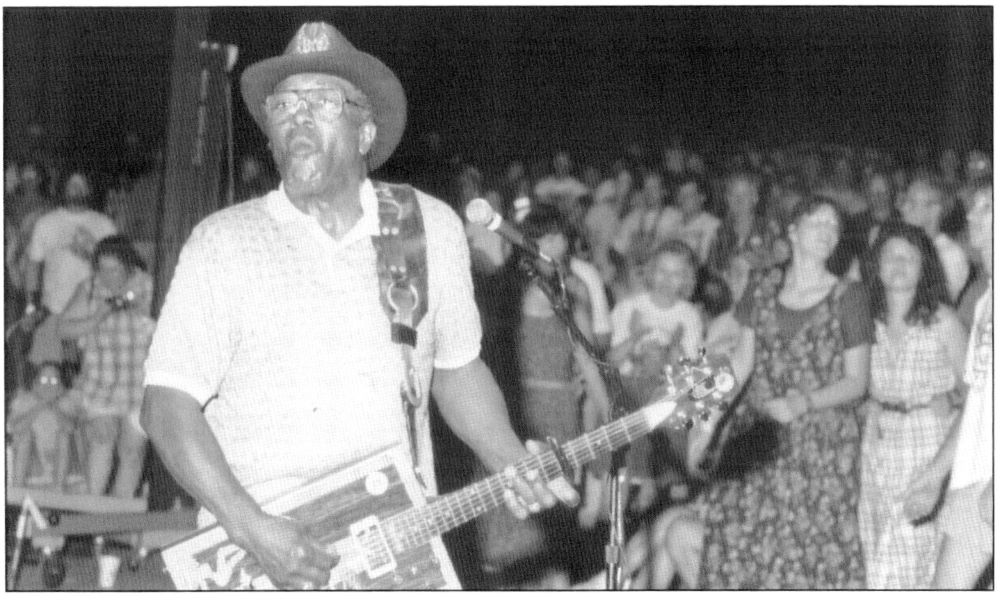

Ellas McDaniel, known as Bo Diddley, paid his respects as a rhythm and blues singer at the Florida Folk Festival for many years. Living in Archer, Florida, the trip was not nearly as long as some that he made, playing concerts for Presidents George Bush, Bill Clinton, and John F. and Jackie Kennedy and traveling the world to perform at tributes and headline concerts. This 1985 photograph shows Diddley with his trademark rectangular guitar. (Florida Photographic Collection, State Archives of Florida.)

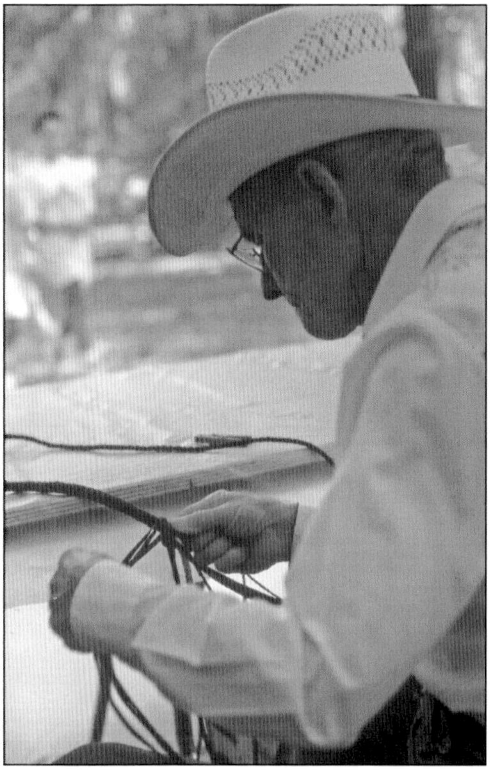

Julian P. "Curly" Dekle grew up on a farm near Lake Butler, Florida, and learned the art of braiding whips from his father, Judge P. P. Dekle. There were two aspects of Dekle's whips that made them different from all others—the belly of the whip was weighted down with SB pellets rolled in duct tape, and the whip was braided from the tip to the handle to eliminate the knot at the end (which might interfere with the cracking action). He performed in a number of rodeos, Wild West shows, fairs, and festivals throughout the southern United States, billed as the "Florida Cracker." By the time of his retirement, he had created quite a striking show. Dekle passed away in 2004 at the age of 92. (Both Florida Photographic Collection, State Archives of Florida.)

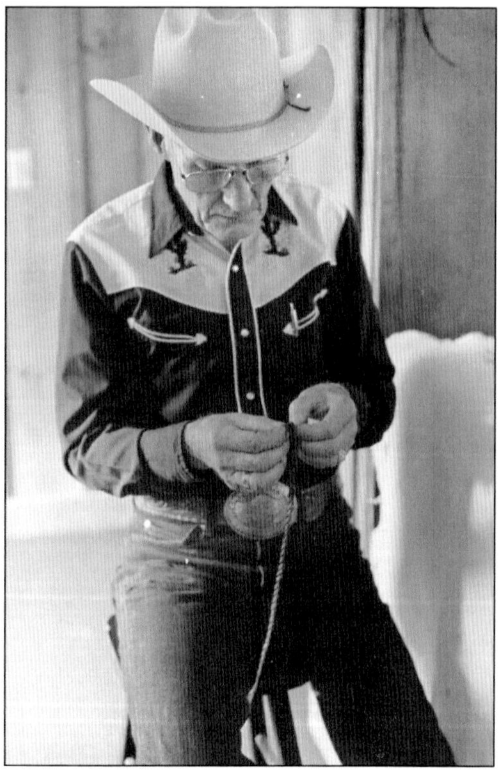

After learning to play the cornstalk fiddle, cigar-box banjo, and a Silvertone guitar in his youth, Don Grooms became a journalist, writing for magazines and newspapers, before going to Gainesville, Florida, to teach journalism at the University of Florida. During this time, Grooms returned to playing the guitar and writing songs, strongly influenced by Will MacLean. Grooms played several festivals, including the Florida Folk Festival, and various small venues throughout Florida. (Florida Photographic Collection, State Archives of Florida.)

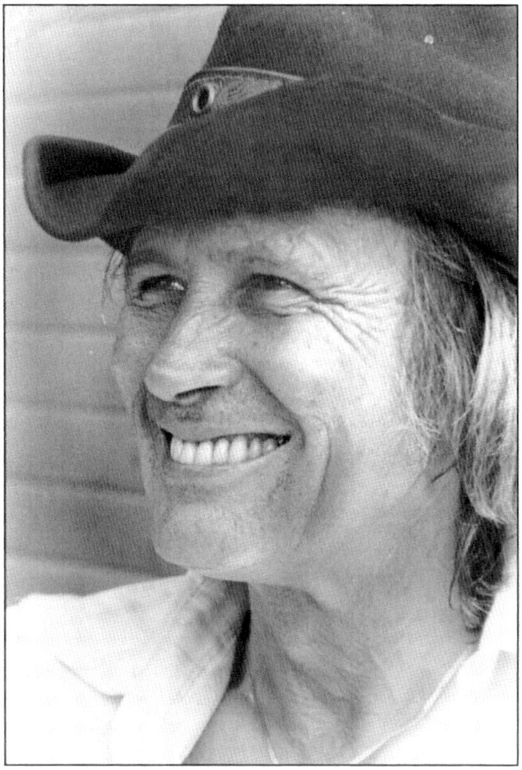

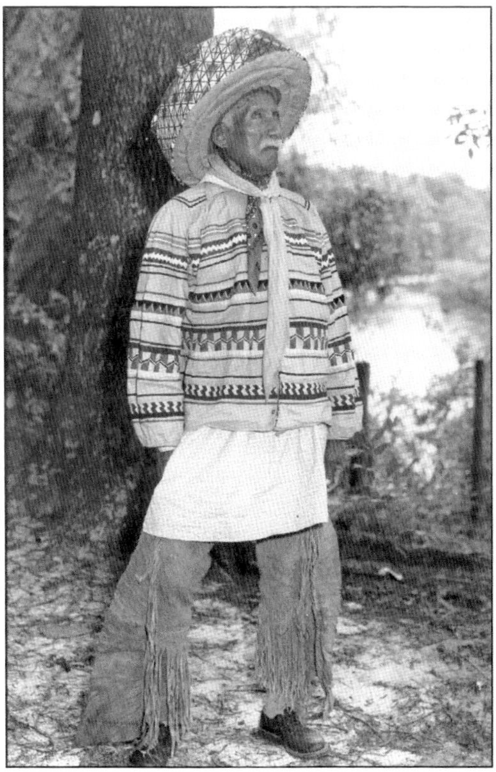

Learning more than 200 words, Billy Bowlegs III used them in such a manner as to command respect. He often attended "white men" events that would gain honor and respect for the Seminole tribe. Although he lived on the Brighton Seminole Indian Reservation, he visited Hamilton County yearly during the Florida Folk Festival to demonstrate dances of the tribes, hunting calls for various animals, and the traditional dress of the Seminoles. (Florida Photographic Collection, Florida State Archives.)